META-COGNITION: A RECENT REVIEW OF RESEARCH, THEORY AND PERSPECTIVES

Meta-Cognition: A Recent Review of Research, Theory and Perspectives

Michael F. Shaughnessy, Marcel V. J. Veenman and Cynthia Kleyn-Kennedy

Editors

Nova Science Publishers, Inc.

New York

16750 96 97

NOTICE TO THE READER

LIBRARY OF CONGRESS CATALOGING-IN-PUBLICATION DATA

Meta-cognition : a recent review of research, theory, and perspectives / Michael F. Shaughnessy, Marcel V.E. Vennemann, and Cynthia Kleyn Kennedy, editors.

  p. cm.
 ISBN 978-1-60456-011-4 (hardcover)
 1. Metacognition.   I. Shaughnessy, Michael F.   II. Vennemann, Marcel V.E.   III. Kennedy, Cynthia Kleyn.
 BF311.M4483 2007 2008
 153--dc22

2007035260

Published by Nova Science Publishers, Inc. ✦ New York

CONTENTS

In: Meta-Cognition: A Recent Review of Research...   ISBN: 978-1-60456-011-4
Editors: M.F. Shaughnessy et al. pp. 1-2   © 2008 Nova Science Publishers, Inc.

Chapter 1

INTRODUCTION

Over the past two decades, the word "metacognition" has become a regularly used part of our language and vocabulary in both psychology and education. Many research articles have been written about it, the conceptualization of this construct has expanded, and conferences abound with investigations and empirical research into various facets of this domain.

This book provides some of the most recent research by scholars from various parts of the world. It includes differing perspectives- some empirical, some theory driven, and some application papers. The book focuses on metacognition and it's relevance to gifted and highly able students. Many of the papers focus directly and specifically on this, others are more tangential in nature.

Michele Helms-Lorenz and Annemieke Jacobse of the University of Groningen discuss the metacognitive skills of the gifted from a cross cultural perspective. Norbert Jausovec of the University of Maribor in Slovenia provides a psychophysiological perspective on metacognition.

Joyce Alexander and her colleagues, Kathy Johnson, Brianna Scott and Rhonda Meyer from Indiana University and Purdue examine the mechanisms for transfer across biological domains.

Carol McGaughey of Houston Baptist University discusses an age old question in her paper and relates it to the concept and practice of "breaking set" and the metacognitive mechanisms involved. The singular process and skill of being able to discern cognitive sets is a singular aspect of metacognition.

Marty Carr and Gita Taasoobshirazi of the University of Georgia, Athens, focus on the connections to expertise that metacognition provides. Scott Hunsaker of Utah State University discusses a specific metacognitive strategy called "marginalia".

Smaragda Kazi, Nikolaos Makris and Andreas Denetriou of Patheon University of Social Science, Greece, the University of Thrace, Greece and the University of Cyprus, in Cyprus discuss the on going developmental process of the self-mapping of cognitive processes from early childhood to adolescence. Their challenging series of experiments are engaging to read, review and examine and the methodologically pristine nature of their research deserves recognition.

David Moshman of the University of Nebraska discusses the realm of epistemic development and the perils of change of operational definitions and how this relates to metacognition and thinking. Virginia Mahan of South Plains College in Texas provides an overview of the realm of metacognition in terms of multicultural education.

Marcel V.J. Veenman of Leiden Univesity delves into the realm of giftedness and discusses the speed of expertise acquisition relative to intellectual ability and the metacognitive skillfulness of novices. The " expert vs. novice " construct is one that has been investigated in metacognitive research for many years.

Seyed Mohammed Alavi and Mayhar Ganjabi have investigated the domain of second language learning and the metacognitive aspects involved in terms of reading comprehension. They indicate areas of needed future research and examine both cognitive and metacognitive strategies.

The book ends with an interview with John Flavell whose pioneering work in the realm of metacognition is well known to us all. This book is dedicated to his initial ground breaking work and we acknowledge a debt of gratitude to him for all of his work over the years.

In: Meta-Cognition: A Recent Review of Research...   ISBN: 978-1-60456-011-4
Editors: M.F. Shaughnessy et al. pp. 3-43   © 2008 Nova Science Publishers, Inc.

Chapter 2

METACOGNITIVE SKILLS OF THE GIFTED FROM A CROSS-CULTURAL PERSPECTIVE

Michelle Helms-Lorenz and Annemieke Elisabeth Jacobse

University of Groningen, Groningen, The Netherlands

ABSTRACT

The paucity of studies concerning metacognitive skills from a cross-cultural perspective is surprising considering the widespread multicultural educational settings in all parts of the modern world. This chapter will provide a short review of the literature concerning the relationship between metacognitive skills and giftedness from a developmental perspective. Data was collected from 103 native (N=34) and migrant (N=69), final year primary school subjects in The Netherlands using the think-aloud assessment procedure. The mean age of the sample was 12.4 years. The sample consisted of regular elementary school subjects; subjects of extreme low IQ were not included. Measures of crystallized and fluid intelligence, measures of school achievement, and background information were also gathered. Using the intelligence measures the sample was subdivided into low, average and highly intelligent groups. The first aim of this study was to compare the metacognitive skills of natives to that of migrants. The second aim was to scrutinize metacognitive skills for each ability group in order to reach conclusions concerning the metacognitive skills of the gifted in a multicultural setting. And, lastly, we investigated the relationship between metacognitive skills, fluid and crystallized intelligence, and school success to compare these relationships between the native and migrant group. Our findings suggest that the concept of metacognitive skilfulness is roughly the same for natives and migrants. The low ability migrant children showed higher levels of metacognitive skills The highly intelligent group showed higher metacognitive skilfulness in both migrants and natives, most profoundly on systematical orderliness. Our results on the study of the relationship between intelligence, metacognitive skilfulness and school performance, suggest that the relationship is influenced by the measures used. Migrants revealed evidence for the independency model (Veenman, 1997) whereas natives revealed evidence for the mixed model. Implications, limitations and suggestions for future research are discussed.

1.1. INTRODUCTION[1]

The knowledge and regulation of one's thought processes is often referred to as "metacognition". Moreover, it is posed by several researchers that metacognitive activities can stimulate learning and problem solving processes (e.g. Davidson & Sternberg, 1998; Malpass, O'Neil & Hocevar, 1999; Swanson, 1992).

Considering the large number of studies on high abilities and giftedness, it is remarkable that this area seems to neglect the role of metacognition in the identification and education of the gifted. Although there is considerable evidence that metacognition plays a role in school performance, there has so far been substantially less research focusing on the metacognitive abilities of the upper range of the intelligence distribution (Carr, Alexander & Schwanenflugel, 1996). A large number of the studies that do assess the relationship between intelligence and metacognition in non-retarded children, exclude predictors of learning performance (Veenman, Kok, & Blöte, 2005b). Thus, assessment of the relationships between metacognition, intelligence and performance of especially young gifted children, compared with children of average and low ability is scarce. The paucity of such research is unfortunate considering the importance of the findings on thought processes of the gifted in accordance with educational and practical purposes, as for instance, the developing of superior instructional methods and strategies in order to nurture expertise in gifted, and supple mentally, average students (Hong, 1999).

In reviewing the relationships between metacognition, high abilities, and performance, the importance of which is argued above, it is important to take a cross-cultural perspective in order to account for the constant growth in the migrant population in the Netherlands and other Western countries. According to prediction by the Dutch 'Centraal Bureau voor Statistiek' (2003), the proportion of non-Western migrants in elementary and secondary education in the Netherlands will increase to about twenty percent by 2020; including western migrants, approximately one third of the children in educational settings within The Netherlands will be of non-Dutch origin. These estimates will differ per country, which affects the sense of urgency to gather knowledge and expertise of multicultural educational settings. Increasing globalisation, however, will add to the sense of urgency all over the world. The relationships between (high) intelligence, metacognition and performance from a cross-cultural perspective, will form the heart of this chapter. Prior to the empirical research to be presented, a review of findings from literature with specific relevance for our study is provided.

1.2. High Ability

1.2.1. Approaches towards Intelligence

In order to assess various conceptions of giftedness or high abilities and come to a definition of use for our study, it is essential to first review the overarching approaches towards intelligence. Three important ones are the psychometric, the cognitive and the biological approach. The biological approach attempts to explain intelligence using biological

---

[1] The chapter is based on the master's thesis of the second author (Jacobse, 2006).

factors. It has its roots in Galton's (1883) ideas about intelligence being observable by certain psychophysical abilities. The measurements in this approach are related to central nervous system functioning, for instance, by assessing EEG (electroencephalography) parameters. Most research using this approach is performed on adults because the assessment of intelligence of children using biological measurements is seen as less useful due to the ongoing dynamic brain maturation of children. Moreover, a shortcoming of the assessment of biological intelligence is that it cannot be assessed in a direct manner, but only as the product of its interaction with the environment where observable (Melis, 1997).

The cognitive approach springs from research on information processing during problem solving. It attempts to assess intelligence by means of studying mental representations and processes. Within this approach, a "cognitive correlates" and a "cognitive components" approach can be discerned. The "cognitive correlates" approach was first introduced by Hunt, Frost and Lunneborg (1973). They correlated scores on relatively simple cognitive tests with scores on broad psychometric intelligence tests. A typical information processing task is the inspection time (IT) task (Nettlebeck, 1982) where subjects are briefly presented with two lines (through a tachistoscope) and have to indicate the longest line. This task generally shows small, but apparent correlations with traditional intelligence measures. The notion of a cognitive-components approach was introduced by Sternberg (1977). In this approach, performance on complex psychometric tasks is subdivided into basic information processing components. Thus, the problem solving is translated in terms of stages of processing which can be defined and used as a measure of the process. The cognitive-components research mainly focuses on inductive reasoning measured by reasoning tests. Some difficulties of this approach consist of methodological and statistical obscurities, the lack of a univocal model of reasoning and unclear assumptions regarding information-processing components (Melis, 1997).

The psychometric approach, on the other hand, attempts to assess cognitive functioning by means of explorative statistical analysis of test responses. This is a bottom-up approach in which statistical measurements by intelligence tests determine the definition of intelligence. Thus, the foundation of this approach is merely statistical and lacks a profound theoretical underpinning, which can be seen as a weakness of the approach. In support of the psychometric tradition, Spearman (1927) discovered a significant phenomenon which he referred to as the "positive manifold" phenomenon. This refers to the repeated finding that results of different ability tests positively correlate with one another. From this phenomenon, Spearman concluded that there had to be a general intelligence factor (G), which represents what all valid tests have in common. Later on, researchers such as Burt (1949), Horn and Cattell (1966), and Vernon (1950) discovered that besides this general factor, group factors are of great importance. These group factors are found by extracting first, second, or even higher order factors in higher-order factor analysis. The group factors found by Horn and Cattell (1966) for instance, include those factors relatively close to the general factor (fluid intelligence), and other factors involving abilities such as crystallized intelligence, verbal comprehension and figural insight which are less closely related to G or general intelligence.

Caroll (1993), after extensive longitudinal research, proposed a multilevel psychometric model of intelligence including a level with narrow, specific abilities (e.g. speed of reasoning, sound discrimination, memory span), a level consisting of group factors (e.g. fluid intelligence, crystallized intelligence, general memory and learning, broad visual perception);

and the level for the G factor. The further that group factors and specific abilities are placed from the G factor in the model, the weaker the relationship with this general factor.

A distinction in intelligence found in psychometric research tradition (e.g. Marshalek, Lohman & Snow, 1983), is the distinction between fluid and crystallized intelligence. Measures of fluid intelligence are dynamic in nature and measure one's ability to reason and to solve problems. These measures seem to be quite close to the general intelligence factor G (e.g. Caroll, 1993; Horn & Cattell, 1966). Measures of crystallized intelligence, on the other hand, measure the ability to apply previously learned information to the problems at hand. The latter measure seems more amenable to background influences, such as culture, experiences, parental support, and so forth (Helms-Lorenz, van de Vijver & Poortinga, 2003; Minnaert & Janssen, 1999). School achievement tests mainly measure crystallized measures of intellectual knowledge and skills learned in education. Traditional intelligence (IQ) tests usually measure a combination of crystallized and fluid intelligence. However, IQ tests differ in the relative proportions of crystallized and fluid intelligence measured. The size of the contribution of both within a given test is often unknown to the user. The Ravens Progressive Matrices is considered to be a test of fluid intelligence (Jensen, 1985).

Reflecting on the inappropriateness of the biological approach for measurement of intelligence of young children and the relative dissension of the findings and methods within the cognitive approach, the psychometric approach is selected for this study. An attempt will be made to discern the role of crystallized and fluid intelligence on performance using two types of intelligence tests. Additionally, to discern the relationship of metacognition, intelligence and school performance, metacognitive skills and school-subject performance measures will be gathered. The focus is on high intelligence and giftedness. Therefore, in the next paragraphs the focus will be shifted towards this subject.

1.2.2. Conceptions of Giftedness

Sternberg (2001) explained that in the assessment of high intelligence, the view one has of the plasticity of giftedness is crucial. There is the more conventional view of abilities as relatively stable traits of individuals as proposed by theoretical contributions by, among others, Binet, Spearman and Galton. From this view the assumption is made that, to a large extent, people are born gifted, and some individuals will be broadly gifted across domains and cultures while others will not. An alternative, more dynamic view, stemming from Vygotskian theories consists of giftedness being associated with an individual's large zone of proximal development. Theorists promoting this view find some individuals to generally have a larger zone of proximal development than others. However besides that, environmental factors such as scaffolding and mediated learning experiences can play a large role in stimulating giftedness. Assessments following this view will typically consist of dynamic assessments of learning whilst being tested.

Through the years, additional factors of potential influence on giftedness have been discussed from different perspectives. Some of the frequently mentioned influences consist of factors such as motivation, creativity, knowledge base and metacognition (Alexander et al, 1995; Carr et al., 1996). Several researchers have attempted to integrate such factors in their view of giftedness. Mönks (1992), for instance, proposed a multi-factorial model in 1985 including high intellectual abilities, motivation and creativity, and the external social factors of family, school and peers. As a result of research with retarded children, Campione and Brown (1978) proposed the ability to generalize information from one situation to another depending on effective executive control as being a hallmark of intelligence. And, in a study by Perleth (1992), some support for this intelligence concept of Campione and Brown was found in transfer abilities of gifted children. In Gardner's (1983) theory of multiple intelligences, the term metacognition or related terms are not encountered. But, rather, creative activities including encoding, combining and comparing new knowledge to existing knowledge, which are closely related to the concept of metacognition which will be discussed in paragraph 1.3.

The triarchic theory by Sternberg (1994) supports the view that metacognitive activities, referred to as metacomponents, are of particular relevance in cognitive performance.

In addition to these viewpoints, several studies connect giftedness to the novice-expert paradigm. For instance, Shore (2000), states that metacognition and flexibility are related to the two parts of expert performance; self-regulation in combination with an extensive knowledge base and the selective use of this knowledge. The author interestingly notes that if novices are thought to be able to become experts by means of appropriate instruction, assuming that parts of giftedness are related to expert performance, the implication would be that some facets of giftedness can be taught. The resemblance between giftedness or high abilities and expert behaviour was found in various studies. In the studies on elementary school children, Shore and his colleagues found that children with high IQ scores solved relatively complex problems using strategies that are also found in expert behaviour such as organizing knowledge hierarchically, planning and using metacognitive skills.

Pelletier and Shore (2003) summarize findings from many areas where there is an overlap between characteristics of high abilities and giftedness, and expert performance. Experts and gifted learners, for example seem to be comparable in being able to accurately use their knowledge base, in monitoring their own processes, in forming representations of information, and in accurate strategy use. A difficulty in comparing experts and gifted children however, is that research on expertise is generally based on the performance of highly trained, experienced, and motivated adults. However, the scarce research available on this subject supports the view of similarities between gifted children and experts, therefore, this might be a fruitful area to examine. De Corte (1995) accordingly states that research on expertise may contribute to a superior understanding of the cognitive activities and processes of exceptional performance, and consequentially of giftedness.

In reference to the concepts described above, and for this study a definition of giftedness is adopted that views giftedness as being partly stable of nature influenced by biological factors, but on the other hand, having a substantial dynamic feature which can be influenced by external factors. Although our study does not focus on expert versus novice behaviour, performance can be seen as the level of expertise one reaches. A model in which high intelligence is conceptualized in such manner, is the theory of "developing expertise" proposed by Sternberg, which is discussed in the next paragraph.

1.2.3. Giftedness as Developing Expertise

By proposing his theory of giftedness as "developing expertise", Sternberg (2001) attempts to integrate the different conceptions of giftedness mentioned in the section above. He defines developing expertise as "the ongoing process of the acquisition and consolidation of a set of skills needed for a high level of mastery in one or more domains of life performance." (p. 160). Thus, abilities can be viewed as developing expertise, both concepts being completely intertwined. This view does not exclude genetic influences on individual differences, but points out that in intelligence tests, this genetic factor is not what is being measured, but rather expressed manifestations thereof, that will potentially lead to later success. In this view, gifted learners are seen as people who develop expertise more rapidly, to a higher level, or to a qualitatively different kind of level than others. In the model of developing expertise, Sternberg has taken up five key elements that fuel the development of expertise: metacognitive skills, learning skills, thinking skills, knowledge and motivation. He notes that gifted individuals will typically excel in the development of expertise by combining some, or all of these elements.

Sternberg's "theory of successful intelligence" in which intelligence is seen as consisting of analytical, creative and practical aspects forms the basis for the developing expertise model. He suggests that in their developing expertise, people can show analytical, creative or practical expertise independently or in different combinations across various domains. It is of practical interest that recent studies show that teaching in accordance to the developing expertise in the triarchic set of analytical, creative and practical aspects, results in superior learning outcomes across ages (e.g., Sternberg, 2001; Sternberg, Grigorenko & Jarvin, 2001). By describing the theory of developing expertise and the instruction model for triarchic teaching, Sternberg and his colleagues have opened the doors for us to expand our notions of ability and giftedness.

From this theory, we derive the expectation that metacognition can be of relevance in the development of expertise measured by instruments for determining school success. We adopt the assumption that metacognition may prove to be a key concept of intelligence, partly supplemental to genetic influences. Additionally, following this theory, the expectation of high ability students to show a higher level of expertise in metacognitive and performance measures seems feasible. In order to provide a framework for the assessment of metacognition, in the next paragraph the definitions, development and differential measurement methods of metacognition will be discussed.

1.3. Metacognition

1.3.1. Defining Metacognition

While reviewing existing literature on the subject of metacognition, one is bound to note the diversity in the description, experiments, and the measurement of the concept metacognition. As Veenman, Van Hout-Wolters and Afflerbach (2006) note, the domain of metacognition seems to lack coherence. However, practically all the literature on the subject of metacognition refers to the pioneering work of Flavell. He introduced metacognition as "knowledge and cognition about cognitive phenomena" (1979), which is also referred to in terms such as "thinking about thinking" or "higher order cognition of cognition" (e.g. Alexander et al., 1995; De Jong, 1992; Hacker, 1998; and Veenman et al., 2006). Flavell defined metacognition as consisting of both a component of knowledge, and experiences and regulation (1979). Building on the contributions of Flavell, Brown shifted the focus to the monitoring and regulatory aspects of metacognition in her articles of the late seventies (e.g. Brown, Campione & Barclay, 1979). On the other hand, Kluwe's articles, published in the eighties, focus on executive control as a key concept within the domain of metacognition in which he makes the distinction between declarative and procedural knowledge (e.g. Kluwe, 1982).

Since these and other early contributions to the discussion about the concept of metacognition, many terms have been developed over the years, for example: metacognitive beliefs, metacognitive awareness, metamemory, executive skills, self-regulation, metacognitive skills and so on (Veenman et al., 2006). Though the diverse conceptualizations have differential focal points, the most common distinction seems to separate metacognitive declarative knowledge (about the interactions between the characteristics of a person, task and strategy), from metacognitive procedural knowledge (exhibited in metacognitive skills concerning the regulation of, and control over cognitive processes and learning) (Veenman, et al., 2005b; 2006). Shraw and Graham (1997) for instance, make the distinction between metacognitive knowledge and metacognitive control. In their view, metacognitive knowledge includes different kinds of metacognitive awareness, and metacognitive control processes consist of skills that help a person use that knowledge to regulate cognitive processes. Alexander et al. (1995) also use a comparable distinction between declarative metacognitive knowledge and a more procedural aspect to which they refer to as cognitive monitoring. Besides these two factors, they have chosen to add a third factor: "strategy regulation and control" which they use as a separate indicator of the metacognition referring to a strategy or task. Yore and Craig (1992) use a definition of metacognition as consisting of the awareness and executive control of cognition.

In this study, we adopt the distinction of Veenman et al. (2005b) of metacognitive declarative knowledge and (procedural) metacognitive skilfulness. Some researchers have argued a reciprocal relationship between these two components of metacognition. For instance, Shraw and Graham (1997) put forth that two components of metacognition, in their study labelled as metacognitive knowledge and metacognitive control, seem to be intercorrelated in a reciprocal manner. Alexander and Schwanenflugel (1996) note that research has suggested metacognitive knowledge to be a possible predictor for the benefits one will have from strategy use, independent of the use of any particular strategy. However, we agree with Veenman et al. (2005b; 2004) that caution is required in suggesting a causal connection between the two because metacognitive knowledge does not automatically lead to appropriate execution of metacognitive skills. Metacognitive skills among themselves however, do seem to be highly interdependent (Veenman, et al. 2005b; Veenman, Elshout, & Meijer, 1997). Since a reciprocal relationship between metacognitive knowledge and skillfulness is not always evident, independent assessment of both aspects seems sensible. In this study, the focal point will be on metacognitive skills.

1.3.2. Development of Metacognitive Skills

In 1987, Garner wrote: "Though we do not have a theory of the developmental mechanisms that move relatively acknowledgeable, non-monitoring, strategically naïve individuals to a more metacognitively sophisticated state, we do have a rich research base documenting that the movement occurs." (p. 31). Since the time of this statement, more research has been done on the development of metacognition. Veenman et al. (2006) summarize recent findings in describing a general developmental sequence. They give notice of a theory of mind developing between the ages of three to five years. In the years after that, metamemory and metacognitive knowledge develop and continue to do so throughout life. At the age of eight to ten years metacognitive skills seem to emerge[2], expanding in the years thereafter. The authors note that certain metacognitive skills, such as monitoring and evaluation, seem to mature later than others.

Hacker (1998) states that with increasing age, people gain in both the amount of knowledge they can hold in memory as in the accuracy of the skills that monitor their knowledge. Likewise, De Jong (1992) cites several studies from which can be concluded that as students (mostly elementary-school children) grow older, their metacognitive knowledge and skills expand.

Kreuzer, Leonard, Flavell and Hagen (1975) for instance, found results which indicated that older children (9-11 years) possess a greater variety of memory strategies and exhibit more systematic thought processes than their younger counterparts (6-7 years) in verbalizing how certain classes of variables interact regarding a retrieval problem. Zimmerman (1989) concludes that older students more frequently take notes, re-read these notes more often, pay more attention to process monitoring and organize their learning more efficiently than younger children.

Alexander et al. (1995) agree that it is likely that metacognition develops over time as a result of children gaining more experience because their experiences will help them to represent factual knowledge about cognitive processes more abstractly and will help them gain superior control over their mental activity. Additionally, as Carr and Biddlecomb (1998) indicate, the development of metacognitive skills of children is influenced by children's social interactions with peers and adults.

The results of a study on secondary school students between around 12-15 years by Veenman and Spaans (2005a) suggest that metacognitive skills, measured by means of systematic observation of thinking-aloud protocols and the assessment of computer log files, initially develop in separate domains (i.e., domain specific) among the first year students, but later on become a more general factor. Shraw and Graham (1997) note that one can expect metacognitive knowledge and regulation to increase as knowledge and expertise within a domain develop. As students initially acquire metacognitive knowledge and skills in different domains, they proceed to construct more general metacognition across domains because they learn how to use their knowledge and skills in a more flexible, less domain-bound manner.

Alexander et al. (1995) have not only assessed the development of metacognition tied to age, but in addition have proposed four possible models for the development of metacognition in relation to intelligence. They elaborated multiple possible hypotheses concerning this development. One is the model of metacognitive abilities that develop in a monotonic fashion, parallel to the increase of intellectual abilities over the years; "the monotonic development hypothesis". In this model, children of high intelligence will maintain monotonic superiority over children of lower intelligence throughout life. Another possible model is provided by the "acceleration hypothesis" in which we see effects of higher intelligence becoming larger with age. The third hypothesis posed is the "ceiling hypothesis" that states that highly intelligent children develop metacognitive skills faster, but effects diminish over time with lower intelligence children catching up eventually. Finally, if there were no coherence between intelligence and metacognitive skills, Alexander, 1995 et al. state,

---

[2] Veenman et al. (2006) add that it is probably more likely that metacognitive knowledge and skills already begin to develop as early as in preschool or early-elementary school years on a very basic level, but only become apparent when educational demands require more direct usage of this repertoire.

no separate theory would be needed. The review of empirical evidence by Alexander, 1995 et al. predominantly suggests acceleration or alternatively, a monotonic relationship between intelligence and metacognition. The monotonic hypothesis seems to be the explanation most in line with the ideas of general intelligence theorists, but most previous research lending support for this hypothesis was done on average and retarded children, and much less on children of high ability. On the issue of strategy use some evidence was found suggesting a possible acceleration hypothesis. Cognitive monitoring, seemed to be similarly difficult for children across intellectual boundaries.

Veenman et al. (2004) found in their research on fourth (mean age 9.5 years) and sixth graders (mean age 11.6 years), that intelligence gave children a head start in metacognitive skilfulness, but did not affect the course of its development, which supports the monotonic hypothesis. In addition, results of Veenman and Spaans (2005a) suggested that metacognitive skills increased with age in a monotonic fashion. Therefore the ceiling and acceleration hypotheses were rejected. Shraw and Graham (1997) argue that metacognitive knowledge and control processes might develop following different trajectories. Though metacognitive knowledge seems to grow monotonic in line with intellectual ability, control processes such as strategy use, on the other hand appear to be more in line with an accelerated growth trend.

Recapitulating the developmental insights discussed in this paragraph, we can expect the students in our empirical study, who have a mean age of 12.4, to be in the initial phase of their development of metacognitive skills. From the findings described by Veenman et al. (2006), it is expected that especially the monitoring and evaluation skills will show minimal development in our sample.

1.3.3. Measuring Metacognitive Skills

In measuring metacognitive skills, most often verbal report techniques are used. These techniques comprise off-line and on-line methods. Off-line methods frequently used in research on metacognitive skills are questionnaires or interviews (compare Chan, 1996; Jakobs, & Paris, 1987; Malpass, et al., 1999; Minnaert & Janssen, 1999; Perleth, 1992; Swanson, 1992; Yore & Craig, 1992). These off-line methods have the advantage that the collection of data is simple and takes relatively less time. Interviews have the additional advantage that it is possible to continue questioning until the meaning of the answer is clear. Disadvantages of both methods however, are the possibility that learners may have forgotten, or simply might not mention, several relevant learning activities. Also, the effects of reflection-skills of students and social pressure may influence the responses. Questionnaires appear to be less suitable for elementary school pupils (Van-Hout-Wolters, 2000).

An on-line method, which is used in assessment of metacognition, is the "thinking-aloud method" in which the students are asked to think aloud during the performance of a task (compare Swanson, 1990; Veenman et al. 1997; 2000; 2004; 2005a;b). The thinking aloud of the subjects is usually recorded and transcribed. These transcriptions are then judged on metacognitive verbalizations. This method is typically used in research but not often in educational practice. Assessment by means of thinking aloud protocols, in which information is gathered during the learning activities, has the advantage that little information is lost (Van Hout-Wolters, 2000). Prins, Veenman and Elshout (2006) argue that the assessment of thinking aloud protocols is suitable for novice as well as advanced learners, as long as the task used is complex enough to prevent automatic execution. Disadvantages of thinking-aloud protocols are found in the fact that the gathering and analyses of data is relatively complex and time-consuming. Therefore, this on-line method is not frequently applied to large groups of subjects. Besides, these measures may also be influenced by social desirability (Van Hout-Wolters, 2000). Additionally, one may argue that on-line measures disrupt and delay learning. However as, among others, Veenman et al. (2005b) argue, merely thinking aloud does not seem to interfere with cognitive and metacognitive processes. Possible exceptions for this statement may be found in thinking aloud assignments over scattered episodes or during strongly routinely executed tasks (Van Hout-Wolters, 2006). Another on-line method which was for instance used by Veenman et al. (2005a, 2004), is the analysis of computer log-files. In this method, the learning of the student is assessed in terms of the duration, quantity, and sequence of working through the computer-task. An advantage of this method is the fact that the data can be gathered on-line relatively easy for larger groups of students, while the learning process is not or minimally disturbed. A weakness of this method, however, is that it only provides quantitative data which can, at most, provide indications of metacognitive activities. Besides, the fact that the tasks are executed on the computer may cause bias, because in education the usage of books is still a more common practice than computer-based learning (van-Hout-Wolters, 2006).

In a review of comparisons of different on-line and off-line methods, Van Hout-Wolters (2006) remarks that on-line methods generally show highly correlated results (compare Veenman et al. 2005b). This is also true for think-aloud protocols in comparison with computer log-files. However, the general off-line questionnaires on learning show low correlations with the on-line thinking-aloud measurements, and the relationship between more specific questionnaires and thinking aloud measures are equivocal. Possibly, off-line methods confer a less clear reflection of the learning activities, or the low correlations are due to the fact that on-line and off-line assessments tend to measure somewhat different constructs. As we have seen, both on-line and off-line methods have their strengths and weaknesses. Van Hout-Wolters (2006; 2000) suggests that we make several practical and content-based considerations when choosing a particular method. Examples of possible concerns are the goal of the assessment, the content referring to the skills and domains to be assessed, the target group, the type of data one wants to collect, and the assessment procedure of preference.

Reflecting on the data collected for the current study, the young age of the children in our sample renders the questionnaire a less suitable measurement instrument. In addition, the fact that, as we have seen in the previous paragraph, the children in our sample are in an early phase of development of skills and will probably show few metacognitive activities makes an on-line method more appropriate. This choice guarantees that the least amount of scarce data will be lost. Veenman et al. (2000) proposed an instrument for systematic observation of thinking-aloud measurements to replace the time-consuming intensive full protocol analysis. Observation using the systematic measure by means of the assessment by means of a list of metacognitive activities, can be executed more efficiently and less laboriously.

Veenman et al. (2000; 2005b) validated this list in a study where the full transcription of thinking aloud protocols were put together with results found using the systematic observation procedure. The two measurements proved to be highly correlated, providing support for the view that measurement using only the systematic observation measure, may adequately replace the method of full transcription. Having taken note of this, the choice was made to indeed assess metacognitive skills through the 'thinking aloud method' using only the systematical observation method in this study.

The sort of skills we want to assess will also be of influence for the measurement method (Van Hout-Wolters, 2006). Veenman et al. (2005b; 2004; 2000) described various important metacognitive activities during different phases of problem solving. For instance, before beginning with a task, a thorough task orientation or task analyses will help a student focus on relevant information in order to be able to build an adequate (mental) representation of the task. While keeping that information in mind, designing an action plan will give the possibility for systematic control of the process. During the execution of the task, a systematic working method may help the student keep track of the progress. Evaluation and monitoring activities may also be used to detect faulty procedures and mistakes. After problem solving has occurred, elaboration activities such as drawing conclusions and reflecting can be valuable for future performance (Veenman et al., 2005b; 2004; 2000).

Van Hout-Wolters (2006) agrees that metacognitive skills contain activities across the phases of orientation, planning, monitoring, adjustment, evaluating and reflecting. Earlier studies also represent a great deal of these categories summed up by Veenman et al. and Van Hout-Wolters. Shraw and Graham (1997), Swanson (1992) and Yore and Craig (1992) cite Jacobs and Paris on three essential phases being exhibited during metacognitive control processes: planning, monitoring and evaluation (see Jacobs, & Paris, 1987). In line with the previous research, Hong (1999) refers to metacognitive activity consisting of acts such as planning or goal-setting and solution monitoring. Minnaert and Janssen (1999) in their study use a metacognitive questionnaire with questions referring to activities in the phases of goal-setting, orienting, planning, monitoring, testing, diagnosing, on-line regulating, evaluating and reflecting. Malpass, et al. (1999) define state metacognition as consisting of awareness, planning, self-checking, and the use of task-relevant cognitive strategies. The systematic observation instrument proposed by Veenman et al. (2000) seems appropriate for reflection on metacognitive skills across important phases in problem-solving processes drawing on the distinctions described above. It discerns metacognitive activities within the phases orientation, systematic orderliness, evaluation and reflection.

Besides choosing the measurement method, it is also necessary to choose a task during which the thinking-aloud measurement can take place. It is expected that, in giving children the freedom to choose their own task from several options of varying complexity, children will be capable of selecting a problem appropriate for their own "threshold of problematicity". The theory of the threshold of problematicity assumes that intelligence has a varying impact on performance depending on task complexity. Following the considerations of Elshout (1987), the upper threshold of problematicity is seen as the point at which metacognitive skills begin to play a prominent role in the problem solving process. Tasks with a level of complexity below this threshold will lead to smooth, internalized and rapid problem solving. Above this threshold, that is, during more complex tasks, learners will be less able to depend solely on their task or domain specific abilities and will be urged to depend more on metacognitive skills to guide their learning process (Prins et al., 2006; Veenman et al., 2005b). Most recent support for the threshold of problematicity theory comes from Prins et al. (2006) who found that first year psychology students working with a computer environment of differing complexity, relied more on their metacognitive skilfulness than on their intellectual ability when operating at the boundary of their knowledge. Drawing on the notion of the threshold of problematicity, in our study different tasks varying in complexity were offered to the children to choose from. All tasks will be of a level that excludes pure automatic and internalized problem solving.

1.4. Cultural Orientations and Influences

Superior performance in learning is generally agreed on, not only to be determined by genetic factors, but by an interplay of cognitive, affective and social factors. Social and emotional issues can facilitate or, in fact, hamper the full use of one's abilities (Passow, Mönks & Heller, 1993). Aspects as self-concept and motivation (see e.g. Chan, 1996; De Corte, 1995; De Jong, 1992; Hacker, 1998; Mönks, 1992; Passow, et al., 1993; Perleth, Lehwald & Browder, 1993; Robinson, 1993; Sternberg, 2001), and family influences (Alexander et al., 1995; Passow et al., 1993; Perleth et al., 1993; Robinson, 2000; 1993; Shore & Kanevsky, 1993) are argued to influence performance.

Factors such as positive and supporting interactions, meaningful stimulation of learning, a variety of experiences, freedom and materials to play and experiment and real emotional support will be positive factors in the development of both abilities and metacognitive skills (Freeman, 1993). Moreover, another factor of interest that may influence metacognitive skills, as well as intellectual abilities, is "'culture". Culture is a package concept that comes as a whole. It influences patterns of relationships, undermining the universality of certain theories and models.

In the education of children from different cultural groups, as we see in most of our schools today, not only are advantages of diversity to be seen, but there are also quite a lot of problems concerning cultural differences. It seems that a variety of barriers exist in the education of minority (migrant) children from diverse cultural backgrounds. In the assessment of intelligence, school performance or any other concept in different cultural settings the validity of score comparisons has been - and still is - the focus of ample scientific research and debate (e.g., Jensen, 1985; Helms-Lorenz & Van de Vijver, 1995, Helms-Lorenz, Van de Vijver & Poortinga, 2003). Subject related factors that can influence test performance of natives and migrants are: verbal abilities, cultural norms and values, test-wiseness, and acculturation strategy. Most tests call for high verbal abilities and skills. Natives and migrants differ in mastery of the native language and cultural knowledge. Test instructions and item phrasing can unintentionally cause bias and reduce the validity of inferences drawn from score comparisons (e.g., Van de Vijver & Poortinga, 1997).

When using conventional test measures in a multicultural educational setting to identify high ability, Sternberg (2001) points out that not all cultures may value the sort of expertise measured by these tests equally. A study by Okagaki and Sternberg (1993) for instance, pointed out that Latino parents viewed social intelligence as being more important, while Asian and Anglo parents stressed cognitive intelligence more. Other factors that may possibly affect test performance are: motivation for success and familiarity with the kinds of tasks in the test. Passow et al. (1993) note that over-reliance on conventional intelligence tests may hinder the development of gifted minority students. In addition, they stress the fact that minority and disadvantaged students sometimes will need more social and affective support than they tend to be given in educational practice. Other possible obstacles mentioned by Frasier (1993) are: less experimental experiences, socioeconomic or racial isolation and deprivation and geographic living conditions. Through similar, and other cultural barriers, students from other cultures may be greatly underestimated. As Passow et al. remark, "currently, there is a clear and widespread recognition that minorities and disadvantaged populations around the world represent the largest reservoir of undeveloped potential available". (p. 899). Taylor (1993), for instance, cites principles for the measurement of giftedness in black secondary school children proposed by Tlale (1991) who suggests measuring metacognitive, as well as cognitive functions in identifying gifted black children. Moreover, as we have seen earlier, using the developing expertise model by Sternberg (2001) in assessment of abilities may prove useful in measuring different areas of expertise viewed from various focus points across cultures.

It is noteworthy that in different programs for the support of black pupils, for instance the Thinking Actively in a Social Context (TASC) program in Africa, the teaching of metacognitive skills is seen to be a great stimulating factor for the development of learning and abilities. This TASC program proceeds from different conceptions of intelligence from Vygotsky and Feuerstein to Sternberg's theory of intelligence. Children are taught how, and when, to use strategies, and are given ample practice in the application of skills and strategies that are significant and relevant to the learners. Several studies have shown that training metacognitive skills can benefit the working method and performance of students. For example, in the intervention-study by Verschaffel, De Corte, Lasure, Van Veerenberg, Bogaerts and Ratinckx (1999), the results point to a significant positive effect of a learning environment aimed at the development of metacognitive strategies in the mathematics curriculum which results in an increase in the upper elementary school pupils' problem solving skills. Furthermore, the metacognition-oriented mathematics method for heterogeneous classrooms 'IMPROVE' by Maverech and Kramarski (1997) showed that seventh grade students who had been working with the method, significantly outperformed the non-treatment control group on measures of mathematics achievement, particularly in mathematical reasoning. The students using this method were instructed in new concepts, metacognitive questioning, previewing, verification and reducing difficulties, and were supported in practice, obtaining of mastery, and enrichment. Veenman et al. (2006) remarked that in supporting students by providing metacognitive instruction, the instruction will have to be embedded in the content matter, must inform learners about the usefulness of metacognitive skills and the training should be of considerable duration to guarantee thorough and maintained appliance. They argue that all successful instructional programs should attend to explaining: What to do, When to do it, Why do it, and How to do it, the so-called "WWW&H rule". Bearing in mind that metacognitive skilfulness appears to positively affect the performance of minority students, similar metacognitive training programs can thus be useful in the stimulation of performance among children with different cultural backgrounds, provided that possible cultural barriers are taken into consideration in instruction and evaluation.

Building on previous findings, our study will not only consider differences among ability groups, but also cultural differences between natives and minorities. Our study will assess if metacognitive skills have an additive positive influence on performance, in addition to intelligence, across ability and cultural groups. A beneficial additive effect will point to the importance of stimulation of metacognitive skills in educational practice. Both a crystallized and a fluid intelligence measure will be used. Fluid measures, which measure nonverbal reasoning abilities, are seen to be especially valuable in evaluating minority and culturally different students who are limited in language skills (Feldhusen & Jarwan, 1993; Frasier, 1993; Perleth et al., 1993).

1.5. Interrelation between High Ability, Metacognitive Skills, and Performance

1.5.1. High Abilities and Metacognitive Skills

Various sources lend support to the idea that children with high abilities perform better in the area of metacognitive skills, although research does not support this idea uniformly. An imperative aspect of metacognitive skilfulness is the use of relevant metacognitive strategies. Veenman et al. (2005b) point out that several researchers have reported significant differences in metacognitive strategy use between highly intelligent and average students. In line with these findings, Sękowski (1995) cites various studies showing that gifted students are more likely to perform strategic actions such as identifying the problem, forming a representation of the information, determining the sources of knowledge, generating solution steps and monitoring problem-solving more accurately than students of lower abilities.; Gifted children seem to use strategies more efficiently and learn new strategies with greater ease. Perleth et al. (1993) cite a study of Waldmann and Weinert suggesting that gifted children use more and better strategies and are better able to substitute more favorable strategies for inappropriate ones if needed. The results of one of Perleth's own studies, using German intelligence tests to discern the gifted, indicate a small superiority of gifted children in grade four concerning strategy use (1992). Additionally, Shore (2000) remarks that elementary school children with higher IQ-scores seem to use more expert-like strategies, and use these strategies more consistently than their peers of lower intelligence.

In spite of these findings, evidence of gifted children having a general advantage in their use of strategies is not conclusive. Carr et al. (1996) argue that over half of the studies of elementary school children have found no giftedness effects on independent strategy use. Exceptions are formed in several studies finding giftedness effects when examining more complex strategies, as some of the studies mentioned above. Alexander et al. (1995) suggest that gifted and non-gifted children might have the same type of strategies in their repertoire, particularly the more simple ones, but gifted children may not always use them appropriately. They may even tend to over regulate their strategies to their disadvantage. Possibly, gifted children will learn to use their strategies in a superior way while they proceed through elementary school and will be able to gain advantage over their peers again towards high school. Perleth (1992) also discusses the contradictive results found in studies of strategy use of the gifted. He argues that the results might be influenced by the differential cultural backgrounds of the investigated samples. Besides, the way giftedness or high abilities is measured, differs across studies and this which may also influence findings (Van Hout-Wolters, 2006). However, following the suggestion of Alexander et al. (1995) that gifted children might regain an advantage towards high school, the expectation is fostered that the late elementary school children in our study might already have gained a small advantage over their low and average ability peers in metacognitive skilfulness.

1.5.2. Models Describing the Relationship between Ability, Metacognitive Skills and Performance

Veenman et al. (2005a;b; 2004; 1997) and Minnaert and Janssen (1999) have described the relationship between intellectual ability and metacognitive skilfulness as predictors of performance using multiple hypothetic models.

Schoolperformance

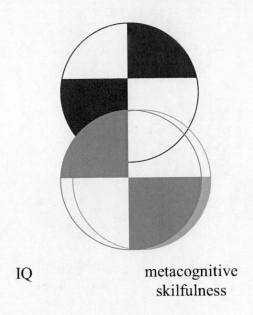

IQ   metacognitive
                         skilfulness

Figure 1.1. Intelligence model.

Schoolperformance

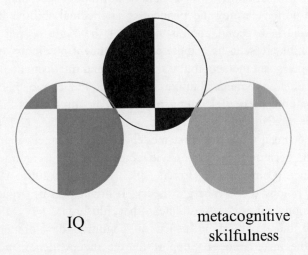

IQ   metacognitive
                         skilfulness

Figure 1.2. Independency model.

Schoolperformance

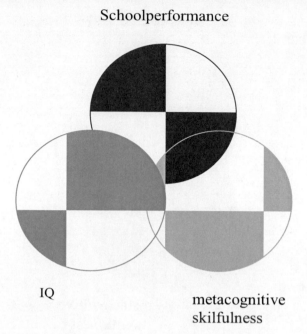

IQ   metacognitive
                                            skilfulness

Figure 1.3. Mixed model.

The first model, also referred to as the *intelligence model*, views metacognition as an integrated part of intellectual ability. Metacognitive skilfulness according to this view cannot have a predictive value for learning independent of intellectual abilities because the two are completely interwoven. In a second, contrasting model, the *independency model,* intelligence and metacognitive skills are seen as completely independent predictors of learning. Finally, the *mixed model* suggests that metacognitive skilfulness and intellectual abilities are related to some extent, but that use of metacognitive skills over and above this relationship has a surplus value in the prediction of learning outcomes. In the figures 1.1 to 1.3 schematic representations of the three models can be found.

According to Veenman et al. the first model is in accordance with the viewpoints of Brown and Sternberg, because these authors view metacognition as an integrated part of their theories of intelligence (Campione & Brown, 1978; Sternberg, 2001; 1994). We however, disagree with this typology of Sternberg's theory. It might also be argued that Sternberg's theory of developing expertise postulates that different key elements, including metacognition, have more or less influence on cognitive development differing across individuals, fitting the mixed model. Support for the independency model was found by Swanson (1990) who, using a metacognitive questionnaire for fourth and fifth grade children, concluded from the findings that it seems that measures of metacognition and abilities tap different forms of knowledge, with metacognition being a significant independent factor stimulating problem-solving. However, follow-up studies showed that metacognition was only partially independent of intelligence (Veenman et al., 2005b). For the mixed model, Veenman and others have found a considerable amount of support, although one must bear in mind that the different instruments for assessment of intelligence, performance and metacognitive skills may cause some bias across comparisons (van Hout-Wolters, 2006). For instance, the study of Veenman et al. (1997) with psychology freshman, indicates that metacognitive skills are not entirely independent of intellectual abilities (measured by the Groninger Intelligence Test) but rather have an extra value, which seems to point to the mixed model. The data analyzed in the study of Minnaert and Janssen (1999), also researching metacognitive activities in freshmen, seemed to be in line with the mixed model as well, although the authors note that, considering the little common variance between intelligence measured by the "AH Group test of high level intelligence" and metacognitive skills, the evidence additionally seems somewhat in favour of the independency model.

Veenman et al. (2004), in their study concerning various age groups from elementary school to university, suggest through overall analysis across the age groups that the majority of results appear to fit the mixed model. Metacognitive skills in their study had an overall predictive value on top of abilities of an additional 14% of the variance. Results of other studies by Veenman et al. (2005a;b) also support the idea that metacognitive skilfulness, here measured by systematic observations and computer log-files, has a part of shared variance with intellectual abilities, but additionally, has it's own predictive value above that. A recent study by Prins et al. (2006) also found results resembling the mixed model. Veenman et al. (2006) state that on the average, intellectual ability will uniquely account for approximately ten percent of variance in learning. The proportion of overlap between intellectual ability and metacognitive skilfulness together will predict about twenty percent of the variance, and metacognition alone will generally have a surplus value in predicting variance in learning performance of around seventeen percent. However, caution is required in the assessment of the relationships between these three factors because, as we have seen in previous paragraphs, other factors for instance, development across ages, domain knowledge and culture, may have mediating influences on the relationships.

Reflecting on the fact that several researchers agree that metacognitive instruction can make meaningful contributions in stimulating performance across different domains (Alexander & Schwanenflugel, 1996; Carr, et al., 1996; De Corte, 1995; Prins et al., 2006; Yore & Craig, 1992), instructional support aimed at stimulating metacognitive skillfulness might therefore in the future prove to be a useful tool in compensating for students' cognitive limitations (Veenman et al., 2006; Alexander & Schwanenflugel, 1996). To investigate possible support for a surplus value of metacognitive skillfulness above intelligence, following the mixed model, or respectively support for one of the other models, the assumptions made in the models will be examined for the sample of our study.

1.6. Research Questions

Having come to various conclusions for our study from the theoretical findings throughout this chapter, our empirical study was designed as follows: the study would assess the metacognitive skills for children of differential intelligence groups, particularly focusing on the skillfulness of children of high ability. Intellectual ability was seen as partly a fixed and partly a dynamic characteristic of individuals which leads to the application of both a more static, crystallized- and a more dynamic, fluid intelligence measure. The fluid measure was viewed as the intelligence measure with relative low cultural loading. Regarding metacognition, the focus will be on the measurement of metacognitive skills using an instrument for systematic observation of thinking aloud protocols. In this, metacognitive behaviour across different problem-solving phases was assessed during the execution of a self-chosen task. Drawing on the 'developing expertise model' by Sternberg, performance measures are seen to measure the degree of expertise children have from an academic viewpoint.

It was expected that, even though metacognitive skilfulness may only be in an early awakening phase of development for late elementary school children comprising the sample, children of high ability might show a small advantage in metacognitive skills over their peers of lower intelligence. Possibly, the scores on monitoring and evaluation activities would be low across ability groups reflecting on the possible later development of such skills. Assumedly, metacognitive skilfulness will have a surplus value above intelligence in prediction of performance. However, cultural barriers in the migrant group might lead to cultural differences across the metacognitive, intelligence and performance measures.

These aspects will be assessed by means of three research-questions:

1. Do students of comparable intelligence across the native and migrant sample score alike on overall metacognitive-skill measurements, or are there cross-cultural differences to be perceived?
2. Are there dissimilarities between the high intelligent group and the other intelligence groups according to the quantity and distribution of metacognitive skill-scores across the different phases of metacognitive activities (orientation, systematic orderliness, evaluation and reflection) and are there cultural differences in this?
3. Which relationship is there between (high) abilities, metacognitive skills and school-performance; does metacognitive skilfulness have an additive predictive value for school-performance on top of intelligence?

2. METHOD

2.1. Sample

All subjects were in their final elementary school year with an average age of 12.1 for the native, and 12.5 for the migrant group. The sample in this study consisted of 103 children; 34 native and 69 migrant. 86 children were born in the Netherlands, 1 in Morocco, 1 in another African country, 3 in Suriname, 2 in an Asian country, 2 in Afghanistan, 2 in Iraq, and for 8 subjects the birth country was unknown. The sample consisted of 57 boys and 46 girls. The children were in their last elementary school year and had a mean age of 12.4 (SD = .53).

2.2. Intellectual Ability

Two intelligence tests were administered: the RAVEN Standard Progressive Matrices and the NIO (Nederlandse Intelligentietest voor Onderwijsniveau). These tests were administered in groups (school classes). The NIO test was evaluated and judged as 'good' on quality of the test material, quality of the manual, norms, test reliability, construct validity, and criterion validity by an independent test screening organization in the Netherlands (Commissie Testaangelegenheden Nederland, of the Dutch Institute for Psychology). From the NIO test, three scores are derived: NIO total, NIO verbal and NIO symbolic. The RAVEN test measures nonverbal reasoning abilities and is seen to be especially valuable in evaluating students who are limited in the dominant language skills (Feldhusen & Jarwan, 1993; Frasier, 1993; Perleth et al., 1993). RAVEN is categorized as a more fluid measure of intelligence since fluid intelligence is defined as the ability to reason and to solve problems (Jensen, 1985), while NIO primarily represents crystallized intelligence representing acquired information influenced by the educational and socio-economic backgrounds of children (compare Minnaert and Janssen, 1999). On the RAVEN test a mean score of 44.72 (SD = 6.49) was obtained, and the mean on the total NIO test was 95.76 (SD = 17.00).

In order to enable comparisons between children of differential abilities, the subjects were spread over a low- (20%), average- (60%), and high (20%) intelligence groups using the frequency distributions of both the RAVEN and the NIO measure of the entire sample.

Admittedly, the percentage representing the high ability group (20%) in this study is a broader range than many researchers propose for comparisons with studies of gifted children in which the cut-off often fluctuates around 3-5%. However, there are researchers that suggest taking in a larger group than mere 3-5% in order to include subjects at the beginning level of the gifted category, being more in line with our distinction. For instance, Gagné (1993) suggests that "an appropriate threshold zone between the gifted or talented and the general population could be described as the top 15–20% of the population" (p. 82) with possibly within that distinction, room for division in different levels of giftedness. Renzulli accordingly argued that children only need to be in the top 20% of ability tests to have the necessary abilities for high achievement. Within that 20%, factors such as creative productivity and motivation come into play affecting possible excellent performance (Carr et al., 1996; Renzulli, 1992).

2.3. School Performance

As an academic performance measure, the scores on the Primary School Leaving test of the National Institute for Educational Measurement (CITO) was used. The test has a language, arithmetic, and an information section. Most schools administer this test around January in the final elementary school year. The mean CITO scores of subjects were used in analysis. On the CITO test, a mean score of 531.31 (SD = 11.35) was obtained in our sample

2.4. Metacognitive Skillfulness

As argued in paragraph 1.3.3, for the required measurements in our study an on-line thinking-aloud method was appropriate. Since Veenman et al. (2000) developed an instrument to systematically observe the thinking aloud protocols which has proven to be reliable, less time consuming and laborious than the usage of full protocol analysis (see paragraph 1.3.3); this instrument was chosen to measure metacognitive skills in our study. This instrument consists of a list of activities which are representative of metacognitive skilfulness in general, and particularly for metacognitive skilfulness during mathematical problem-solving. These activities contain skills across different phases of the problem-solving process namely: orientation, systematic orderliness, evaluation and reflection. Thus, the instrument provided the opportunity to assess metacognitive skilfulness in all activities, and additionally, across different phases.

We chose to rate the activities on a five-point scale ranging from '0' (activity not present), through 1 (small initiation of activity), 2 (activity partly present), and 3 (activity present, but not executed to the fullest) to '4' (activity fully present). In order to enhance reliability, two judges performed the assessment together, discussing until agreement was reached (compare e.g. Veenman et al., 2005b; 2004; 2000). Activities were judged only on the quality of the metacognitive rendering, not on cognitive correctness. After the rating, sum scores were calculated for the whole range of activities, and additionally, for the series of activities representing different phases of the problem-solving process (i.e. orientation, systematic orderliness, evaluation, reflection).

The instrument of Veenman et al. (2005b, p. 200,201) which had been somewhat extended since the first version, was used in this study, consisting of the list of 15 activities shown below.

	Orientation phase					
1	Entirely reading the problem statement (as incomplete task analysis leads to trial-and-error behaviour);	0	1	2	3	4
2	Selection of relevant data (task analysis);	0	1	2	3	4
3	Paraphrasing of what was asked for (task analysis and goal setting);	0	1	2	3	4
4	Making a drawing related to the problem (task analysis);	0	1	2	3	4
5	Estimating a possible outcome (goal setting);	0	1	2	3	4
	Systematic orderliness					
6	Designing an action plan before actually calculating (planning);	0	1	2	3	4
7	Systematically carrying out such plan (to avoid haphazard behaviour);	0	1	2	3	4
8	Calculation correctness (avoid sloppiness);	0	1	2	3	4
9	Avoiding negligent mistakes (such as inattentively switching numbers);	0	1	2	3	4
10	Orderly note-taking of problem solving steps (in order to keep an overview of problem-solving steps and create an opportunity for checking outcomes);	0	1	2	3	4
	Evaluation phase					
11	Monitoring the on-going process;	0	1	2	3	4
12	Checking the answer;	0	1	2	3	4
	Reflection phase					
13	Drawing a conclusion (recapitulating);	0	1	2	3	4
14	Reflecting on the answer (referring to the problem statement);	0	1	2	3	4
15	Relating to earlier problems solved (reflection with the aim to learn from one's experiences).	0	1	2	3	4

Activities 1-5 represent a subjects' orientation to the problem. Activities 6-10 express the systematic orderliness shown during the task. Activities 11 and 12 outline evaluation processes, and lastly, activities 13-15 embody reflections after solving the problem. These groups of activities are referred to as phases of metacognitive skilfulness.

2.4.1. Metacognitive Task

In this study, mathematical problem solving tasks were presented to the sample. The mathematical tasks consisted of four different word problems varying in complexity, of which one problem had to be chosen to solve. The four tasks (Dutch version) can be found in Jacobse (2006). By giving the children the freedom to choose a task, it was assumed that they would select a problem appropriate for their own threshold of problematicity (see paragraph 1.3.3). After choosing the task, the child had to perform the mathematical word problem whilst thinking aloud. Individual video recordings were made for later assessment. Test leaders had been previously instructed to let the children perform the task independently. The comments they were permitted to make consisted of direct instructions prior to the problem solving, and reminders to the children to keep them thinking aloud. As we have seen in paragraph 1.3.3, merely thinking aloud generally does not interfere with cognitive and metacognitive processes. In Table 2.1, the percentage of the natives and migrants choosing each task is presented. Tasks 1 to 4 have an increasing level of complexity[3] (gas being the easiest, followed by wolf, followed by jaguar, and with balloon being the most difficult task).

Both the migrant and the native subjects of the low IQ group tended to choose the more difficult tasks. The native average IQ group slightly preferred the easier tasks, and the migrant average IQ slightly preferred the more difficult tasks. In both the native and migrant high ability group, roughly one third of the group preferred to do the easier tasks. In Table 2.2 the mean metacognitive scores and standard deviations of the natives and the migrants are tabulated per chosen task and RAVEN IQ level.

In searching for the most appropriate task per ability level the assumption was made that an appropriate task (at the threshold of problematicity) should elicit higher metacognitive scores with low dispersion (SD) compared to less appropriate tasks. No clear pattern emerges from Table 2.2. The highest mean metacognitive sumscores often have the greatest variance. The inspection is not fully possible since the low IQ group did not choose to do the easiest task. For the high ability group, the highest mean metacognitive sum scores were obtained for the easier tasks accompanied by the highest standard deviations. Valid conclusions as to the most appropriate task per ability group based on these results are therefore not possible.

**Table 2.1. Native (left) and migrant (right) task choices (in percentages)
for three ability levels**

RAVEN IQ level	Native				Migrant			
	GAS	WOLF	JAGUAR	BALLOON	GAS	WOLF	JAGUAR	BALLOON
Low		28.6	71.4		4.2	8.3	70.8	16.7
Average	44.4	11.1	22.2	22.2	22.2	14.8	55.6	7.4
High	14.3	14.3	47.6	23.8	10	20	55	15

---

3 The complexity was rated by two judges who counted the number of mental operations needed to solve the problems.

Table 2.2. Mean metacognitive scores (and standard deviations) of native (left) and migrant (right) per chosen task for three ability levels

RAVEN IQ level	Native				Migrant			
	GAS	WOLF	JAGUAR	BALLOON	GAS	WOLF	JAGUAR	BALLOON
Low		5 (2.8)	7.8 (2.9)		19	10.5 (.71)	8.7 (4.4)	11 (8,2)
Average	16.7 (8.6)	13	5 (1.4)	10 (0)	17,5 (6.2)	10 (2.2)	11.5 (5.7)	4.5 (2.1)
High	14.7 (4.0)	20 (4.4)	13.5 (6.4)	15.4 (2.9)	19.5 (7.8)	11.2 (2.9)	12.7 (4.8)	8.7 (2.1)

2.5. Information on Individual Background

Information on background variables concerning age, gender and culture were gathered and used.

Table 3.1. Correlational matrix of performance, ability, and metacognitive skill measures of natives (below the diagonal) and migrants (above the diagonal)

	Mean CITO	RAVEN total	NIO total	NIO verbal	NIO symbolic	Sumscore mc
mean CITO	–	.252*	.707**	.703**	.585**	.363**
	.	.045	.000	.000	.000	.003
	31	64	61	61	61	66
RAVEN total	.773**	–	.308*	.289*	.286*	.204
	.000	.	.015	.023	.024	.098
	31	34	62	62	62	67
NIO total	.855**	.792**	–	.938**	.908**	.243
	.000	.000	.	.000	.000	.053
	31	34	34	64	64	64
NIO verbal	.779**	.679**	.921**	–	.707**	.435*
	.000	.000	.000	.	.000	.010
	31	34	34	34	64	34
NIO symbolic	.775**	.774**	.908**	.673**	–	.546**
	.000	.000	.000	.000	.	.001
	31	34	34	34	34	34
Sumscore mc	.524**	.516**	.535**	.212	.239	–
	.002	.002	.001	.093	.057	–
	31	34	34	64	64	34

Note: Performance measure: mean CITO = mean score on CITO test, ability measures: RAVEN total = total RAVEN score, NIO total = total NIO score, NIO verbal = score on NIO verbal, NIO symbolic = score on NIO symbolic, metacognitive skill measure: Sumscore mc = sumscore on metacognitive skills.
** Correlation is significant at the 0.01 level (2-tailed).
* Correlation is significant at the 0.05 level (2-tailed).

3. RESULTS

In Table 3.1 correlations of the native and the migrant sample between the performance, ability, and metacognitive skill measures are presented.

For the native sample, the fluid and crystallized intelligence measures RAVEN and NIO total, verbal, and symbolic, are all significantly correlated at the .01 level, and for the migrant sample, the two intelligence measures are significantly correlated at the .05 level. In the migrant group, no significant correlations were found between the RAVEN and the NIO total with the metacognitive skill measure. In the native group, this measure does not significantly correlate with the verbal and the symbolic part of the NIO. Drawing upon this finding in both groups the fluid and crystallized measures show significant correlations, liberty was taken to occasionally merely perform analysis using one of the intelligence measures; the RAVEN, specifically in reference to it's presumed low cultural loading.

3.1. Cross-cultural Differences regarding Metacognitive Skill Scores

Assessment of differences between the cultural groups on the metacognitive skill measured by means of an independent samples t-test, points out that the difference between natives and migrants in the low ability group is just short of significance with a p value of .07, in favour of the migrants. In the average- and high ability groups, no significant differences were found. This is illustrated in Figure 3.1.

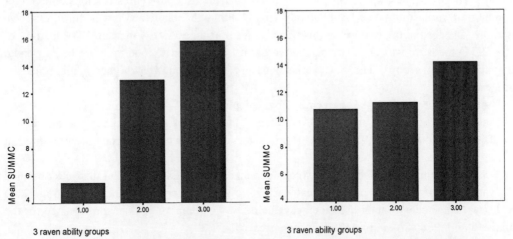

Note: x: RAVEN low (1), average(2), and high(3) ability group, y: mean metacognitive skill score.

Figure 3.1. Graphic representation of mean scores on the whole metacognitive skill measure across RAVEN ability groups per cultural group; natives (left) and migrants (right).

**Table 3.2. Explanatory factor analysis: factor loadings
of natives (left) and migrants (right)**

	Component		Component
	1		1
mean CITO	.916	mean CITO	.826
RAVEN total	.879	RAVEN total	.384
NIO total	.970	NIO total	.970
NIO verbal	.859	NIO verbal	.913
NIO symbolic	.896	NIO symbolic	.872
Sumscore mc	.637	Sumscore mc	.376

Note: Performance measure: mean CITO = mean score on CITO test, ability measures: RAVEN total =
total RAVEN score, NIO total = total NIO score, NIO verbal = score on NIO verbal, NIO symbolic
= score on NIO symbolic, metacognitive skill measure: Sumscore mc = sumscore on metacognitive
skills.

Exploratory factor analysis was performed to determine the factor structure of the
cognitive and metacognitive measures. The extraction method was a principal component
analysis with the rotation method varimax. One component was extracted for the native as
well as the migrant sample. The component of the natives has a total eigenvalue of 4.499
explaining 75% of the variance, and for the migrant group a total eigenvalue on the first
component of 3.506 explaining 58% of the variance. In both representations, the factor
loading of metacognition was relatively small, although somewhat larger for the native
sample, and for the migrant group this was also true for the RAVEN measure. The loading of
the CITO measure was larger for the native group, with the NIO total measure having equal
impact in both groups. The NIO verbal measure has a somewhat higher loading for the
migrant group.

Assessment of factorial agreement by calculation of Tucker's phi (Tucker, 1951),
revealed that the factors of both the native and the migrant group are comparable with a
coefficients per factor of .95 and .94. The factor loadings per cultural group are presented in
Table 3.2.

When forcing the extraction of two components, the rotated component matrices obtained
by varimax rotation with Kaizer normalization, show the following picture presented in Table
3.3. Here, the second factor has an eigenvalue of .684 explaining 11% of the variance for the
natives, and .968 explaining 16% for the migrants.

When a division over two components takes place, for the native sample the variables
composing the first component are the CITO and NIO measures. The contribution of
metacognition is relatively small for the first factor. Within the second extracted component
of the native group, metacognition has the greatest contribution influence. This is also true for
the migrant group in which the first component is also mainly affected by the CITO and NIO
measures while the metacognitive measure, and additionally the RAVEN component, have
the highest loading on the second factor.

Table 3.3. Explanatory factor analysis:
component matrix of natives (left) and migrants (right)

	Component				Component	
	1	2			1	2
mean CITO	.857	.330		mean CITO	.768	.305
RAVEN total	.796	.372		RAVEN total	.188	.606
NIO total	.945	.272		NIO total	.977	.151
NIO verbal	.904	.09		NIO verbal	.913	.159
NIO symbolic	.807	.390		NIO symbolic	.886	.116
Sumscore mc	.252	.952		Sumscore mc	.08	.863

Note: Performance measure: mean CITO = mean score on CITO test, ability measures: RAVEN total = total RAVEN score, NIO total = total NIO score, NIO verbal = score on NIO verbal, NIO symbolic = score on NIO symbolic, metacognitive skill measure: Sumscore mc = sumscore on metacognitive skills.

3.2. Differences in Quantity and Distribution of Metacognitive Skill Scores

To assess the quantity and distribution of metacognition-scores across the different phases as used by Veenman et al. (e.g. 2005b), descriptives were calculated for the different ability groups (RAVEN) for both natives and migrants. Graphic representations of the differences across phases are shown below in Figure 3.2 through Figure 3.5.

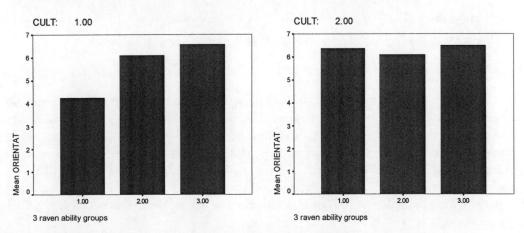

Note: x: RAVEN ability groups; low (1),average (2),high (3), y: mean orientation score.

Figure 3.2. Orientation phase scores of natives (left) and migrants (right) by ability group.

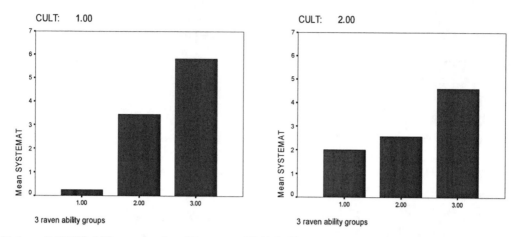

Note: x: RAVEN ability groups; low (1),average (2),high (3), y: mean systematical orderliness score.

Figure 3.3. Systematic orderliness phase scores of natives (left) and migrants (right) by ability group.

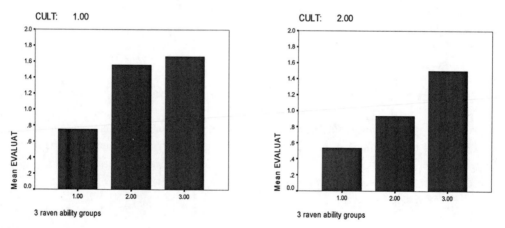

Note: x: RAVEN ability groups; low (1),average (2),high (3), y: mean evaluation score.

Figure 3.4. Evaluation phase scores of natives (left) and migrants (right) by ability group.

During the orientation phase, in which a maximum of 20 points was possible, the graphic representation of mean scores reveals some differences in scores across cultural and ability groups, with students of the high ability group across cultures attaining the largest mean scores. However, an independent samples t-test reveals that all the differences on orientation scores are not significant. In further assessment of differences between ability-groups by means of a one-way ANOVA, the advantage of the high ability group as a whole appears not to be significantly higher in reference to the scores of the of the average- and low ability group.

In terms of systematic order, the maximum possible score is also 20 points. The low ability migrant group scores higher than the low ability native group with a mean score of 2.00 (SD = 2.58) versus .25 (SD = .50) respectively. An independent samples t-test reveals that the difference between the migrant and the native low ability groups is significant (p=.02). The difference between the native and the migrant high- and average ability groups is not significant. Across the ability groups, the high ability group yields significantly higher scores than the average- (p = .01) and low ability (p = .00) groups, as calculated by means of a one-way ANOVA.

In the evaluation phase, a maximum of 8 points could be attained. The low ability native and migrant group mean scores were both beneath one point, and the mean score of the average migrant group was also small (.93, SD = 1.14). The average native group had a mean of 1.56 (SD = 1.65) on evaluation activities. The differences between scores of the natives and migrants in the average group, assessed through means of an independent samples t-test, are just short of being significant (p = .07). Between the other ability groups, differences yielded no significance. Analyzing the differences between the ability groups using one-way ANOVA, reveals a close to significant advantage of the high ability group over the low ability group (p = .07), but not over the average ability group.

The reflection phase mean scores produce a quite different pattern compared to other phases which, excluded one exception in the orientation phase for the migrant group, all have a rising pattern as ability increases. Here a maximum of 12 points could be obtained. An independent samples t-test points out that the cultural differences between the average- (p = .07) and the high (p = .09) ability group are just short of significance in favour of the native group. The average ability natives yielding a mean sore of 1.89 (SD = 1.49) and the migrants of 1.61 (SD = 1.67). Within the high ability group, the natives have a mean score of 1.75 (SD = 1.60), and the migrant children of high ability obtained a mean score of 1.60 (SD = .84). However, a one-way ANOVA showed no significant benefits of the high ability group over the other groups.

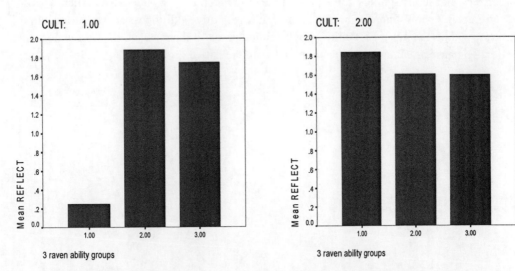

Note: x: RAVEN ability groups; low (1),average (2),high (3), y: mean reflection score.

Figure 3.5. Reflection phase scores of natives (left) and migrants (right) by ability group.

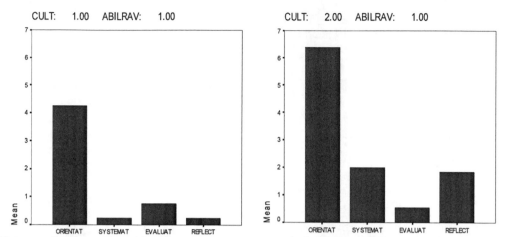

Note: x: orientat = orientation phase, systemat = systematical orderliness phase, evaluat = evaluation phase, reflect = reflection phase, y: mean score.

Figure 3.6. Distribution of mean metacognitive skill scores of RAVEN low ability group of natives (left) and migrants (right).

To provide a combined picture of the findings described above across phases, see graphs as presented in Figures 3.6 through 3.8. Figure 3.6 shows that although differences are small, the pattern of scores on systematic orderliness, evaluation and reflection is somewhat different for natives and migrants in the low ability group. The difference in the systematic orderliness phase, is significant in favour of the migrant children as indicated earlier.

Figure 3.7 shows more similarity in mean metacognitive skilfulness scores across cultural groups within the average ability group, although dissimilarities in the evaluation- and reflection phase are almost significant in favour of the native group.

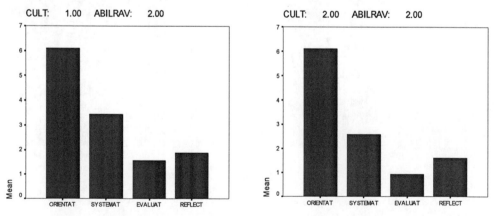

Note: x: orientat = orientation phase, systemat = systematical orderliness phase, evaluat = evaluation phase, reflect = reflection phase, y: mean score.

Figure 3.7. Distribution of mean metacognitive skill scores of RAVEN average ability group of natives (left) and migrants (right).

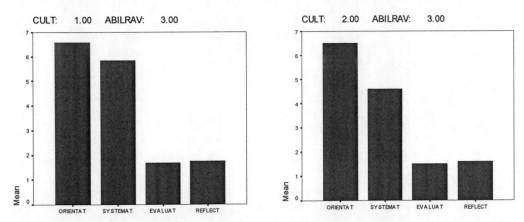

Note: x: orientat = orientation phase, systemat = systematical orderliness phase, evaluat = evaluation
    phase, reflect = reflection phase, y: mean score.

Figure 3.8. Distribution of mean metacognitive skill scores RAVEN high ability group of natives (left)
and migrants (right).

Moreover, as illustrated in figure 3.8, the high ability group shows a quite similar pattern
of mean metacognitive skill scores for both natives and migrants, although the natives have a
close to significant benefit in the reflection phase.

In comparing the distribution of scores across ability groups, it is apparent that in all
ability groups, the orientation activities yield relatively high scores. On the other hand,
particularly the scores in the evaluation and the reflection phase are relatively small. The only
phase in which the pattern of the high ability group as a whole shows a clear advantage is the
systematic orderliness phase, consisting of activities like planning and note-taking, in which
significant differences in favour of the high ability group were found.

3.3. Interrelationship between High Abilities, Metacognitive Skills and School-Performance

Using the method employed by Veenman et al. (2005a;b; 2004; 1997), a correlational
analysis among the different intelligence measures is performed. Some relevant correlations
which were already discussed above were utilized; additionally the semi-partial correlations
were calculated to investigate the individual effects of intelligence and metacognitive
activities on the performance measure. Also, the shared variance was calculated: r^2 shared $= r^2$
total $-$ (semi-part MC) ^{2} - (semi-part IQ) ^{2}. The results are presented in Table 3.4.

For migrants, metacognitive skilfulness was found to have unique significant value,
reflected by the semi-partial metacognitive skill score, in predicting CITO scores whilst
controlling for RAVEN scores (at the .01 level), and both parts of the NIO test (at the .05
level), while the total NIO test yielded a almost significant value with a p of .06. Reflecting
on the portion of shared variance of the different measures (r^2 shared), it seems that for the
migrant children, intelligence and metacognitive skill measures generally have less variance
in common, suggesting greater independence of those two factors in the prediction of school
performance than found in the native sample.

Table 3.4. Correlational analysis of intelligence measures, metacognitive skills and performance

Natives

	IQ	MC	Semi-part mc	Semi-part IQ	R² Shared
RAVEN IQ					
CITO	.77**	.52**	.24	.69**	.12
MC	.52**				
NIO IQ					
CITO	.86**	.52**	.20	.80**	.09
MC	.54**				
NIO Verbal IQ					
CITO	.78**	.52**	.38*	.73**	.07
MC	.44*				
NIO Symbolic IQ					
CITO	.78**	.52**	.22	.69**	.12
MC	.55**				

Migrants

	IQ	MC	Semi-part mc	Semi-part IQ	R² Shared
RAVEN IQ					
CITO	.25*	.36**	.35**	.19	.03
MC	.20				
NIO IQ					
CITO	.71**	.36**	.25 (p .06)	.69**	.03
MC	.24				
NIO Verbal IQ					
CITO	.70**	.36**	.27*	.69**	.02
MC	.21				
NIO symbolic IQ					
CITO	.59**	.36**	.26*	.56**	.03
MC	.24				

Performance measure: CITO, ability measures: RAVEN, NIO (total), NIO verbal, NIO symbolic, metacognitive skill measure: mc.

** Correlation is significant at the 0.01 level (2-tailed).

* Correlation is significant at the 0.05 level (2-tailed).

Table 3.5. Analysis of variance for subjects in the RAVEN low, average and high ability-groups with low or high metacognitive skills

RAVEN IQ	LOW MC (SD)	HIGH MC (SD)	t-test
Low (whole group) (N = 11+ 4)	525.00 (10.0)	528.25 (9.6)	-.56
Low (natives) (N = 4 + 0)	521.25 (13.6)	-	-
Low (migrants) (N = 7 + 4)	527.14 (7.7)	528.25 (9.6)	-.21
Average (whole group) (N = 33 + 29)	524.76 (9.8)	534.00(8.9)	-3.88[**]
Average (natives) (N = 8 + 9)	533.25 (9.2)	538.11 (7.3)	-1.21
Average (migrants) (N = 25 + 20)	522.04 (8.4)	532.15 (9.0)	-3.88[**]
High (whole group) (N = 6 + 14)	542.17 (5.7)	542.36 (9.4)	-.05
High (natives) (N = 3 + 7)	545.00 (4.6)	547.86 (3.6)	-1.07
High (migrants) (N = 3 + 7)	539.33 (6.0)	536.86 (10.4)	.38

Low mc = low metacognitive skills (scores 0 - 11), high mc = high metacognitive skills (scores > 11).
[**] Correlation is significant at the 0.01 level (2-tailed).
[*] Correlation is significant at the 0.05 level (2-tailed).

Table 3.6. Analysis of variance for subjects in the NIO total low, average and high ability-groups with low or high metacognitive skills (low mc/high mc)

NIO IQ	LOW MC (SD)	HIGH MC (SD)	t-test
Low (whole group) (N = 13 + 2)	517.54 (6.8)	531.50 (10.6)	-2.57[*]
Low (natives) (N = 2 + 0)	517.0 (1.4)	-	-
Low (migrants) (N = 11 + 2)	517.64 (7.4)	531.50(10.6)	-2.33[*]
Average (whole group) (N = 31 + 29)	529.06 (8.7)	531.69 (9.1)	-1.15
Average (natives) (N = 9 + 8)	529.89 (10.4)	537.38 (7.5)	-1.68
Average (migrants) (N = 22 + 21)	528.73 (8.1)	529.52 (8.8)	-.31
High (whole group) (N = 4 + 13)	545.75 (4.0)	546.15 (4.3)	-.17
High (natives) (N = 4 + 8)	545.75 (4.0)	547.38 (3.62)	-.70
High (migrants) (N = 0 + 5)	-	544.20 (4.9)	-

Low mc = low metacognitive skills (scores 0 - 11), high mc = high metacognitive skills (scores > 11).
[**] Correlation is significant at the 0.01 level (2-tailed).
[*] Correlation is significant at the 0.05 level (2-tailed).

Table 3.7. Analysis of variance for subjects in the NIO verbal low, average and high ability-groups with low or high metacognitive skills (low mc/high mc)

NIO Verbal IQ	LOW MC (SD)	HIGH MC (SD)	t-test
Low (whole group) (N = 21 + 10)	518.90(6.5)	527.20 (8.9)	-2.95**
Low (natives) (N = 4 + 0)	516.0 (4.3)	-	-
Low (migrants) (N = 17 + 10)	519.59 (6.8)	527.20 (8.9)	-2.50**
Average (whole group) (N = 18 + 18)	530.78 (7.5)	531.89 (7.3)	-.45
Average (natives) (N = 5 + 7)	536.60 (5.9)	536.43 (7.5)	.04
Average (migrants) (N = 13 + 11)	528.54 (7.0)	529.00 (5.7)	-.18
High (whole group) (N = 9 + 16)	540.11 (8.4)	546.00 (4.1)	-2.36*
High (natives) (N = 6 + 9)	539.83 (9.8)	547.00 (3.6)	-2.04 (p .06)
High (migrants) (N = 3 + 7)	540.67 (6.7)	544.71 (4.7)	-1.11

Low mc = low metacognitive skills (scores 0 - 11), high mc = high metacognitive skills (scores > 11).
** Correlation is significant at the 0.01 level (2-tailed).
* Correlation is significant at the 0.05 level (2-tailed).

Additionally, calculations were made following a method used by Minnaert and Janssen (1999). In this analysis of variance, using intelligence measures and within that the associated ability groups, the additive stimulating effect of low or respectively high metacognitive skill scores is assessed. The distinction of high and low metacognitive skill scores is made by dividing the scores in two groups of approximately 50%, resulting in a group with low metacognitive skillfulness yielding scores between 0 and 11 (54%), and a high metacognitive skilful group with scores > 11 (51%). Calculations were made across the whole group and in addition over the group split for natives and migrants, although occasionally some of the measures for the spilt groups could not be calculated due to a small sample size. The findings are presented in Tables 3.5 through 3.8.

For the RAVEN average ability group, metacognitive skillfulness for the whole- and the migrant group had a significant effect on the CITO-scores. Assessing the total NIO test, metacognitive skills had significant value for performance scores for the low NIO ability group. Reviewing the findings on the NIO-verbal measure, metacognitive skilfulness has a significant additive effect on the whole, and migrant low NIO ability group, and, subsequently, on the total high ability group, while in the high ability native group, a close to significant effect (p .06) is found. Using the distinction by the NIO symbolic test, metacognitive skills were found to have only a significant additive effect on performance for children in the low ability group.

Table 3.8. Analysis of variance for subjects in the NIO symbolic low, average and high ability-groups with low or high metacognitive skills (low mc/high mc)

NIO Symbolic IQ	LOW MC (SD)	HIGH MC (SD)	t-test
Low (whole group) (N = 20 + 7)	519.30 (7.8)	527.71 (7.5)	-2.47[*]
Low (natives) (N = 4 + 0)	517.50 (6.6)	-	-
Low (migrants) (N = 16 + 7)	519.75 (8.2)	527.71 (7.5)	-2.19[*]
Average (whole group) (N = 16 + 18)	529.50 (7.5)	532.17 (10.1)	-.86
Average (natives) (N = 5 + 2)	534.60 (6.1)	535.50 (12.0)	-.14
Average (migrants) (N = 11 + 16)	527.18 (7.1)	531.75 (10.2)	-1.28
High (whole group) (N = 12 + 19)	537.83 (8.8)	542.58 (7.1)	-1.66
High (natives) (N = 6 + 14)	540.50 (10.8)	543.36 (7.0)	-.71
High (migrants) (N = 6 + 5)	535.17 (6.1)	540.40 (7.8)	-1.26

Low mc = low metacognitive skills (scores 0 - 11), high mc = high metacognitive skills (scores > 11).
[**] Correlation is significant at the 0.01 level (2-tailed).
[*] Correlation is significant at the 0.05 level (2-tailed).

4. CONCLUSION AND DISCUSSION

An attempt will be made to derive possible directions for the answers on the research questions by assessing our outcomes in the light of previous research findings, if available.

1. Do students of comparable intelligence across the native and migrant sample score alike on overall metacognitive-skill measurements, or are there cross-cultural differences to be perceived?

At first sight, the general pattern in mean scores on metacognitive skilfulness appears to be similar across the cultural groups in the average and high ability group by means of visual inspection of graphic representations of the scores. Also, the factor structure of both cultural groups is similar, as reflected in the factorial agreement between the two. On the other hand, a closer examination reveals more detailed information. When extracting two factors, metacognition loads on a second component in both cultural groups. Yet, in this bi-factorial solution the RAVEN test score behaves differently in both cultural groups. For the natives, the RAVEN test loads highly on the first factor and for the migrants it loads highly on the second factor. It seems to be that crystallized and fluid intelligence measures tap the same latent variable in the native group and different latent variables in the migrant group. To speak in Sternberg's terms, one can say that natives develop their true potential (fluid IQ) more than migrants do.

Although differences between the natives and the migrants in the average- and high ability group were not found to be significant, there is a tendency for natives to have slightly higher scores compared to migrant children. This was expected as is presumably the result of difficulties experienced in the area of the Dutch language, less familiarity with the Dutch cultural values and norms, lack of test taking skills and familiarity and inhibiting acculturation strategies. A specific dissimilarity across the cultural groups in metacognitive skilfulness was found. In the low-ability group, the migrant children showed an almost significant metacognitive advantage, yielding a mean score of about twice the size of the score of the native sample. Perhaps these low-ability migrant children have accustomed themselves more to the implementation of metacognitive skills compared to their native low-ability peers because they rely more strongly on them for compensation of their culture and language related disadvantages. Another possible explanation is that these findings may be the result of extra (meta)cognitive instruction these children may have received, since lately a lot of attention has been given to the support of high-risk groups of students such as migrant, low-ability children in the Dutch educational system.

2.   Are there dissimilarities between the high intelligent group and the other intelligence groups according to the quantity and distribution of metacognitive skill-scores across the different phases of metacognitive activities (orientation, systematic orderliness, evaluation and reflection) and are there cultural differences in this?

Although the mean scores of the three ability groups in our sample were relatively small, presumably due to the early phase of development of the age group in the study, the high ability group almost consistently showed a tendency towards slightly higher scores on metacognitive skills compared to the other ability groups. In the evaluation phase, the high ability group had a close to significant advantage over the low ability group. But the advantage of the children with high abilities over the average- and the low ability group is most apparent in the systematical orderliness phase in which the high ability group significantly outperformed both other ability groups. Perhaps the fact that benefits of the high ability group over other groups are not profound in all phases, is influenced by the relatively small sample or perhaps the tasks the children in the high ability group chose were not always appropriate for their threshold of problematicity. Although not all differences were found to be significant, the advantage of the high ability children in this study on usage of metacognitive strategies is in line with findings by Veenman et al. (2005b), Sękowski (1995), Perleth (1992), and Shore (2000). The suggestion of Alexander et al. (1995) that gifted children start to gain advantages towards high school is in line with our findings, too.

In reference to the issues discussed in paragraph 1.3.2; it may be possible that the highly intelligent children will show accelerated or monotonic growth of metacognitive skills in the years hereafter, following the hypotheses posed by Alexander et al. (1995). Similar developmental issues would be interesting to assess through further research.

An exception to the advantage of high intelligent children, is found in the reflection phase where the results are equivocal across ability and cultural groups. This may be an indication of the developmental rate of these skills which might be delayed compared to the other phases (i.e., a later growth of development in this area). Although during the other phases, more clear patterns were found, the scores in all phases were quite small with maximal scores ranging from about 15 to 35 percent of the maximum points possible. This finding seems in line with the assumptions of Veenman et al. (2006) that metacognitive skills just start to emerge at late elementary school age (eight to ten years).

Thus, although the findings seem to support our expectations that children of higher abilities have some advantage in metacognitive skilfulness, only the benefits on systematical orderliness were significantly supported by our data. Further investigation, with a larger sample and with tasks suitable for the intelligence levels of interest, would be needed to corroborate a possible advantage of the high ability group in other phases

3. Which relationship is there between (high) abilities, metacognitive skills and school-performance; does metacognitive skilfulness have an additive predictive value for school-performance on top of intelligence?

For both the native and the migrant group, significant relationships were found for the metacognitive skill measure and performance and also for ability measures and performance. Intelligence measures additionally were related to metacognitive skilfulness for the natives, but no significant relationships were found between ability and metacognition in the migrant group. This is supported by the finding from correlational analysis that intelligence and metacognitive skills have a small shared variance in predicting performance of migrant children.

Semi-partial correlations show that for migrants, support is found for the independency model posed by Veenman et al., undermining the intelligence model in which metacognitive skills and intellectual ability completely overlap. However, although the overlap with intelligence is relatively small, the fact that there is some shared variance in predicting performance, also lends some support for the mixed model (Minnaert & Janssen 1999; Veenman et al., 2005a;b; 2004; 1997).

In the native sample, metacognitive skills have some independent value in stimulating performance but mostly not significant, with cognitive abilities playing a far greater role. Additionally, metacognitive skills and intelligence show more overlap than for the migrant sample, excluding the independence model for the natives. Our results seem to imply that for native children metacognitive skills have a small surplus value in prediction of performance, above a portion of overlap with intellectual abilities, which is most in line with the assumptions of the mixed model.

In assessing the impact of higher levels of metacognitive skills on performance, our findings suggest that, especially children of low ability, benefit from an additive effect of metacognitive skilfulness on top of intelligence. The fluid and crystallized ability measures again, yield varying results. The migrant low ability (using crystallized IQ measures only) children executing higher levels of metacognitive skills show significantly higher performance. For all high ability children, a surplus effect of metacognitive skills is only found using a crystallized-, verbal intelligence measure. Using the fluid measure, the average ability group significantly profits from a higher level of metacognitive skilfulness. Based on this study, we conclude that the relationship between IQ, metacognitive skills and school performance depends on the IQ tests used, the metacognitive measures applied, and the cultural background of the subjects involved. Further investigations across domains and cultural groups with larger samples are needed to map these influences in order to validate the universality of the models proposed by Veenman (1997) and the research findings often conducted within a single cultural group.

In reference to the practical implications of our study, reflection on the results suggesting some advantages in metacognitive skills for children of all ability groups, implies that instruction in order to stimulate further expansion of metacognitive skills could be an interesting factor in the educational improvement of children of all ability levels and cultural backgrounds.

SUGGESTIONS FOR FUTURE RESEARCH

One major caveat in this line of research is the lack of a validated and normed instrument to measure metacognitive skilfullnes. Beginning with the issue of appropriateness of tasks for various IQ levels should be the focus of future research. To pinpoint the threshold of problematicity a large sample of the full IQ range should be presented with a number of tasks of different complexity levels within a knowledge domain (e.g. Mathematics). The elicited metacognitive skills should then be used to determine suitable tasks for each ability group. This should be done for a number of age and cultural groups. In this way, a normed metacognitive instrument can be designed for accurate measurement of metacognitive skills across age groups. With such an instrument, the developmental course of metacognitive skills can be traced longitudinally. Furthermore, it will add to the body of knowledge concerned with mediating influences in the relationship between concepts of IQ, school performance and metacognitive skillfulness. Uniformity in the measurement of metacognitive skills would greatly enhance this area of research and would be of significant use in educational settings.

REFERENCES

Alexander, J. M., & Schwanenflugel, P. J. (1996). Development of metacognitive concepts about thinking in gifted and nongifted children: Recent research. *Learning and Individual Differences, 8*(4), 305-326.

Alexander, J. M., Carr, M., & Schwanenflugel, P. J. (1995). Development of metacognition in gifted children: Directions for future research. *Developmental Review, 15*(1), 1-37.

Brown, A. L., Campione, J. C., & Barclay, C. R. (1979). Training and self-checking routines for estimating test readiness: Generalization from list learning to prose recall. *Child Development, 50*, 501-512.

Burt, C. (1949). The structure of the mind: a review of the results of factor analysis. *British Journal of Educational Psychology, 19*, 176-199.

Campione, J. C., & Brown, A. L. (1978). Toward a theory of intelligence: Contributions from research with retarded children. *Intelligence, 2*, 279-304.

Carr, M., Alexander, J. M., & Schwanenflugel, P. J. (1996). Where gifted children do and do not excel on metacognitive tasks. *Roeper Review, 18*(3), 212-217.

Carr, M., & Biddlecomb, B. (1998). Metacognition in mathematics from a constructivist perspective. In D. J. Hacker, J. Dunlosky, & A. C. Graesser (Eds.), *Metacognition in educational theory and practice* (pp. 69-92). Mahwah, New Jersey: Lawrence Erlbaum Associates, Publishers.

Carroll, J. B. (1993). *Human cognitive abilities: A survey of factor-analytic studies*. Cambridge: Cambridge University Press.

Centraal Bureau voor Statistiek (2003, 7 april). In 2020 één op de drie leerlingen allochtoon. Requested 20 July 2006, from http://www.cbs.nl/nl-nl/menu/themas/dossiers/allochtonen/publicaties/artikelen/archief/2003/2003-1164-wm.htm

Chan, L. K. S. (1996). Motivational orientations and metacognitive abilities of intellectually gifted students. *Gifted Child Quarterly, 40*(4), 184-193.

Creative Quotations (z.j.). William Feather. Requested 25 August, 2007. http://creativequotations.com/cgi-bin/sql_search3.cgi?keyword=william+feather&boolean=and&frank=all&field=all&database=all

Davidson, J. E., & Sternberg, R. J. (1998). Smart problem solving: How metacognition helps. In D. J. Hacker, J. Dunlosky, & A. C. Graesser (Eds.), *Metacognition in educational theory and practice* (pp. 47-68). Mahwah, New Jersey: Lawrence Erlbaum Associates, Publishers.

De Corte, E. (1995). Learning and high ability: A perspective from research in instructional psychology. In M. W. Katzko, & F. J. Mönks (Eds.), *Nurturing talent, individual needs and social ability* (pp. 148-161). Assen: Van Gorcum.

Elshout, J. J. (1987). Problem solving and education. In E. De Corte, H. Lodewijks, R. Parmentier, & P. Span (Eds.), *Learning and instruction* (pp. 259-273). Oxford, UK/Leuven, Belgium: Pergamon Books, University Press.

Feldhusen, J. F., & Jarwan, F. A. (1993). Identification of gifted and talented youth for educational programs. In K. A. Heller, F. J. Mönks, & A. H. Passow (Eds.), *International handbook of research and development of giftedness and talent* (pp. 233-254). Oxford: Pergamon.

Flavell, J. H. (1979). Metacognition and cognitive monitoring. A new area of cognitive – developmental inquiry. *American Psychologist, 34*(10), 906-911.

Frasier, M. M. (1993). Issues, problems and programs in nurturing the disadvantaged and culturally different talent. In K. A. Heller, F. J. Mönks, & A. H. Passow (Eds.), *International handbook of research and development of giftedness and talent* (pp. 685-692). Oxford: Pergamon.

Freeman, J. (1993). Parents and families in nurturing giftedness and talent. In K. A. Heller, F. J. Mönks, & A. H. Passow (Eds.), *International handbook of research and development of giftedness and talent* (pp. 669-684). Oxford: Pergamon.

Gagné, F. (1993). Constructs and models pertaining to exceptional human abilities. In K. A. Heller, F. J. Mönks, & A. H. Passow (Eds), *International handbook of research and development of giftedness and talent* (pp. 69-88). Oxford: Pergamon.

Galton, F. (1883). *Inquiry into human faculty and i's development*. London: MacMillan.

Gardner, H. (1983). *Frames of mind: The theory of multiple intelligences*. New York: Basic Books.

Garner, R. (1987). *Metacognition and reading comprehension*. Norwood, New Jersey: Ablex.

Hacker, D. J. (1998). Definitions and empirical foundations. In D. J. Hacker, J. Dunlosky, & A. C. Graesser (Eds.), *Metacognition in educational theory and practice* (pp. 1-23). Mahwah, New Jersey: Lawrence Erlbaum Associates, Publishers.

Helms-Lorenz, M. (In preparation, NOW nr. 411-01-012). *Metacognitive skills, IQ and elementary school success, an empirical cross-cultural study in the Netherlands.* Groningen: GION, Gronings Instituut voor Onderzoek van Onderwijs, Opvoeding en Ontwikkeling. Rijksuniversiteit Groningen.

Helms-Lorenz, M. (2001). *Assessing cultural influences on cognitive test performance: A study with migrant children in the Netherlands.* Tilburg: Faculty of Social & Behavioral Sciences, Tilburg University.

Helms-Lorenz, M., & Harskamp, E. (In preparation, NWO nr. 411-01-012). *Towards valid assessment and inferences of metacognitive skills in a multicultural elementary school setting.* Groningen: GION, Gronings Instituut voor Onderzoek van Onderwijs, Opvoeding en Ontwikkeling. Rijksuniversiteit Groningen.

Helms-Lorenz, M., van de Vijver, F. J. R., & Poortinga, Y. H. (2003). Cross-cultural differences in cognitive performance and Spearman's hypothesis: G or c? *Intelligence, 31,* 9-29.

Hong, E. (1999). Studying the mind of the gifted. *Roeper Review, 21*(4), 244-252.

Horn, J. L., & Cattell, R. B. (1966). Refinement and test of the theory of fluid and crystallized intelligence. *Journal of Educational Psychology, 57,* 253-270.

Hout-Wolters, van, B. H. A. M. (2006). Leerstrategieën meten. Soorten meetmethoden en hun bruikbaarheid in onderwijs en onderzoek. Paper voor de onderwijsresearchdagen, Vrije Universiteit Amsterdam: in press.

Hout-Wolters, van, B. H. A. M. (2000). Assessing active self-directed learning. In P. R. J. Simons, J. van der Linden, & T. Duffy (Eds.), *New learning* (pp. 83-101). Dordrecht: Kluwer.

Hunt, E. B., Frost, N., & Lunneborg, C. (1973). Individual differences in cognition: a new approach to intelligence. In G. Bower (Ed.), *The psychology of learning and motivation* (pp. 87-122). New York: Academic Press.

Jacobs, J. E., & Paris, S. G. (1987). Children's metacognition about reading: Issues in definition, measurement, and instruction. *Educational Psychologist, 22(3&4),* 255-278.

Jacobse, A. E. (2006). Are gifted children also metacognitively more skilled? *An empirical study in a multi-cultural educational setting.* Master's thesis, University of Groningen, The Netherlands.

Jensen, A. R. (1985). The nature of the black-white difference on various psychometric tests: Spearman's hypothesis. *The Behavioral and Brain Sciences, 8,* 193-263.

Jong, de, F. P. C. M. (1992). Zelfstandig leren. Regulatie van het leerproces en leren reguleren: een procesbenadering. Tilburg: Gianotten.

Kluwe, R. H. (1982). Cognitive knowledge and executive control: metacognition. In D. R. Griffin (Ed.), *Animal mind – human mind* (pp. 201-224). New York: Springer- Verlag.

Kreuzer, M. A., Leonard, C., Flavell, J. H., & Hagen, J. W. (1975). An interview study of children's knowledge about memory. *Monographs of the Society for Research in Child Development, 40*(1), pp.1-60.

Malpass, J. R., O'Neil, J. H. F., & Hocevar, D. (1999). Self-regulation, goal orientation, self-efficacy, worry, and high-stakes math achievement for mathematically gifted high school students. *Roeper Review, 21*(4), 281-289.

Marshalek, M., Lohman, D. F., & Snow, R. E. (1983). The complexity continuum in the radex and hierarchical models of intelligence. *Intelligence, 7,* 107-127.

Melis, C. J. (1997). *Intelligence: A cognitive-energetic approach.* Wageningen: Ponsen & Looijen BV.

Mevarech, Z. R., & Kramarski, B. (1997). IMPROVE: A multidimensional method for teaching mathematics in heterogeneous classrooms. *American Educational Research Journal, 34*(2), pp. 365-395.

Minnaert, A., & Janssen, P. J. (1999). The additive effect of regulatory activities on top of intelligence in relation to academic performance in higher education. *Learning and Instruction, 9,* 77-91.

Mönks, F. J. (1992). Development of gifted children: The issue of identification and programming. In F. Mönks, & W. Peters (Eds.), *Talent for the future* (pp. 191-202). Assen/ Maastricht: van Gorcum.

Nettlebeck, T. (1982). Inspection time: Index for intelligence? *Quarterly Journal of Experimental Psychology, 34A,* 299-312.

Okagaki, L., & Sternberg, R. J. (1993). Parental beliefs and children's school performance. *Child Development, 64,* 36-56.

Passow, A. H., Mönks, F. J., & Heller, K. A. (1993). Research and education of the gifted in the year 2000 and beyond. In K. A. Heller, F. J. Mönks, & A. H. Passow (Eds.), *International handbook of research and development of giftedness and talent* (pp. 883-903). Oxford: Pergamon.

Pelletier, S., & Shore, B. M. (2003). The gifted learner, the novice, and the expert: Sharpening emerging views of giftedness. In D. Ambrose, L. M. Cohen, & A. J. Tannenbaum (Eds.), *Creative intelligence, toward theoretic integration* (pp. 237-281). Cresskill, NJ: Hampton Press.

Perleth, C. (1992). Strategy use and metamemory in gifted and average primary school children. In K. A. Heller, & E. A. Hany (Eds), *Competence and responsibility, the third European conference of the European council for high ability* (pp. 46-52). Seattle: Hogrefe & Huber.

Perleth, C., Lehwald, G., & Browder, C. S. (1993). Indicators of high ability in young children. In K. A. Heller, F. J. Mönks, & A. H. Passow (Eds), *International handbook of research and development of giftedness and talent* (pp. 283-310). Oxford: Pergamon.

Prins, F. J., Veenman, M. V. J., & Elshout, J. J. (2006). The impact of intellectual ability and metacognition on learning: New support for the threshold of problematicity theory. *Learning and Instruction, 16*(4), 374-387

Renzulli, J. S. (1992). A general theory for the development of creative productivity in young people. In F. Mönks, & W. Peters (Eds.), *Talent for the future* (pp. 51-72). Assen/ Maastricht: van Gorcum.

Robinson, N. M. (2000). Giftedness in very young children: How seriously should it be taken? In R. C. Friedman, & B. M. Shore (Eds.), *Talents unfolding: Cognition and development* (pp. 7-26). Washington, DC: American Psychological Association.

Robinson, N. M. (1993). Identifying and nurturing gifted, very young children. In K. A. Heller, F. J. Mönks, & A. H. Passow (Eds.), *International handbook of research and development of giftedness and talent* (pp. 507-524). Oxford: Pergamon.

Sękowski, A. (1995). Metacognition and achievements of gifted students. In M. W. Katzko, & F. J. Mönks (Eds.), *Nurturing talent, individual needs and social ability* (pp. 114-119). Assen: Van Gorcum.

Shore, B. M. (2000). Metacognition and flexibility: Qualitative differences in how gifted children think. In R. C. Friedman, & B. M. Shore (Eds.), *Talents unfolding: Cognition and development* (pp. 167-187). Washington, DC: American Psychological Association.

Shore, B. M., & Kanevsky, L. S. (1993). Thinking processes: Being and becoming gifted. In K. A. Heller, F. J. Mönks, & A. H. Passow (Eds.), *International handbook of research and development of giftedness and talent* (pp. 133-147). Oxford: Pergamon.

Shraw, G., & Graham, T. (1997). Helping Gifted students Develop Metacognitive Awareness. *Roeper Review, 20*(1), 4-8.

Spearman, C. (1927). *The abilities of man.* New York: MacMillan.

Sternberg, R. J. (2001). Giftedness as developing expertise: A theory of the interface between high abilities and achieved excellence. *High Ability Studies, 12*(2), 159-179.

Sternberg, R. J. (1994). Intelligence. In R. J Sternberg (Ed.), *Thinking and problem solving* (pp. 263-288). San Diego: Academic Press, Inc.

Sternberg, R. J. (1977). *Intelligence, information processing, and analogical reasoning: The componential analysis of human abilities.* Hillsdale, NJ.: Erlbaum.

Sternberg, R. J., Grigorenko, E. L., & Jarvin, L. (2001). Improving reading instruction: The triarchic model. *Educational Leadership, 58*(6), 48-52.

Swanson, H. L. (1992). The relationship between metacognition and problem solving in gifted children. *Roeper Review, 15*(1), 43-49.

Swanson, H. L. (1990). Influence of metacognitive knowledge and aptitude on problem solving. *Journal of Educational Psychology, 82*(2), 306-314.

Taylor. (1993). Programs and practices for identifying and nurturing giftedness and talent in Africa. In K. A. Heller, F. J. Mönks, & A. H. Passow (Eds.), *International handbook of research and development of giftedness and talent* (pp.833-847). Oxford: Pergamon.

Tlale, C.D. (1991). Principles for the design of a culturally relevant instrument to identify gifted black secondary school children. *Dissertation Abstracts International, 52*(4A), pp. 1301-1302.

Tucker, L. R. (1951). *A method for synthesis of factor analysis studies* (Pesonnel Research Section Report No. 984). Washington, DC: Department of the Army.

Van de Vijver, F. J. R., & Poortinga, Y. H. (1997). Towards an integrated analysis of bias in cross-cultural assessment. *European Journal of Psychological Assessment, 13*(1), 29-37.

Veenman, M. V. J., Kerseboom, L., & Imthorn, C. (2000). Test anxiety and metacognitive skillfulness: Availability versus production deficiencies. *Anxiety, Stress, and Coping, 13*, 391-412.

Veenman, M. V. J., & Spaans, M. A. (2005a). Relation between intellectual and metacognitive skills: Age and task differences. *Learning and Individual Differences, 15*, 159-176.

Veenman, M. V. J., Kok, R., & Blöte, A. W. (2005b). The relation between intellectual and metacognitive skills in early adolescence. *Instructional Science, 33*, 193-211.

Veenman, M. V. J., Elshout, J. J., & Meijer, J. (1997). The generality vs domain-specificity of metacognitive skills in novice learning across domains. *Learning and Instruction, 2*, 187-209.

Veenman, M. V. J., Van Hout-Wolters, B. H. A. M., & Afflerbach, P. (2006). Metacognition and learning: Conceptual and methodological considerations. *Metacognition Learning, 1*, 3-14.

Veenman, M. V. J., Wilhelm, P., & Beishuizen, J. J. (2004). The relation between intellectual and metacognitive skills from a developmental perspective. *Learning and Instruction, 14*, 89-109.

Vernon, P. E. (1950). *The structure of human abilities*. London: Methuen.

Verschaffel, L., De Corte, E., Lasure, S., Van Vaerenberg, G. Bogaerts, H., Ratinckx, E. (1999). Learning to solve mathematical application problems: A design experiment with fifth graders. *Mathematical Thinking and Learning, 1*(3), 195-229.

Yore, L. D., & Craig, M. T. (1992). *Middle school students' metacognitive knowledge about science reading and science text: Objective assessment, validation and results*. East Lansing, MI: National Center for Research on Teacher Learning. (ERIC Document Reproduction Service No. ED356134)

Zimmerman, B. J. (1989). Models of self-regulated learning and academic achievement. In B. J. Zimmerman & D. H. Schunk (Eds.), Self-regulated learning and academic achievement. *Theory, research and practice* (pp 1-25). New York: Springer- Verlag.

Chapter 3

METACOGNITION –
A PSYCHOPHYSIOLOGICAL PERSPECTIVE

Norbert Jaušovec[*]
Univerza y Manboru, Manbor, Slovenia

> To know that one knows what one knows, and to know that one doesn't know what one
> doesn't know, there lies true wisdom.
> *Confucius (ca. 551–479 B.C.E.), Chinese sage*

ABSTRACT

This chapter describes two pilot studies. The aim of the first study was to use EEG measures as moderating variables for analyzing metacognition. Alltogether the EEG data suggest that respondents confronted with tasks requiring metacognitive processes more involved their left than right hemisphere. This seems reasonable, because functions that are predominantely mediated by the left hemisphere are; letters, words, language related sounds, complex voluntary movements, verbal memory, speech, reading, writing, and arithmetic. Whereas, functions that are predominately mediated by the right hemisphere are ; faces, complex geometric patterns, non-language environmental sounds, music, tactile recognition of complex patterns, Braille, movements in spatial patterns, non verbal memory, geometry, sense of direction, and mental rotation of shapes.

The aim of the second study was to use EEG measures as moderating variables for resolving a controversy in the relationship between metacognition and intelligence. There are three mutually exclusive models for describing the relation between intellectual ability and metacognitive skillfulness. The first model regards metacognitive skillfulness as a manifestation of intellectual ability. In a second contrasting model, intellectual ability and metacognitive skillfulness are regarded as entirely independent. Finally, according to the mixed model, metacognitive skillfullness is related to intellectual ability to a certain extent,

---

[*] Univerza v Mariboru, Pedagoška fakulteta, Koroška 160, 2000 Maribor, Slovenia. Fax: +386 2 218180; Email: norbert.jausovec@uni-mb.si

but it also has a surplus value on top of intellectual ability. The data obtained in the second study lend further support to the assumption that intelligence and metacognition represent distinct components of the cognitive architecture. The two studies reported suggest that EEG measures as moderating variables could be a useful methodology for studying metacognition.

DEFINITIONS

The term 'metacognition' was introduced by John Flavell in the early 1970s based on the term 'metamemory' previously conceived by the same author (Flavell, 1971). Flavell (1979) viewed metacognition as learners' knowledge of their own cognition, defining it as 'knowledge and cognition about cognitive phenomena' (p. 906). Metacognition is often referred to in the literature as 'thinking about one's own thinking', or as 'cognitions about cognitions'. It is usually related to learners' knowledge, awareness and control of the processes by which they learn (Brown, 1987, Garner & Alexander, 1989), and the metacognitive learner is thought to be characterized by ability to recognize, evaluate and, where needed, reconstruct existing ideas (Gunstone, 1991).

Metacognition consists of two components: knowledge and control. Metacognitive knowledge pertains to one's knowledge about how one's cognition operates ("I know that I do not memorize names well"), whereas metacognitive control pertains to how one controls one's cognitive operations. Nelson and Narens (1990,) conceptualized metacognition as operating at two levels: the objective level and the meta-level. The objective level carries out cognitive operations, whereas the meta-level controls activities that occur at the objective level. Flavell's definition was followed by numerous others, often portraying different emphases on mechanisms and processes associated with metacognition. Paris and his colleagues, for example (Paris & Jacobs, 1984, Cross & Paris, 1988, Paris & Winograd, 1990), identified two essential features in their definition of metacognition: 'self-appraisal' and 'self-management' of cognition. 'Metalearning' (White & Gunstone, 1989), 'deutero-learning' (Bateson ,1983) and 'mindfulness' (Salomon & Globerson, 1987) are terms also used in the literature to describe metacognition. The number of definitions, terms and analyses of what metacognition stands for has been the cause for some confusion in the literature. Weinert (1987), for instance, spoke of a 'vague' and 'imprecise' working definition of metacognition.

In an attempt to clarify some of the obscurity covering what metacognition stands for, Flavell (1987) proposed a taxonomic categorization of the components of metacognition. In doing so he distinguished between (a) 'metacognitive knowledge' and (b) 'metacognitive experience'. 'Metacognitive knowledge' is that part of one's knowledge that refers to cognitive matters. It comprises knowledge of person variables (knowledge concerning what human beings are like as cognitive organisms), task variables (referring to knowledge about how the specific information encountered affects and constraints the way in which one deals with it) and strategy variables (knowledge about cognitive strategies or procedures for achieving various goals). 'Metacognitive experience', on the contrary, comprises conscious experiences that can be either cognitive or affective and are pertinent to an ongoing cognitive situation or endeavor.

METACOGNITIVE RESEARCH

Research on metacognition has its roots in two distinct areas of research: developmental psychology and cognitive psychology (Schwartz & Perfect, 2002). Metacognitive research in the area of developmental psychology can be traced back to the theory proposed by Jean Piaget. However, metacognitive research in a pure form did not emerge until the 1970s, when Flavell and colleagues investigated children's knowledge of their own cognitions (Schneider & Lockl, 2002). In the area of cognitive psychology, work on metacognition was initiated by Hart (1965) with his investigation on feeling of knowing experiences (FOKs). However, according to Schwartz and Perfect (2002), research on metacognition did not become mainstream cognitive psychology until recently.

Research in metacognition has covered mainly three components: (a) knowledge about strategies, (knowledge about when, where and why different strategies should be used); (b) strategy use, (the actual use of metacognitive strategies); and (c) cognitive monitoring, (an acquisition procedure needed for evaluating and changing strategy use and for determining the limits of the knowledge (Chmiliar, 1997). Among the conclusions reached by metacognitive research to date are that: (a) knowing about knowing develops, (b) both children and adults often fail to monitor cognitions, and (c) some strategies are difficult to learn and easy to abandon (Garner & Alexander, 1989).

The fact that the link between metacognition and thinking skills encouraged application of the former to improve the latter has resulted in a number of researchers focusing on groups with learning difficulties. Feuerstein et al. (1980), for instance, worked with disadvantaged underachieving children in employing their Instrumental Enrichment, while Campione et al. (1982) studied metacognition mainly in relation to students with learning problems and sometimes with mentally retarded children. The view that metacognitive processes of self-monitoring and self-regulation are fundamental determinants of competent functioning in the real world has resulted in several research studies relating metacognitive dysfunction to schizophrenia (Koren, et al., 2006; Moritz et al., 2006; Lysaker et al. 2005).

Others, on the contrary, focused on the importance of metacognition for general aptitude and giftedness (for an overview see, Steiner and Carr, 2003). Several researchers (Cheng, 1993; Hannah & Shore, 1995; Span & Overtoom-Corsmit, 1986; Shore & Dover, 1987; Zimmerman & Martinez-Pons, 1990) have reported significant differences in metacognitive strategy usage between intellectually gifted and average students. Allon et al. (1994), on the other hand, reported low correlations between WISC-R intelligence and metacognition obtained retrospectively by questioning participants about their problem solving activities. Moreover, Swanson (1990) obtained support for the independency notion with children performing two Piagetian tasks. His experimental design, however, which forced intelligence and metacognition to be orthogonal 140 factors, does not permit the conclusion that both predictors are fully independent (see Veenman & Elshout, 1991). Indeed, follow-up studies (Maqsud, 1997; Swanson et al., 1993) showed that metacognition was only partially independent of intelligence.

METHODS AND TECHNIQUES USED IN ANALYZING METACOGNITION

The central problem related to metacognition research is its estimation in the individual's cognitive process while solving a problem or learning. This is a practical obstacle caused by the fact that metacognition is an inner awareness or process rather than an overt behavior (White, 1986), and because individuals themselves are often not aware of these processes (Rowe, 1991). In employing interviews for educational purposes, for instance, there is difficulty in judging whether a pupil who takes some time before replying to a question is unsure and unconfident about his/her response, or whether that silent interval is a sign of one's effort to reflect back on his/her learning and retrieve the answer in a metacognitive manner.

The most frequently used approach is thinking aloud methodology, where the respondents are asked to verbalize their thoughts as they work on a problem. This method was used by many early investigators. It gained popularity in problem solving studies during the 1960s. Use of the method in information processing research led to its utilization in many related areas of psychological research. The thinking aloud method requires no more than that the subjects during their thinking activity provide an account of what they are doing. The subjects thus report problem solving behaviors, rather than mental states. The later being the characteristic of introspection and retrospection which require the subjects to analyze the composition of thought processes. The comparison of introspective and thinking aloud methodology revealed several characteristics being in favor of the thinking aloud methodology. The thinking aloud protocols are more complete and contain more information than the introspective protocols. A second characteristic is that the thinking aloud protocols are more present oriented, have a more elliptical form, and contain more indefinite referents.

Although there is evidence to suggest that the instruction to think aloud does not significantly alter the sequence of cognitive process (Ericson & Simon, 1984), the method has its limitations: verbal protocols include only the events and operations of which the subject is aware at the time; additionally, they are sensitive only to sequential operations. Another source of error could be the analysis of thinking aloud protocols with different taxonomies. No matter how carefully designed, the chosen scheme for both data collection and data analysis will influence not only what the investigator observes, but will to some degree determine the regularities and laws which might be identified.

It seems that these methodological shortcomings affect above all research into metacognition (Dörner, 1979). Metacognitive processes occur infrequently in thinking aloud protocols (about 1% of all statements can be identified as metacognitive).

A different method for investigating the individual's metacognitions during problem solving was introduced by Metcalfe and Wiebe, (1987). The technique requires the subjects to give judgments repeatedly about how close they feel to the solution of problems - called feeling-of-warmth (FOW) judgments - in the course of the problem solving. These judgments are called "warmth" judgments after the searching game in which one person hides an object and then directs others to where the object is by telling them that they are getting warmer - closer to the object, or colder - farther away. Subjects are asked to indicate how near they believe they are to the solution. The "feeling of warmth" procedure was used to examine the subjective phenomenology of different problems. It could be shown that the patterns-of-warmth ratings differed for insight and non-insight problems. Non-insight problems showed a more incremental pattern in the course of their solving than did insight problems. The conclusion drawn from these findings was that insight problems were solved by some non-analytic, sudden process, in contrast to an analytic process of reducing the difference between the initial and goal state, which characterized the solution of non-insight problems. Some researchers opposed this conclusion as being rather vague and speculative. The finding that subjects cannot predict their performance on insight problems does not logically necessitate that solutions to such problems occur as a sudden flash of illumination.

A similar technique to study metacognition requires subjects to make assessments about the likelihood that they know the answer to a question, or will be able to solve a problem (feeling-of-knowing judgments – FKJ). These judgments are based on episodic memory which, for its optimal function, requires a subsidiary monitoring and control system that assesses the familiarity of incoming events, and adjusts attention. Cognitive energy is assigned to events on the basis of novelty-- devoting little energy to old and already well known events, and much attention to novel events. It is assumed that the values of novelty assessed by such a monitoring-control system are feelings that are available to consciousness, and that they may be used for making feeling-of-knowing judgments. Many researchers have stressed the importance of such a judging system for creativity, especially for problem finding. Identifying differences between a schema and the environment is also important for the process of conceptualization.

To get a deeper inside into metacognition the tip-of-the-tongue states (TOTs refer to the experience of feeling certain that one knows a word, but being unable to retrieve it) were also studied (Brown & McNeill, 1966). In the metacognitive view, TOTs are viewed as an imperfect monitor of ongoing cognitive processes. That is, TOTs are subjective experiences that allow rememberers to monitor and control their retrieval processes (Schwartz, 1999, 2002) when lexical retrieval breaks down. However, as mentioned earlier, it is difficult to observe these processes, and defining them with FOW ratings and FKJs is a circular endeavor.

To overcome the mentioned methodological problems related to FOW, FKJ and thinking aloud methodology some researchers suggested the use of moderating variables (Kuhman et al., 1985). Activation parameters like heart rate and blood pressure or even electroencephalograms (EEG) were used as moderating variables.

In one of our earlier studies (Jaušovec, 1996) the FOW ratings were combined with heart-rate while respondents solved different problem types. The data obtained showed a continuous increase in heart rate during the solution of interpolation problems, suggesting an incremental approach, but a sudden increase when the solution to insight problems (described as illumination) was reached. Budson et al., (2005) on the other hand, used event-related potentials (ERPs) to investigate the neural processes underlying the distinctiveness heuristic— a response mode in which participants expect to remember vivid details of an experience and make recognition decisions based on this metacognitive expectation. Based on the EEG data the authors suggested that the distinctiveness heuristic is a retrieval orientation that facilitates reliance upon recollection to differentiate between item types. Both studies suggest that moderating variables, like heart rate or EEG could be a useful technique for studying metacognition.

PILOT STUDY 1

The aim of the first study was to use EEG measures as moderating variables for analyzing metacognition. Thirty-three students participated in the study. They solved 80 tasks (40 verbal and 40 figural), involving the respondent's working-memory. According to Oberauer et al., (2003) the tasks mainly involved supervision processes (also referred to as executive processes) – the monitoring of ongoing cognitive processes an actions, the selective activation of relevant representations and procedures, and the suppression of irrelevant, distracting ones. Task set switching is regarded as one of the prototypical executive tasks (Meiran, 1996), because a supervisory attentional process must suppress the most active action schema (i.e., the task set used before) and select another one instead (Baddeley, 1986).

The verbal tasks used nouns as stimuli. They either required a semantic classification into animal versus plant, or a syntactical classification according to the number of syllables (one or two). The figural tasks used arrows as stimuli that appeared at varying locations within the frame (one cell in a 2x2 matrix), and pointed to varying directions. For the up-down tasks, participants had to react to the direction in which an arrow pointed (up or down). For the above-below task, they had to base their decision on the location of the arrow (upper or lower half of the frame). Each stimulus appeared in one of the four cells of a 2x2 matrix, and the instruction specified that the first decision criterion had to be applied in the two upper cells, whereas the second criterion had to be applied in the two lower cells. For example, if a noun appeared in the upper left cell, participants had to decide whether it was a plant or animal and press a key (1 or 2) on the STIM response pad. If a noun appeared in the bottom left cell, participants had to decide whether it had one or two syllables. Successive stimuli appeared in adjacent cells, shifting from cell to cell in a regular clockwise order. Therefore, a switch from one decision criterion to the other was required every two trials. This design provided 50% switch trials (ST), and 50% non-switch trials (nST).

While respondents solved the tasks presented on a computer monitor their EEG was recorded. EEG was recorded using a Quick-Cap with sintered electrodes. Using the Ten-twenty Electrode Placement System of the International Federation, the EEG activity was monitored over nineteen scalp locations (see Figure1).

The 19 EEG traces were digitized online at 1000 Hz and stored on a hard disk. Epochs were comprised from the 1500 ms preceding and 2000 ms following the stimulus presentation and automatically screened for artifacts. The presentation sequence is shown in figure 2.

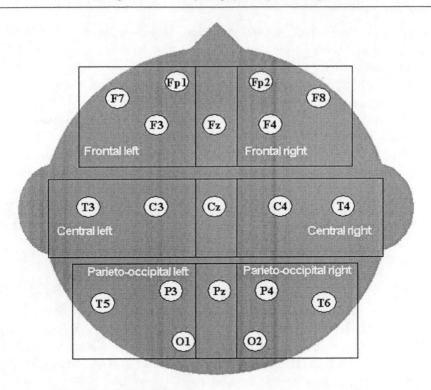

Figure 1. Ten-twenty Electrode Placement System of the International Federation with a schematic presentation of the collapsed ERD/ERS values.

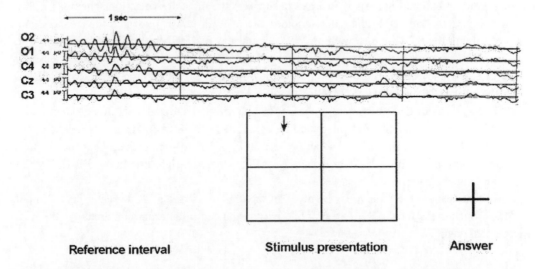

Figure 2. The presentation sequence for the figural tasks. The respondent, had to press '2' on the response pad, because the arrow appeared in the upper left cell and was pointing down (see explanation in text). The EEG data were used to calculate the ERD/ERS values which were defined as the percentage change of the power at each sample point (A_j), relative to the average power in the resting 1000 ms reference interval (R) preceding the stimulus onset (−1500 ms to −500 ms):

$$ERD_{(j)} \% = \frac{R - Aj}{R}.$$

Because EEG measurement requires collection of a huge amount of data which are unusable in raw form they are subjected to data reduction methods. In the present study the event-related desynchronization/synchronization (ERD/ERS) method was used. The quantification of ERD/ERS requires a number of event-related EEG trials (in our study 80 trials were used), synchronously triggered by an event (see Figure 2, the event is the presentation of the matrix). In the first step the frequency band of interest is selected and each trial is bandpass filtered. In a second step each sample is squared to obtain power values. ERD is defined as the percentage change of the power at each sample point or an average of some samples relative to the average power in a reference interval preceding the stimulus onset. A positive ERD indicates a power decrease, and a negative ERD a power increase (Pfurtscheller, 1999). The ERD/ERS values were collapsed for different electrode locations, distinguishing the hemispheres as well as frontal, central and parietal brain areas (see figure 1).

The alpha frequency bands were individually determined. On average, this method resulted in a band of 10.03 – 12.02 Hz for the upper alpha band, a band of 8.03 – 10.02 Hz for the lower-2 alpha, and a band of 6.03 – 8.02 Hz for the lower-1 alpha. These bands were chosen because research has identified their relationship to different cognitive functions. The upper alpha (10-12 Hz) activity is modulated by semantic memory processes (Klimesch, 1997). The lower-1 and lower-2 alpha (6-10 Hz) bands are related to attentional task demands. The lower-1 alpha band is mainly related to the level of alertness, whereas the lower-2 alpha band is more related to expectancy (Klimesch, 1999). Evidence further indicates that alpha power is inversely related to mental effort (e.g., Nunez, 1995). Because the switching tasks (ST) in comparison to the non-switching tasks (nST), required a supervisory attentional process which had to suppress the most active action schema (i.e., the task set used for the nST), and select another one instead, it was expected that respondents while solving the ST would show more ERD (greater mental activity) than while solving the nST . This hypothesis was tested using a general-linear model (GLM) for repeated measures for each frequency band. The factors and their levels were: TASK (ST, nST); HEMISPHERE (Left, Right); AREA (Frontal, Central, Parietal).

The analysis of ERD/ERS data in the lower-1 alpha band showed a significant interaction effect between the factors hemisphere and task ($F(1, 32) = 9.58$; $p < .004$), as well as area and task ($F(2, 64) = 3.97$; $p < .024$) . As can be seen in figure 3, respondents solving the ST to a greater extent involved the left hemisphere (less ERS) than the right one (more ERS). For the nST an opposite pattern was observed.

With respect to the brain areas involved in solving the ST and nST, a greater involvement of the frontal areas for the ST, and more activity in the central and parietal areas for the nST were observed.

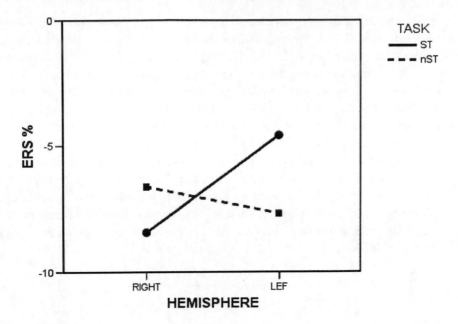

Figure 3. ERD/ERS in the lower-1 alpha band for the ST and nST in the left and right hemisphere.

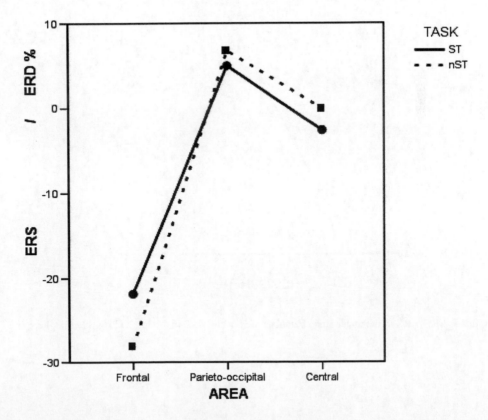

Figure 4. ERD/ERS in the lower-1 alpha band for the ST and nST in the frontal, parieto-occipital and central brain areas.

A similar ERD/ERS pattern was also observed in the upper-alpha band. The conducted GLM for repeated measures showed a significant interaction effect between the factors hemisphere and task $F(1, 32) = 6.31$; $p<.017$). Respondents solving the ST to a greater extent involved the left hemisphere (more ERD) than the right one (less ERD).

All together the EEG data suggest that respondents confronted with the switching tasks (requiring metacognitive processes) more involved their left than right hemisphere. This seems reasonable, because functions that are predominantly mediated by the left hemisphere are: letters, words, language related sounds, complex voluntary movement, verbal memory, speech, reading, writing, and arithmetic. Whereas, functions that are predominantly mediated by the right hemisphere are: faces, complex geometric patterns, nonlanguage environmental sounds, music, tactile recognition of complex patterns, Braille, movements in spatial patterns, nonverbal memory, geometry, sense of direction and mental rotation of shapes (Kolb & Whishaw,1986). The data further suggest that EEG as a moderating variable could be a useful tool in metacognitive research.

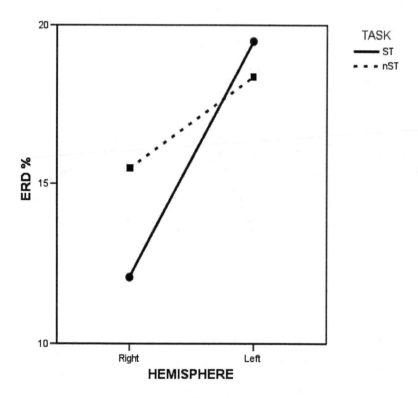

Figure 5. ERD/ERS in the upper alpha band for the ST and nST in the left and right hemisphere.

PILOT STUDY 2

The aim of the second study was to use EEG measures as moderating variables for resolving a controversy in the relationship between metacognition and intelligence. There are three, mutually exclusive models for describing the relation between intellectual ability and metacognitive skillfulness (Veenman & Elshout, 1991; Veenman et al., 1997). The first model regards metacognitive skillfulness as a manifestation of intellectual ability. In a second, contrasting model, intellectual ability and metacognitive skillfulness are regarded as entirely independent. Finally, according to the mixed model, metacognitive skillfulness is related to intellectual ability to a certain extent, but it also has a surplus value on top of intellectual ability.

Swanson (1990) investigated whether high levels of metacognitive knowledge about problem solving could compensate for overall aptitude. He found that highly metacognitive students outperformed less metacognitive students in problem-solving regardless of their overall aptitude level. In fact, he reported that high-metacognitive/low aptitude children performed significantly better than low-metacognitive children with higher overall aptitude scores. He hence concluded that high performance on the problem solving tasks is more closely related to children's performance on the metacognitive measures than on the overall aptitude measures.

The research design used in the first part of the second pilot study was similar to the one of Swanson (1990). Compared were 12 high-metacognitvie and average intelligent (HMCAIQ) students to 12 low-metacognitive and high intelligent students (LMCHIQ). The metacognitive competence of students was based on several switching tasks involving the monitoring of ongoing cognitive processes, whereas the IQ of students was determined with the WAIS-R test (see Table 1).

The procedure, EEG and statistical analysis were the same as in the first study. Significant differences related to the factor group were only observed in the two lower alpha bands. They were more pronounced in the lower-2 alpha band. In the lower-1 alpha band a significant interaction effect between the factors group, area and task were observed $F(2, 44)$ = 4.45; p<.017). High-metacognitive individuals solved the switching tasks with less mental effort (more ERS) than did the Low-metacognitive individuals. The differences were especially pronounced over the parieto-occipital brain areas (see Figure 6).

In the lower-2 alpha band a significant interaction effect between the factors group and task were observed $F(1, 22)$ = 21.22; p< 1.4E-04). As can be seen in Figure 7, the high and low metacognitive individuals displayed an opposite pattern of ERD in relation to the task type. HMCAIQ individuals solved the ST tasks with less mental effort than LMCHIQ individuals.

Also significant were the interaction effects between the factors group, task and hemisphere $F(1, 22)$ = 25.89; p< 4.3E-05), and group, task and area $F(2, 44)$ = 5.10; p< .01). The HMCAIQ individuals while solving the ST task showed lower ERD in both hemispheres than did the LMCHIQ individuals, who showed more ERD in both hemispheres and a greater involvement of the left hemisphere. The interaction with the factor area showed a similar pattern as for the lower-1 alpha band.

Because the lower-2 alpha band is related to expectancy (Klimesch, 1999), the ERD patterns observed in high-metacognitive individuals suggest that their expectancy while solving the nST tasks was higher than when solving the ST tasks. With respect to the presentation sequence in the study this seems to be an adequate metacognitive strategy. The presentation sequence of tasks was always the same: ST-nST-ST-nST-...., therefore anticipating a strategy change while solving the nST (more ERD displayed by high-metacognitive individuals), seems a more reasonable metacognitive approach than anticipating a strategy change while solving the ST tasks (more ERD displayed by low-metacognitive individuals). It could further point to faster and more automatized mental activity in high-metacognitive individuals as compared to low-metacognitive individuals. The data further support the model put forward by Swanson (1990), namely that intellectual ability and metacognitive skillfulness are independent.

The aim of the second part of the study was to further investigate this question. For that purpose 16 high-metacognitive (HMC) and 16 low-metacognitive (LMC) individuals of equal (above average) intelligence sowed ST and nST tasks (the same as in study 1) while their EEG was recorded. (see Table 2).

The conducted GLM showed an interaction effect between the factors group and task $F(1, 30) = 6.34; p< .017)$. As can be seen in Figure 8, the high and low metacognitive individuals displayed an opposite pattern of ERD in relation to the task type. As in the first part of the study, HMC individuals solved the ST tasks with less mental effort than did the LMC individuals. These data lend further support to the assumption that intelligence and metacognition represent distinct components of the cognitive architecture.

Table 1. Means, SD and t-test, for the WISC-R IQ scores and metacognitive performance scores for the HMCAIQ and LMCHIQ groups of respondents

	Group	Mean	SD	t-test
IQ	HMCAIQ	98.75	.452	36.200
	LMCHIQ	127.50	2.714	p< 2.65E-13
Metacognition	HMCAIQ	109.50	6.544	5.790
	LMCHIQ	94.75	5.926	p< 8.01E-06

Table 2. Means, SD and t-test, for the WISC-R IQ scores and metacognitive performance scores for the HMC and LMC groups of respondents

	GROUP	Mean	SD	t-test
IQ	HMC	110.50	12.45	.13
	LMC	111.50	17.55	N.S.
Metacognition	HMC	111.38	6.05	5.68
	LMC	87.38	10.10	p< 1.08E-04

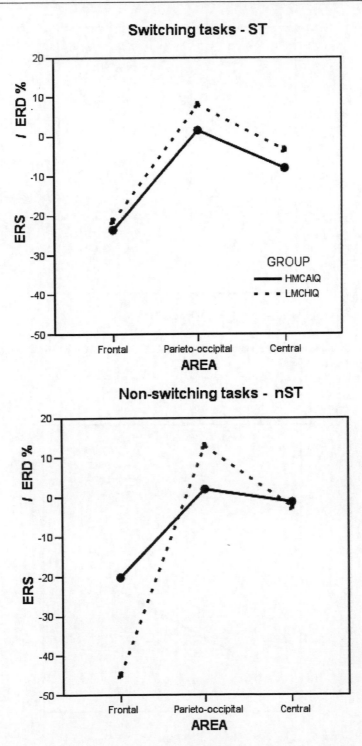

Figure 6. ERD/ERS in the lower-1 alpha band for the ST and nST in the frontal, parieto-occipital and central brain areas for the HMCAIQ and LMCHIQ groups of respondents.

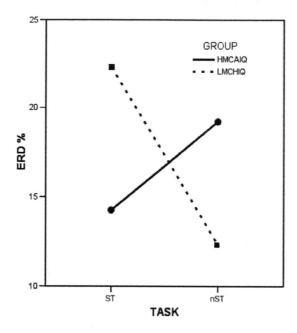

Figure 7. ERD/ERS in the lower-2 alpha band of the HMCAIQ and LMCHIQ LMC individuals while sowing the ST and nST.

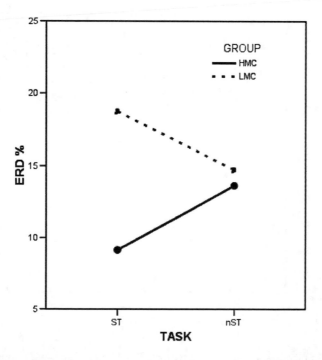

Figure 8. ERD/ERS in the lower-2 alpha band of the HMC and LMC individuals while sowing the ST and nST.

CONCLUSION

The two studies reported suggest that EEG measures as moderating variables could be a useful methodology for studying metacognition.

REFERENCES

Allon, M., Gutkin, T. B., and Bruning, R. (1994). The relationship between metacognition and intelligence in normal adolescents: Some tentative but surprising findings. *Psychology in the Schools, 3*, 93–97.

Baddeley, A. (1986). *Working memory.* New York: Oxford University Press.

Bateson, G. (1983). *Steps to an Ecology of the Mind.* London: Paladin.

Brown, R., & McNeill, D. (1966). The "tip of the tongue" phenomenon. *Journal of Verbal Learning and Verbal Behavior, 5*, 325–337.

Brown, A. (1987). Metacognition, executive control, self-regulation, and other more mysterious mechanisms, In: F.E.Weinert, R.H. Kluwe (Eds.), *Metacognition, Motivation, and Understanding* (pp. 65–116). Hillsdale, NJ: LEA.

Budson, A.E.,Droller, D.B.J. Dodson C.S., Schacter, D.L., Rugg, M.D., Holcomb, P.J. and Daffner, K.R. (2005). Electrophysiological dissociation of picture versus word encoding: The distinctiveness heuristic as a retrieval orientation. *Journal of Cognitive Neuroscience,17*, 1181-1193.

Campione, J.C., Brown, A.L. & Ferrara, R.A. (1982). Mental retardation and intelligence. In R.J. Sternberg, Ed, *Handbook of human intelligence* (pp. 392–490). Cambridge: Cambridge University Press.

Cheng, P. (1993). Metacognition and giftedness: The state of the relationship. *Gifted Child Quarterly, 37*, 105–112.

Chmiliar, L. (1997). Metacognition and giftedness. *Agate, 11*, 28–34.

Cross, D. R. and Paris, S. C. (1988). Developmental and instrumental analysis of children's metacognition and reading comprehension. *Journal of Educational Psychology, 80*, 131–142.

Dörner, D.(1979). Problemloesen als Informationsverarbeitung. Mainz: Kohlhammer.

Ericsson, K. and Simon, H. A. (1980). Verbal reports as data. *Psychological Review, 87*, 215–251.

Feuerstein, R., Rand, Y., Hoffman, M. and Miller, M. (1980). *Instrumental enrichment: An intervention programme for cognitive modifiability.* Baltimore, MD: University Park Press.

Flavell, J.H. (1979). Metacognition and cognitive monitoring: A new area of cognitive-developmental inquiry. *American Psychologist, 34*, 906-911.

Flavell, J. H. (1971). First discussant's comments. What is memory development the development of? *Human Development, 14*, 272–278.

Flavell, J. H. (1987). Speculations about the nature and development of metacognition. In F. E. Weinert and R. H. Kluwe (Eds.) M*etacognition, motivation, and understanding* (pp. 21-29). Hillsdale, NJ: Lawrence Erlbaum.

Garner, R. and Alexander, P. A. (1989). Metacognition: answered and unanswered questions. *Educational Psychologist, 24*(2), 143–158.

Gunstone, R. F. (1991). Constructivism and metacognition: theoretical issues and classroom studies. In R. Duit, F. Goldberg and H. Niedderer (Eds), R*esearch in physics learning: Theoretical issues and empirical studies* (pp. 129-140). Bremen: IPN.

Hannah, C. L., and Shore, B. M. (1995). Metacognition and high intellectual ability: Insights from the study of learning disabled gifted students. *Gifted Child Quarterly, 39*, 95–109.

Hart, J. T. (1965). Memory and the feeling-of-knowing experience. *Journal of Educational Psychology, 56*, 208–216.

Jaušovec, N., (1996). What can heart rate tell us about processes involved in problem sowing? In E. Baumgartner and W. Baumgartner (Eds.), P*henomenology and cognitive science* (pp. 151-160). Dettelbach: J.H. Roll.

Klimesch, W.(1997) EEG-alpha rhythms and memory processes. *International Journal of Psychophysiology, 26*, 319-340.

Klimesch, W. (1999). EEG alpha and theta oscillations reflect cognitive and memory performance: a review and analysis. *Brain Research Reviews. 29*, 169-195.

Kolb, B., and Whishaw, I.Q. (1996). *Fundamentals of human neuropsychology.* New York: W. H. Freeman and Company.

Koren, D., Seidman, L.J., Goldsmith, M., and Harvey, P.D., (2006). Real-World Cognitive— and Metacognitive—Dysfunction in Schizophrenia: A New approach for Measuring (and Remediating) More "Right Stuff". *Schizophrenia, Bulletin, 32*, 310-326

Kuhman, W., Lachnit, W. and Vaitl, D. (1985). The quantification of experimental load: Methodological and empirical issues. In A. Steptoe, H. Rueddel, and H. Neus (Eds.), *Clinical and methodological issues in cardiovascular psychophysiology* (pp. 45-52). Berlin: Springer-Verlag.

Lysaker, P.H., Carcione, A., Dimaggio, G., Johannesen, J.K., Nicol, G., Procacci, M., Semerari, A. (2005). Metacognition amidst narratives of self and illness in schizophrenia: associations with neurocognition, symptoms, insight and quality of life. *Acta Psychiatrica Scandinavia, 112*, 64–71.

Maqsud, M. (1997). Effects of metacognitive skills and nonverbal ability on academic achievement of high school pupils. *Educational. Psychologist, 17*, 387–397.

Meiran, N., (1996). The reconfiguration of processing mode prior to task performance. *Journal of Experimental Psychology: Learning, Memory, & Cognition, 22*, 1423-1442.

Metcalfe, J and Wiebe, D. (1987). Intuition in insight and noninsight problem solving. *Memory Cognition, 15*, 238-246.

Moritz, S., Woodward, T.S., Chen, E. (2006). Investigation of metamemory dysfunctions in first-episode schizophrenia. *Schizophrenia Research, 81*, 247– 252.

Nelson, T.O. and Narens, L. (1990). Metamemory: a theoretical framework and new findings. In Bower, G.H., Ed., *The psychology of learning and motivation* (pp.125–173). New York, NY: Academic Press.

Nunez, P.L. (1995). Mind, brain, and electroencephalography. In P. L. Nunez (Ed.), *Neocortical dynamics and human EEG rhythms* (pp. 133-194). NY: Oxford University Press.

Oberbauer, K. Sus, H.M., Wilhelm, O. and Wittman, W. (2003). The multiple faces of working memory storage, processing, supervision and coordination. *Intelligence, 31*, 167-193.

Paris, S. G. and Jacobs, J. E. (1984). The benefits of informed instruction for children's reading awareness and comprehension skills. *Child Development, 55*, 2083–2093.

Paris, S. G. and Winograd, P. (1990). How metacognition can promote academic learning and instruction. In B. F. Jones and L. Idol (Eds.), *Dimensions of thinking and cognitive instruction* (pp. 15–51). Hillsdale, NJ: Lawrence Erlbaum.

Pfurtscheller, G. (1999). Quantification of ERD and ERS in the time domain. In G. Pfurtscheller & F.H. Lopes da Silva (Eds.), *Handbook of electroencephalography and clinical neuropsychology, Vol. 6: Event-related desynchronization* (pp. 89-105). Amsterdam: Elsevier.

Rowe, H. A. H. (1991). Observing thinking and learning processes. In G. Evans (Ed.) *Learning teaching cognitive skills* (pp. 9-26). Melbourne: A.C.E.R..

Salomon, G. and Globerson, T. (1987). Skill may not be enough: the role of mindfulness in learning and transfer. *Journal of Educational Research, 11*, 623–637.

Schneider,W., & Lockl, K. (2002). The development of metacognitive knowledge in children and adolescence. In T. J. Perfect & B. L. Schwartz (Eds.), *Applied metacognition* (pp. 224–257). Cambridge, England: Cambridge University Press.

Schwartz, B. L., & Perfect, T. J. (2002). Introduction: Toward an applied metacognition. In T. J. Perfect & B. L. Schwartz (Eds.), *Applied metacognition* (pp. 1–11). Cambridge, England: Cambridge University Press.

Schwartz, B. L. (1999). Sparkling at the end of the tongue: The etiology of tip-of-the tongue phenomenology. *Psychonomic Bulletin & Review, 6*, 379–393.

Schwartz, B. L. (2002*). Tip-of-the-tongue states: Phenomenology, mechanism, and lexical retrieval*. Hillsdale, NJ: Erlbaum.

Shore, B. M., and Dover, A. C. (1987). Metacognition, intelligence, and giftedness. *Gifted Child Quarterly, 3*, 37–39.

Span, P. and Overtoom-Corsmit, R. (1986). Information processing by intellectually gifted pupils solving mathematical problems. *Educational Studies of Mathematics, 17*, 273–295.

Steiner, H.H. and Carr, M. (2003). Cognitive development in gifted children: Toward a more precise understanding of emerging differences in intelligence. *Educational Psychology Review, 15*, 215-245.

Swanson, H. L. (1990). Influence of metacognitive knowledge and aptitude on problem solving. *Journal of Educational Psychology, 82*, 306–314.

Swanson, H.L, Christie, L and Rubadeau, R.J. (1993). The relationship between meta-cognition and analogical reasoning in mentally retarded, learning disabled, average, and gifted children. *Learning Disability Research, 8*, 70–81.

Veenman, M.V.J. and Elshout, J.J. (1991). Intellectual ability and working method as predictors of novice learning. *Learning and Instruction, 1*, 303–317.

Veenman, M.V.J., Elshout, J.J. and Meijer, J. (1997). The generality vs. domain-specificity of metacognitive skills in novice learning across domains. *Learning Instruction, 7*, 187–209.

Weinert, F. E. (1987). Metacognition and motivation as determinants of effective learning and understanding. In F. E. Weinert and R. H. Kluwe (Eds.), *Metacognition, motivation, and understanding* (pp. 1–16).Hillsdale, NJ: Lawrence Erlbaum.

White, R. T. (1986). Origins of PEEL. In J. R. Baird and I. J. Mitchell (Eds.), *Improving the quality of teaching and learning: An Australian case study – the PEEL Project* (pp. 1- 7). Melbourne: Monash University.

Zimmerman, B.J. and Martinez-Pons, M. (1990). Student differences in self-regulated learning: Relating grade, sex, and giftedness to self-efficacy and strategy use. *Journal of Educational Psychology, 82*, 51–59.

In: Meta-Cognition: A Recent Review of Research...   ISBN: 978-1-60456-011-4
Editors: M.F. Shaughnessy et al. pp. 63-83   © 2008 Nova Science Publishers, Inc.

Chapter 4

STEGOSAURUS AND SPOONBILLS: MECHANISMS FOR TRANSFER ACROSS BIOLOGICAL DOMAINS

Joyce M. Alexander[*]
Indiana University, USA
Kathy E. Johnson
Indiana University-Purdue University Indianapolis, USA
Brianna Scott
Indiana University, USA
Rhonda D. Meyer
Alliance for School Choice, USA

ABSTRACT

This chapter examines the state of the literature regarding transfer across domains built primarily of declarative knowledge, with a particular emphasis on domains related to biology. We propose that expertise in declarative knowledge domains can transfer to other related domains, but not through typical strategy use or procedural knowledge platforms. Transfer between domains related to biology seems to be facilitated by an increased level of attention to perceptual and behavioral features in the expert domain. Although there is a significant literature documenting transfer across declarative knowledge domains in adults, evidence for transfer in children has been more difficult to obtain. The present chapter presents a model of the types of knowledge which would be prone to transfer effects in children and reviews research on the factors that most likely facilitate that transfer.

We argue that transfer in children, when it does occur, is often implicit and unaccompanied by metacognitive awareness, and we provide relevant evidence through an analysis of children's performance on a referential communication task. Finally,

[*] Correspondence and requests for reprints should be directed to Joyce Alexander, Department of Counseling and Educational Psychology, 201 N. Rose Ave., Bloomington, IN 47405. E-mail: joalexan@indiana.edu

methods for supporting the development of metacognitive knowledge about concepts are explored, as well as future directions for research.

Although children frequently are depicted as universal novices (Brown & DeLoache, 1978), there are groups of child experts who, because of interest or experience, have come to know more about a domain than many adults will ever know (e.g., Alexander, Johnson, & Schreiber, 2002; Chi, 1978). A child expert's superior performance is facilitated by a well-organized and rich semantic network of domain-specific knowledge (e.g., Gobbo & Chi, 1986). Attempts to glean evidence that components of expert skill transfer to unfamiliar domains have invariably met with failure in the adult and child skilled performance literature (e.g., Chi, Glaser, & Farr, 1988; Glaser, 1987). These failures may be attributable to the types of domains that have been investigated. Research on expertise has been devoted predominantly to domains dependent on strategic performance and procedural knowledge (e.g., chess, computer programming, Go). In domains such as these, the strategies that are used to increase proficiency are inextricably linked to conceptual knowledge pertaining to the domain.

Mastery of domains characterized by knowledge of object categories (e.g., dinosaurs, rocks) is rooted in category differentiation and the learning of features and dimensions along which category members may be grouped, rather than in the development of knowledge-dependent heuristics. As such, it is possible that expertise may exert effects on categorization and perceptual discrimination in less familiar but related domains, particularly if such domains share theoretical similarity (e.g., two different biological domains). The potential role of metacognition and other individual difference variables in facilitating such transfer is not known, particularly for young children.

The present chapter will review evidence from studies of child experts and explore questions such as: What types of knowledge transfer from one biological domain to another? How extensive is the transfer? What factors facilitate this transfer? The remainder of the chapter addresses these questions through 4 sections. In the first, we review the literature surrounding the effects of expertise and the extent of transfer typically seen. Next, we review the literature that examines child experts and the transfer of their knowledge, proposing a model for the transfer of expertise across domains. Following, we review the literature on factors that support transfer across domains such as IQ and metacognitive knowledge. Finally, we examine our model with a set of data from 4- to 9-year-old dinosaur experts and conclude with future directions for research.

EXPERTISE

Although expertise exists along a continuum, individuals who are considered to be experts typically have acquired vast amounts of domain-specific knowledge and the ability to perform domain-relevant pattern-based retrieval in their area of expertise (Chase & Simon, 1973; Ericsson & Lehman, 1996). Experts display highly organized knowledge (Chi, Glaser, & Rees, 1982; Hoffman 1992) and generally represent problems in their domain of expertise in terms of general principles rather than surface elements (Chi, Feltovich, & Glaser, 1981).

For example, research on expertise effects in the domain of physics has shown that novices tend to focus on the explicit information given in a problem (objects, surface structure of the problem,) while experts tend to focus more on non-obvious principles acquired through inferences, classifying physics problems in terms of physical principles aligned with problem solutions. In addition, the automaticity of access to information within the domain reduces the role of memory search and general processing skills in experts' problem solving (Glaser, 1987).

Experts also understand the conditions under which their knowledge might be useful and know how to regulate problem solving within the domain (Chi et al., 1981). Importantly, however, performance quality is not solely related to time spent in the domain but instead likely relates to the role of deliberate practice and the factors that lead some individuals to engage in sustained, deliberate practice more than others (Ericsson & Charness, 1995; Ericsson, Krampe, & Tesch-Romer, 1993). Interestingly, expertise in a domain is not necessarily related to high scores on measures of general intelligence (Chase & Simon, 1973).

Child Experts

Children who are experts on domains such as dinosaurs and chess, while not likely to reach the pinnacle of consistent performance described by Ericsson and Lehman (1996) or Glaser (1987), still know more about a domain than most adults will ever know. Research in this area has suggested that child experts possess, a) improved memory for domain-relevant information; b) better understanding of causal relations; c) knowledge of many words denoting concepts learned within the relevant domain; d) improved processing efficiency, and e) hierarchically-organized domain knowledge (e.g., Chi, 1978; Chi, Hutchinson & Robin, 1989; Chi & Koeske, 1983; Gobbo & Chi, 1986; Johnson & Mervis, 1994).

Child experts present a unique opportunity for studying the relation between developmental processes and the increased processing efficiency that accompanies the acquisition of expertise. Typically age and knowledge levels covary throughout childhood. Thus, older children know more than do younger children. In addition, older children have more strategies available to support their learning than do younger children, as well as higher levels of metacognitive knowledge. The availability of child experts allows researchers to test the degree to which increases in domain-specific knowledge can account for changes in performance normally attributed to cognitive developmental processes (Carey, 1985). Researchers can capitalize on the availability of child experts to address a range of questions pertaining to knowledge effects, transfer, and potential mechanisms for such transfer.

Expertise on Domains Related to Biology

The term "domain" is used by different groups of researchers to mean different things (Hirschfeld & Gelman, 1994). Some researchers use this term to refer to extremely broad areas of cognitive competencies, such as the representation of number or causal relations. Others use the term "domain" to denote theories, or coherent clusters of beliefs pertaining to areas such as biology, physics, or music (Carey, 1985; Gopnik & Meltzoff, 1997; Karmiloff-Smith, 1992). We have adopted the use frequently seen in the expertise literature, where "domain" tends to have a considerably narrower focus, typically referring to particular areas of specialization such as chess, numerical digit span, or birds (Ericsson & Smith, 1991).

Domains that are related to biological concepts are composed primarily of declarative knowledge. These domains are organized taxonomically through hierarchical inclusion relations that support induction (Berlin, Breedlove, & Raven, 1973; Malt, 1995; Waxman, Lynch, Casey, & Baer, 1997), and they encompass a rich array of perceptual and behavioral features that vary in terms of the degree to which they are extended across categories or category members (Shipley, 1993; 2000). Mastery of domains related to biological concepts thus requires category differentiation and the learning of features and dimensions by which members can be grouped. Across most object domains (whether related to biology or not), concepts may be represented at multiple levels of specificity: *superordinate* (e.g., animal, vehicle); *basic* (e.g., bird, car); *subordinate* (e.g., sparrow, sedan), and *sub-subordinate* (e.g., chipping sparrow, Pontiac sedan). *Basic* level concepts are most perceptually and pragmatically salient and have been shown to be the most common level at which items are categorized (e.g., Gelman, 2003; Neisser, 1987; Rosch, Mervis, Gray, Johnson, & Boyes-Braem, 1976).

Domains related to biological knowledge consist primarily of *subordinate* concepts (e.g., kinds of dinosaurs, kinds of birds). Categorization at subordinate levels is considerably more difficult for young children than categorization at the basic level because of the similarities among category members (e.g., all kinds of dinosaurs look alike and function similarly relative to basic level contrasts among dinosaurs, birds, and cetaceans; Callanan, 1989; Mervis & Crisafi, 1982; Mervis, Johnson, & Mervis, 1994). This difficulty in subordinate level categorization is one of the first obstacles that must be overcome by a developing child expert.

At an even deeper and more abstract level, biological concepts are embedded within larger knowledge systems or theories (Keil & Lockhart, 1999; Medin, 1989; Murphy, 2001) – most notably a framework theory of biology (Barrett, Abdi, Murphy, & Gallagher, 1993; Carey, 1985; Johnson, Scott, & Mervis, 2004; Wellman, 1990). Framework theories help to define the ontology of domains by highlighting causally relevant properties that lend organizational structure to the knowledge base. Such theories also help to specify the kinds of theoretical explanations that are appropriate. For example, it would be appropriate to attribute an increase in the size of an animal to growth processes, but inappropriate to attribute an increase in building size to growth.

Much research related to the issue of how expert knowledge impacts categorization has been focused on biological concepts, such as trees (Lynch, Coley, & Medin, 2000; Medin, Lynch, Coley, & Atran, 1997; Proffitt, Coley, & Medin, 2000), birds (Bailenson, Shum, Atran, Medin, & Coley, 2002; Boster, 1988; Boster, Berlin, & O'Neill, 1986; Johnson & Mervis, 1997, 1998), and fish (Boster & Johnson, 1989; Medin et al., 2006). A sizeable literature from the field of cognitive anthropology precipitated much of this work, beginning with Berlin, Breedlove, and Raven's (1973) seminal explorations of folk classification of plants and animals, and the extent to which people's everyday categorization converges with scientific taxonomy (see Malt, 1995 for a review).

Generally this research has provided evidence that for experts, the subordinate level of categorization begins to function as the basic level, in that it is the preferred level for identifying and categorizing objects (Johnson & Mervis, 1997; Tanaka & Taylor, 1991). Furthermore, experts' knowledge has been shown to reorganize (Johnson & Mervis, 1994), such that experts are essentially freed from relying predominantly on perceived similarity when classifying and reasoning about objects (Coley, Shafto, Stepanova, & Baraff, 2005). Knowledgeable experts can use a variety of causal, thematic, and ecological relations to guide inductive inferences. Abstract goals or ideals also become increasingly salient in determinations of prototypicality (Lynch, et al., 2000). In general, expertise tends to increase one's understanding of multiple relations among entities, and the ability to apply this understanding in context-specific ways (Shafto & Coley, 2003). Whether these tendencies remain constrained to the domain of expertise, or whether they generalize to other domains related to biology will be considered throughout the remainder of this chapter.

TRANSFER OF EXPERTISE

Expertise is generally thought to be largely domain-specific. Ericsson and Charness (1999) have argued that the acquisition of expertise depends upon approximately 10 years of deliberate practice and study. Interestingly, Glaser (1987) has suggested that certain domains may lend themselves more to generalizability than others. When domain structures are sufficiently similar such that structural alignment and analogical thinking are tenable, aspects of expertise might transfer to the structurally similar domain (Gentner & Gentner, 1983). In general, however, transfer from the domain of expertise to other domains is very rare.

The basic assumption behind transfer is that knowledge or skills from the expert domain is directly applied to other domains (DeCorte, 2003). *Near transfer*, or the transfer of skills or knowledge between very similar contexts (as when a garage mechanic transfers knowledge of a particular car model's engine to a newer model) occurs fairly readily (Perkins & Salomon, 1988). However, evidence for *far transfer*, or the transfer of skills across contexts that on the surface seem very dissimilar (as in the application of chess strategies to political or military campaigns), has consistently been difficult to obtain (Bransford & Schwartz, 1999; Thorndike & Woodworth, 1901). Though the transfer of knowledge across domains that are related to biology would seem more challenging than generalizing from one car model's engine to that of a newer model, it fits more closely with Perkins and Salomon's (1988) notion of near transfer. Clearly, examples of near and far transfer exist along a continuum of opportunities for transfer (Barnett & Ceci, 2002).

Perkins and Salomon (1988) have argued that any type of transfer is more likely under certain conditions. First, the initial knowledge or skills should have been thoroughly learned and already practiced across multiple contexts. Transfer can also be facilitated through an explicit abstraction process whereby the learner reflects on underlying principles that are acquired in one situation and then applies those de-contextualized principles to a new situation, otherwise known as "high road transfer." Typically the learner's metacognitive knowledge or the explicit use of analogies by a teacher can play a significant role in facilitating high road transfer.

Bransford and Schwartz (1999; p. 66) have noted that, "prevailing theories and methods of measuring transfer work well for studying full-blown expertise, but they represent too blunt an instrument for studying the smaller changes in learning that lead to the development of expertise. New theories and measures of transfer are required." Bransford and Schwartz go on to propose that these new theories of transfer need to concentrate on the effects of current learning on the subsequent learning of new information, not on the direct application of information from one situation to another. In other words, how well are the individuals "prepared for future learning?" They argue that a focus on preparation for future learning (PFL) may enable researchers to notice instances of positive transfer that would normally be hidden. Transfer may also need to be studied through the implicit transfer of information between domains (Alexander, Johnson, Albano, Freygang, & Scott, 2006; Johnson & Mervis, 1998), which we turn to next.

Transfer across Domains Related to Biology

Previous research with adults has revealed a clear attentional shift with expertise from relying on surface features to relying on more abstract behavioral features or even features supporting causal/ecological reasoning (Coley, Shafto, Stepanova, & Baraff, 2005; Proffitt, et al., 2000; Shafto & Coley, 2003). Work by Johnson and Mervis (1998) suggests that this attentional shift may generalize to other biological domains. They found that adult bird experts based similarity decisions on deep features related to taxonomic membership for both familiar (bird) and less familiar (tropical fish) stimuli. Bird experts also rated perceptual features indicative of taxonomic categories in fish (e.g., fin shape) as perceptually more salient than did novices. In a separate study involving both adults and children, Johnson, Scott and Mervis (2004) found that adult dinosaur experts were significantly more likely to infer correct functional correlates for shorebird features than were adult dinosaur novices. Adult dinosaur experts also were likely to accept morphed, hypothetical dinosaurs with novel combinations of features as plausible, providing reasonable explanations for why such features could have co-evolved. Finally, although not based in a biological domain, research by Smeeton, Ward, and Williams (2004) found that experts in field hockey are more likely to transfer pattern recognition skills to similarly structured sports such as soccer but not to sports with different structures such as volleyball (Smeeton, et al., 2004). Thus, some evidence suggests that adult experts are capable of extending at least some aspects of their category-based knowledge to other similar domains.

Assessments of child experts generally have not revealed evidence for direct application of information from one domain to another. Instead, the evidence suggests that high levels of domain-specific knowledge may culminate in the child's better preparation for future learning of related information and an increased likelihood of focusing on diagnostic features in the new domain. This typically happens without the child being explicitly aware of their relative advantage. For example, Johnson and Mervis (1994) reported a case study in which one 4-year-old child's existing knowledge of passerine birds facilitated his rate of learning about (unfamiliar) shorebirds, relative to other children who began with less knowledge.

Chi et al. (1989) found that child dinosaur experts were more likely than novices to transfer their dinosaur knowledge to novel dinosaurs by comparing the novel dinosaurs to known dinosaurs and families in order to draw inferences about expected behaviors. Finally, Johnson and Eilers (1998) found that children with expertise on dinosaurs described differences between unfamiliar shorebird pairs more analytically by emphasizing more subtle perceptual differences than did children with less knowledge.

On the other hand, very little evidence exists in support of explicit transfer of knowledge-dependent strategies in children. Alexander, et al. (2002) found that children with high levels of dinosaur knowledge did not deploy strategies more effectively within a less familiar, but related, biological domain (sea creatures). Their task involved presenting children with pairs of 3-dimensional models behind a screen – children were free to explore the models haptically, but could not see the models. Children were asked to simply decide whether the pair included identical creatures (e.g., 2 tyrannosaurs) or not (a tyrannosaur and an allosaurus). While child experts demonstrated an advantage within the expert domain on haptically identifying the initial model in the pair (even being seen to "count" the number of toes on models using their fingers), younger child experts performed very similarly to same-aged novices (and more poorly than older novices) when completing the cross-model comparison task within both the expert and novice domain. In other words, high levels of knowledge did not override 4-to 6-year-old children's tendency to perform poorly on the strategy-laden comparison between difficult pairs on the haptic exploration task.

Similarly, Johnson et al. (2004) found little evidence of transfer on a task that depended more heavily on explicit conceptual knowledge as bases for relations among dinosaur features. Children aged 7 to 9 years were presented with two tasks. In the first, they viewed pictures of hypothetical dinosaurs created by "morphing" dinosaur species together to create feature combinations that were either plausible (e.g., a sauropod with a horned structure on its head; many scientists believe that the horned structures played a communication function, meaning any species of dinosaurs could have evolved with them) or not plausible (e.g., a carnosaur with a set of spikes on its back; large predatory dinosaurs rarely would have needed defense mechanisms as they were typically the animal at the top of the food chain). During a series of interview questions, children were asked to decide whether the hypothetical dinosaurs could have evolved, and to justify why or why not. Invariably children indicated that the hypothetical dinosaurs could not have evolved – typically because they had never seen a dinosaur like that before. This is in keeping with Inhelder and Piaget's (1958) assertion that school-aged children have difficulty with reasoning about the hypothetical – in this case, even when relevant knowledge is quite high. In the second task, children were asked to explain why features of both dinosaurs and shorebirds were functionally important. Although children regularly mentioned relevant properties for dinosaurs (linking body parts to behavioral correlates involving diet, defense, or thermoregulation), children had difficulty making similar inferences for less familiar shorebirds. It may be that the attentional shift described for similarity judgment tasks (Johnson & Mervis, 1994, 1998) precedes the development of explicit awareness concerning why such features are functionally significant. Of course it is also possible that children understand something about the functional significance of the perceptual features that they construe as most salient – yet they have difficulty verbalizing what they know.

In sum, we offer these preliminary conclusions regarding expertise and transfer across object domains. First, what evidence there is for transfer between expert and novice object domains in children appears to be due to a shift in attention to more subtle attributes of objects. Research by Sheya and Smith (2006) suggests that surface perceptual features may play a significant role in the understanding of behavioral or role properties of basic level objects, beginning early in childhood. In fact, Rakinson (2003) and Booth and Waxman (2002) have suggested that highly diagnostic features at the basic level may be important anchors in the conceptual system that serve to focus attention and memory and link the instance in question to relevant conceptual knowledge beginning in infancy. For child-experts, this shift in attention to more subtle attributes of *subordinate* kinds is likely driven by a low-level perceptual learning mechanism and seems to operate largely outside the realm of explicit awareness, though the role of metacognition in this process has not been thoroughly tested.

It seems possible that this perceptually-driven learning mechanism could facilitate transfer between domains at multiple levels. First, an expert in one domain who is just beginning to learn about a second domain might notice how clusters of surface features tend to co-occur in the new domain in ways that are analogous to feature covariation in the expert domain. For example, sharp teeth and two-leggedness tend to co-occur in the dinosaur domain while a median notch in the tail tends to co-occur with flukes and not caudal fins when comparing sea creatures. Second, experts might begin to notice that surface features tend to relate to behaviors or functions similarly across the two domains. The presence of sharp teeth tends to co-occur with eating meat in the dinosaur domain and with eating fish in sea creatures. Experts might also notice that clusters of behavioral properties also tend to co-occur. Eating meat tends to be associated with running fast (as predators must outrun their prey) and preying on relatively large fish also tends to co-occur with faster swimming speeds. Developing experts might also begin to notice that certain properties tend to form a cohesive set of explanations for behaviors such as diet, thermoregulation, and locomotion. These explanations might eventually cohere into a causal underlying framework or theory in the expert domain that could be applied to the newly learned domain. Any of this knowledge might facilitate preparation for future learning in the transfer domain.

Table 1 summarizes these possibilities. It is plausible that the aspects of expertise listed may transfer to other related domains, at least implicitly. We have organized the table such that transfer is more likely to occur at the lower levels of complexity of knowledge (those rows at the top of the table). In other words, current literature suggests that transfer of the understanding of the importance of diagnostic features in domains related to biology (Johnson & Mervis, 1998) would be more likely than transfer of causal relations inherent within an underlying framework theory (Johnson, et al., 2004).

Table 1. Aspects of Child Expertise and their Potential for Transfer

Type of Knowledge	Potential for Transfer
Diagnostic Perceptual Features (or Feature Clusters)	Implicitly Increases Attention to Analogous Types of Features in Related Domains
Behavioral (or Functional) Features	Implicitly Increases Attention to Analogous Types of Features in Related Domains
Causal Relations Between Perceptual and Behavioral (or Functional) Features	Implicitly Increases "Preparedness to Learn" and Analogous Relations in Related Domains
Bases for Taxonomic Relations	Implicitly Increases Attention to Analogous Bases in Related Domain
Framework Theoretical Knowledge	Aspects may Implicitly or Explicitly Generalize to Related Domains, Particularly for Older Children and Adults

FACTORS THAT FACILITATE TRANSFER

A second aim of this chapter is to consider the effects of individual difference factors on transfer between biological domains - with a particular emphasis on IQ and metacognition. We first define metacognition and briefly review the literature on IQ and its relation to metacognition and transfer. We then concentrate particularly on the role of one type of declarative metacognitive knowledge - metaconceptual knowledge – in facilitating transfer effects.

The exact definition of metacognition has been debated in the literature for decades (c.f. Brown, Bransford, Ferrara, & Campione, 1983; Flavell, 1979). Alexander, Carr, and Schwanenflugel (1995) suggested a definition that includes three elements: 1) declarative metacognitive knowledge; 2) cognitive monitoring; and 3) regulation of strategies. Each of these elements has been shown to improve with age (Alexander et al, 1995). Metacognitive knowledge is an umbrella term typically encompassing "meta" information about many different types of cognitive processes. The current chapter focuses on the role of declarative metacognitive knowledge about concepts in predicting transfer across conceptual domains.

Individuals with higher IQ scores consistently have been found to be more apt to transfer what they know – particularly across more disparate domains (Alexander, et al., 1995). In addition, children with higher IQs tend to have higher declarative metacognitive knowledge throughout development. Thus, we assume IQ would facilitate the transfer of knowledge from one biological domain to another. Unfortunately, this has typically been difficult to test. Most of the child expert studies we have reviewed have reported above-average IQ scores in children with the highest levels of knowledge (e.g., Alexander, et al., 2002; Johnson & Mervis, 1994, Johnson & Eilers, 1998). Thus, the exact nature of the relation between these variables may present a unique measurement dilemma for the field. Data we will present below are from a more representative sample, though the average IQ is still one standard-deviation above the normed mean.

Work by Veenman, Wilhelm, and Beishuizen (2004) has been aimed at understanding the interplay of IQ and metacognition developmentally in more knowledgeable and less knowledgeable domains. Their work suggests that metacognition is independent of IQ and tends to play a larger role in task performance when individuals are performing in a novice domain. They argue that the metacognitive skills of experts in a domain are well integrated with domain-specific knowledge whereas the metacognitive skills of novices are not as well integrated with domain knowledge. They also advance the idea that metacognition can be a person-related characteristic, not just dependent on domain knowledge. In fact, metacognitive skillfulness is one important factor that contributes to transfer.

Unfortunately, the majority of studies examining the role of metacognition in transfer have addressed the transfer of skills rather than knowledge and online monitoring of performance rather than declarative metacognitive knowledge. Virtually no work has concentrated on knowledge of domains of object categories or whether domain knowledge in an expert domain could enhance preparation for future learning (PFL) in related domains. Indeed, Alexander, et al. (2006) suggest that when examining performance within conceptual domains, using declarative *metaconceptual* knowledge as a predictor of later performance is more appropriate than using a general metacognitive knowledge measure. Metaconceptual knowledge, as defined by Alexander, et al. (2006), is a series of related meta-information concerning the structure and function of taxonomically-organized concepts (e.g., prototypicality, feature centrality, inclusion relations; Murphy, 2002). It also includes one's knowledge concerning how an entity representation can be affected by high levels of knowledge.

Alexander, et al. (2006) found that metaconceptual knowledge develops steadily between the ages of 5 and adulthood. In addition, IQ is consistently related to metaconceptual knowledge scores throughout development. Finally, although finding a direct connection between high levels of declarative metacognitive knowledge and appropriate task behaviors has been difficult (Veenman, et al., 2004), Alexander et al (2006) found that metaconceptual scores significantly predicts performance on a twenty-questions task designed to tap categorical knowledge. Alexander et al. (2006) argue that the development of metaconceptual knowledge might reflect a transitional step between implicit understandings of conceptually-related strategies, and explicit, on-line articulation of knowledge pertaining to the deployment of such strategies. Interview items assessing metaconceptual knowledge seem to tap some level of general knowledge about conceptual issues, even if it cannot be articulated verbally after the completion of a task. In the next section, we report data that explores the potential role of metaconceptual knowledge and IQ in facilitating transfer across biological domains on a referential communication task for which knowledge of category structure should be quite salient.

EXPLORING TRANSFER BETWEEN BIOLOGICAL DOMAINS: THE CASE OF REFERENTIAL COMMUNICATION

Young children's referential communication skills tend to be relatively poor (Whitehurst & Sonnenschein, 1985). In referential communication situations, the speaker constructs a message in order to direct the listener's behavior, ideally tailoring the message to the particular characteristics of the listener. Referentially precise messages should meet the intent of the speaker and be comprehensible to the listener. Research has shown that the content knowledge of the least knowledgeable partner constrains what can be shared (Whitehurst & Sonnenschein, 1985). Domain-specific knowledge has also been shown to be related to the kinds of communication questions asked in the game of twenty questions (those that address surface characteristics versus deep-level characteristics; Alexander, et al., 2006; Alexander, Johnson, Leibham, & DeBarge, 2005). Metaconceptual knowledge and IQ have both been shown to play important roles in communication tasks (Alexander et al, 2006), though metaconceptual knowledge has been found to be a more important predictor of good communication among children whose IQ is average or slightly below average than for children whose IQ are above average.

Task Procedures

We examined performance on a referential communication task across two domains – one "expert" for which children were reported by parents to be highly familiar (dinosaurs), and one novice (sea creatures). Participants included 35 children (mean age 6.9, range 4.9 to

9.8). Children were recruited through newspaper advertisements and through a Children's Museum exhibit on dinosaurs.

During the task, the child sat at a low table on which two rows of four museum-quality models were randomly placed. One model was placed on a brightly colored mat that designated it to be the "target." Models ranged from 8 to 21 cm long and from 5 to 14 cm high and were readily graspable. Children completed three trials involving models from each of the two domains (dinosaurs and sea creatures), with trials matched across domains in terms of difficulty level. Difficulty level was reflected in the degree of feature overlap between the target and the other models in the array, with more difficult trials involving higher proportions of shared features.

Referential communication tasks typically entail both a speaker and a listener. Because of the logistical difficulties of scheduling a second child to serve as the "listener"- coupled with our inability to experimentally control that listener's level of domain knowledge - we adapted the task by having each child provide messages to a tester, who then proceeded to type the message into a laptop computer. The researcher told the child that the computer knew which eight dinosaurs/sea creatures were laid out on the table and was going to try to guess which model had the mat under it based on the child's clues. The researcher encouraged the child to pick the best possible clues so the computer could figure out as quickly as possible which model was placed on the mat. The researcher told the child that they could not use the model's name but could tell the computer anything else about the animal. In addition, the children were free to explore and pick up any of the models in front of them if they thought it would help them create better clues. The child completed one training trial followed by three trials in both domains. For each trial, children were permitted up to three attempts at helping the computer to guess the correct model (with determinations of success actually made by the tester, who pressed a programmed key at that point to make the computer appear to "guess correctly"). Only the data from the last attempt for each trial are reported here, though the number of attempts required for successful differentiation of the target model was recorded.

During a second session scheduled one week later in the child's home, we administered assessments of children's knowledge of dinosaur names and attributes (modeled after those used by Gobbo & Chi, 1986) to verify that all 35 children possessed at least moderate levels of dinosaur knowledge in the domain of expertise. IQ was then assessed with the Kaufman Brief Intelligence Test (K-Bit; Kaufman & Kaufman, 1990). Finally, metaconceptual knowledge was evaluated using a nine-item interview designed to tap children's knowledge concerning the structure and function of taxonomically-organized concepts, as described by Alexander et al. (2006). We also administered a "clue rating" task to gauge children's metaconceptual sensitivity to the relative usefulness of particular cues. The child's own clues generated for the most difficult trials in each of the two domains were embedded within a standardized list of 16 cues. Children were shown a photograph of each 8-model array along with a close-up photo of the target animal and reminded of the "game" that they had played a week earlier with the computer. Children were asked to rate how useful they thought each clue was on a 4-point scale (4 ="very good") that was anchored by faces varying in terms of level of positive affect.

Data Reduction and Analysis

For each child, the number of attempts required to correctly differentiate the three target models in each domain was recorded. In addition, each clue produced by a particular child was given a distinctiveness score reflecting how well the clue discriminated among models in the array. Scores for each clue were based on the number of exemplars present that could be eliminated with the child's clue. The maximum distinctiveness score was "7" (reflecting that all non-target models could be eliminated; in other words, a completely unambiguous clue), and the lowest score was "0" (reflecting that none could be eliminated, or a very ambiguous clue). Distinctiveness scores were summed across the three final clues generated on each trial (composite scores could range from 0 to 21).

Children's level of strategy use was determined based on the number of trials within a domain for which either verbal and/or nonverbal evidence of contrastive behavior was observed. Videotapes of each testing session were used to code nonverbal evidence, and responses to a standard declarative metaconceptual question were used to record verbal evidence. At the end of each trial the child was asked, "How did you think of such good clues? How did you know those would be the best clues? Why were they better than other clues?" If the child responded by indicating that they had deliberately contrasted the target model with other models in the array (e.g., "It's the only one that has X." "I looked at all of them and then decided to say Y."), one point was awarded for that trial (only five children were this explicit in their strategy awareness, and only in the expert domain). Nonverbal evidence included cases where the child picked up more than one model and obviously engaged in contrastive exploration, or instances of the child looking back and forth between the target model and at least one of the non-targets. Children could receive up to one point for each type of evidence observed in relation to a set of three clues, and scores were then summed across trials within each domain (range: 0-6 points). Evidence for transfer was expected to take the form of similar levels of performance across the two domains. In addition, we were interested in whether intelligence or level of metaconceptual knowledge was predictive of children's performance in the novice (sea creature) domain.

Paired-samples t-test results indicated that strategy scores were higher and total distinctiveness scores were higher in the more familiar dinosaur domain than in the sea creature domain. In contrast, the total number of trials required to successfully differentiate the target was actually higher in the expert than novice domain (see Table 2 for descriptive information). Further analysis revealed that this pattern was attributable to the fact that children typically concentrated their descriptions on features of dinosaurs (e.g., sharp teeth) that were perceptually and behaviorally important – yet were not unique to the target model and therefore did not uniquely discriminate it from the array.

Despite these domain differences, there were similarities between performance measures across domains. Total distinctiveness scores were positively correlated between the dinosaur and sea creature domains, r (35) = .50, p < .01. This correlation remained unchanged even when IQ was partialled out. Thus, there were similarities in the distinctiveness levels of the features children attended to across domains. In addition, those similarities did not seem to be solely due to advantages in central processing speed or verbal ability, as indicated by maintenance of the correlation when IQ was partialled out.

Table 2. Mean Levels of Performance Across Expert and Novice Domain Trials of Referential Communication Task as well as predictor factors

Variable	Dinosaur		Sea Creature		Paired-samples t-test
	Mean	sd	Mean	sd	
Number of Trials needed (max 9)[1]	4.22	0.94	3.71	1.13	t (34) = 2.11, p < .05
Total of Maximum Distinctiveness Scores[2]	44.65	7.79	41.63	9.37	t (34) = 2.12, p < .05
Strategy Score[3]	2.50	1.45	1.94	1.47	t (34) = 2.33, p < .05
IQ	116.26	10.91			
Metaconceptual Knowledge	9.09	2.71			

[1] Lower scores represent more sophisticated performance.

[2] Number of distractors (out of 63 across three trials) successfully eliminated with clues.

[3] Maximum Score = 6, Higher scores represent both verbal and nonverbal behavior reporting an examination of multiple items in the array and a contrastive strategy for clue generation.

Table 3. Correlations across Performance Variables for Transfer to Novice Domain Trials of Referential Communication Task

Performance Variable	Metaconceptual Knowledge	IQ
Number of Trials[1]	-.44**	-.32
Total Maximum Distinctiveness Scores [2]	.27	.34*
Strategy Scores [3]	.24	.42**

* p < .05, ** p ≤ .01.

[1] Lower scores represent more sophisticated performance.

[2] Number of distractors (out of 63 across three trials) successfully eliminated with clues.

[3] Maximum Score = 6, Higher scores represent both verbal and nonverbal behavior reporting an examination of multiple items in the array and a contrastive strategy for clue generation.

We next considered factors that were predictive of performance in each of the two domains. Neither IQ nor metaconceptual scores were related to total distinctiveness or strategy use scores in the expert domain, r (35) = .08 and .18, respectively for IQ; r (35) = .21 and .25, respectively for metaconceptual scores. Both factors, however, did help to predict transfer to the novice domain (see Table 3). IQ was related to total distinctiveness scores in the sea creature domain r = .34, p < .05 as well as strategy scores in the sea creature domain, r (35) = .42, p = .01. Metaconceptual knowledge scores were significantly related to number of trials in the sea creature domain, r (35) = -.41, p = .01. Interestingly, age was not significantly related to any performance measure in either domain (all r's = -.21 to .27)

In addition, qualitative analysis of the children's clues revealed evidence that children were attempting to apply their expert knowledge to the less familiar domain. For example, one child reported that the target sea creature (orca) had "both plant eater and meat eater teeth." Although this information is not accurate, the child is clearly relying on an important feature that discriminates meat-eating from plant-eating dinosaurs. Another child told the computer that the whale shark had a "sharp tail that can attack enemies." Again, this is not accurate information, but the same child had recently characterized the euoplocephalus (target dinosaur) as having "spiky things on its tail." Most children's books clearly note that this spike was likely used for defense and attack behaviors. In fact, 39% of the children's clues for the less familiar domain were rated by researchers as pertaining to three of the main behavioral organizing dimensions in the dinosaur domain (hunting, defense, and diet). Given that the children had little supporting biological knowledge in the sea creature domain, we would predict they would focus almost exclusively on perceptual information when generating clues. Instead, 39% of the children's clues were related to hunting, defense, or diet, suggesting they are aware that perceptual properties are related to underlying biological functions, even if their inferences were not entirely accurate.

Finally, we considered whether children's estimates of clue usefulness reflected their level of general metaconceptual knowledge. Declarative metaconceptual knowledge scores were significantly and positively correlated with children's clue usefulness ratings for both the standardized list of clues (dinosaurs: $r = .48$; sea creatures: $r = .38$) and for their own previously generated clues (dinosaurs: $r = .38$; sea creatures: $r = .44$, all p's $< .05$). This suggests that the metaconceptual interview did tap into children's understanding of the relative quality of the clues they were generating.

In summary, when children engage in message construction for a referential communication task involving highly familiar stimuli, few individual differences relate to behavior. These findings are similar to those of Veenman, Wilhelm, and Beishuizen (2004) and suggest that expertise in a domain facilitates attention to important perceptual features regardless of level of IQ or metacognitive knowledge. Our data show that expert children generate highly distinctive referential communication clues and they tend to focus on distinctive features even when confronted with stimuli from a less familiar domain. The children can also draw inferences about distinctive features in the sea creature domain and (sometimes incorrectly) use them to differentiate the target from the other exemplars in the array. On the other hand, children's clue generation in the novice domain is predicted both by metaconceptual knowledge and IQ. Finally, age is not related to task performance measures, even though it is related to metaconceptual interview scores, $r (35) = .62, p < .001$. Although age is certainly playing a significant role in the metaconceptual scores, it is not directly playing a significant role in performance measures in the novice domain (see correlations in Table 3).

AN INTEGRATION AND SUGGESTIONS FOR FUTURE RESEARCH

Our survey of the literature focused on expertise aligned with domains of biological kinds suggests that both children and adults acquire domain-specific vocabulary and a vast repertoire of feature knowledge that can be recruited to afford flexible bases for categorization and induction. In the context of children's referential communication, we have provided evidence that expert knowledge may support the construction of less ambiguous messages in a novel, but related domain. Our review also suggests that, although children and adults differ in terms of the potential for transfer of domain-specific knowledge, both seem to shift their attention to relatively subtle perceptual features that are particularly diagnostic of taxonomic relations (or salient behaviors). This attentional shift seems to readily generalize to biological domains that are relatively unfamiliar. Our data also suggest that children attempt to apply their knowledge of behavioral features to less familiar, but related biological domains. In the present data set, the distinctiveness scores of these 4- to 8-year old children's referential communication "clues" were highly correlated ($r = .50$) across expert and non-expert domains and approximately 40% of their clues pertained to behavioral features in the novice domain.

This shift in attention to subtle perceptual features seems to be quite implicit for children. Admittedly, few studies have explicitly asked children or adults whether they are aware of the perceptual shift. We hypothesize that adults may more readily reflect explicitly on why such features are important across domains and use that information to guide induction. For example, Shafto and Coley (2003) found that adults restricted the use of their framework theories to the expert domain and to appropriate situations in the novice domain (reasoning about diseases instead of reasoning about blank predicates). Thus, adults seem to be able to flexibly and knowingly use their domain knowledge to assist learning at appropriate times. Data on children have not supported such flexible uses of domain knowledge in novice domains.

Similar to the suggestion by Alexander et al. (2006), the present data support the importance of metaconceptual awareness in transfer. Metaconceptual knowledge does not seem to explicitly affect task performance, as few children were explicitly aware of how to generate effective clues when asked directly after the task. Instead, metaconceptual knowledge seems to be playing an implicit role, possibly facilitating the transition from implicit awareness of diagnostic features to more explicit awareness. Alexander et al., (2006) found that metaconceptual knowledge was related to referential communication skill in a large sample of 6 year olds, with higher levels of metaconceptual knowledge resulting in less ambiguous communication messages. In addition, the present study found correlations between ratings of clue goodness and metaconceptual knowledge as well as a relation between metaconceptual knowledge and number of trials required to do well on the communication task. Both relationships suggest an implicit role for metaconceptual knowledge in facilitating task performance. This implicit awareness may eventually lead to more explicit application and deployment of effective referential communication skills across domains, much as we see in adults.

There are at least two possible explanations for why children seem relatively unaware of the applicability of their knowledge from the expert to novice domain. Children may acquire their knowledge through the brute force of relatively effortful associative processes, whereas adults may be "prepared for learning" in a related domain by virtue of the mediated effects of related schemata. Data consistent with this hypothesis was presented in Bransford and Schwartz (1999). They asked students to generate questions about what they would need to research in order to design effective recovery plans for eagles. Although the fifth graders tended to focus on features of individual eagles, the college students focused on issues of interdependence between the eagles and their habitats. As Bransford and Schwartz concluded, "Because they had not studied eagles directly, the college students were presumably generating questions framed by other aspects of biology that they had learned. So, by this alternative form of transfer test, it would appear that the college students had learned general considerations that would presumably help shape their future learning if they chose to pursue this topic." (p. 66-67).

It may also be the case that adults' more pronounced transfer effects are mediated through the development of metaconceptual knowledge (a "high road transfer") which supports the establishment of domain-general strategies for category learning and transfer. Such strategies may be executed whenever experts confront novel categories that are organized in ways similar to their expert domain. Children may be capable of such explicit strategy control only once sufficient levels of relevant metaconceptual knowledge become available.

Although it may be difficult to foster the development of metacognitive knowledge in young children, recent research has shown that metacognitive skills training can support transfer at least with older children. Georghiades (2000) found that metacognitive instruction is feasible with primary school children under every day circumstances (though difficult and time consuming). Secondly, students who received metacognitive instruction performed better on written assessments about the topic (electricity) than those without metacognitive training. In a follow-up report, Georghiades (2004) found that 5th grade students with metacognitive training gained an even stronger advantage at a time-delay of eight months. Thus, the durability of the conceptual understandings was greater with metacognitive instruction.

It seems that there are multiple opportunities for parents or teachers to share metacognitive information about attention ("Pay attention to this, not that.") and memory ("So, how can we remember these six things?"). But, how often do adults have metacognitively rich conversations about categories with their children? How might children acquire metaconceptual knowledge? Some feedback about concepts may come as children interact with parents about "things" in the world. For example, if a child is attempting to solicit help in reaching one of several dinosaurs from a shelf in a toy store, the helper may request more specific information such as "Which dinosaur?" (or may inadvertently retrieve a dinosaur different from the one the child wanted, thereby providing feedback that the child's message was ambiguous). This may help the child realize that subordinate labels for objects afford precise communication, and that different people may identify the same object in different ways. Other forms of metaconceptual knowledge (e.g., inclusion relations) have been shown to take longer to master (Alexander et al., 2006). Limitations in exposure to a domain built on subordinate kinds and/or working memory limitations may contribute to these problems (Johnson et al., 1997). Additionally, some parents may include more metacognitive information about strategies in their discussions with children than others (Neitzel & Stright, 2003; Stright, Neitzel, Sears, & Hoke-Sinex, 2001); similar findings could be true regarding the embedding of metaconceptual information in everyday activities with children.

Finally, our survey of research also has highlighted some methodological challenges associated with addressing interactions among metacognition, expertise, and knowledge transfer in children that should be considered in future research. First, declarative metaconceptual knowledge is difficult to assess reliably, as children must verbally articulate what they know in a structured interview context. This issue is pertinent to almost all evaluations of metacognition that depend on children providing verbal explanations in relation to particular vignettes. While this issue obviously does not impact children who demonstrate explicit knowledge of conceptual structure and function, it remains possible that children who demonstrate little metaconceptual knowledge are actually more capable than they seem. Limitations in verbal skills may be limiting our awareness of understandings children do have.

In addition, it remains an open question to what extent the implicit forms of transfer described in the present chapter reflect actual shifts in attentional preferences as a result of domain-specific knowledge acquisition, as opposed to more stable individual difference characteristics. For example, it may be the case that children who manifest high levels of interest in dinosaurs tend to have a more analytic cognitive style than children less interested in dinosaurs. Alternatively, one could conduct longitudinal studies in which children are evaluated across multiple domains both before and after training in the "expert" domain. While this is undoubtedly the ideal design for investigating interactions among knowledge, IQ, and metacognition and the potential for knowledge transfer, it carries with it costs associated with longitudinal research, more generally. Multiple samples would be needed to investigate patterns aligned with near vs. far transfer. It would also be difficult to evaluate developmental changes unless longitudinal-sequential variations were implemented. Future researchers must devise novel and creative approaches to dealing with these issues.

ACKNOWLEDGEMENTS

This research was supported by grants BCS-9907865 and BCS-0217466 from the National Science Foundation. We thank Shannon Brown and numerous research assistants at IUPUI and IU for their assistance on this project. We also wish to thank the children and parents who participated in this study, Mudge Morris for her expertise on dinosaurs, and Allison Douglas for her expertise on dolphins, whales, and sharks.

REFERENCES

Alexander, J. M., Carr, M., & Schwanenflugel, P. J. (1995). Development of metacognition in gifted children: Directions for future research. *Developmental Review, 15,* 1-37.

Alexander, J. M., Johnson, K. E., Albano, J., Freygang, T., & Scott, B. (2006). Relations between intelligence and the development of metaconceptual knowledge. *Metacognition and Learning, 1,* 51-67.

Alexander, J. M., Johnson, K. E., Leibham, M. E., & DeBauge, C. (2005). Constructing domain-specific knowledge in kindergarten: Relations among knowledge, intelligence, and strategic performance. *Learning and Individual Differences, 15,* 35-52.

Alexander, J. M., Johnson, K. E., & Schreiber, J. B. (2002). Knowledge is not everything: Analysis of children's performance on a haptic comparison task. *Journal of Experimental Child Psychology, 82,* 341-366.

Bailenson, J. N., Shum, M. S., Atran, S., Medin, D. L., & Coley, J. D. (2002). A bird's eye view: Biological categorization and reasoning within and across cultures. *Cognition, 84,* 1-53.

Barnett, S. M., & Ceci, S. J. (2002). When and where do we apply what we learn? A taxonomy for far transfer. *Psychological Bulletin, 128,* 612-637.

Barrett, S. E. Abdi, H. Murphy, G. L., & Gallagher, J. M. (1993). Theory-based correlations and their role in children's concepts. *Child Development, 64,* 1595-1616.

Berlin, B., Breedlove, D. E., & Raven, P. H. (1973). General principles of classification and nomenclature in folk biology. *American Anthropologist, 75,* 214-242.

Booth, A. E., & Waxman, S. (2002). Object names and object functions serve as cues to categories for infants. *Developmental Psychology, 38,* 948-957.

Boster, J. S. (1988). Natural sources of internal category structure: Typicality, familiarity, and similarity of birds. *Memory & Cognition, 16,* 258-270.

Boster, J. S., Berlin, B., & O'Neill, J. (1986). The correspondence of Jivaroan to scientific ornithology. *American Anthropologist, 88,* 569-583.

Boster, J. S., & Johnson, J. C. (1989). Form or function: A comparison of expert and novice judgments of similarity among fish. *American Anthropologist, 91,* 866-889.

Bransford, J. D., & Schwartz, D. L. (1999). Rethinking transfer: A simple proposal with multiple implications. *Review of Research in Education, 24,* 61-100.

Brown, A. L., Bransford, J. D., Ferrara, R. A., & Campione, J. C. (1983). Learning, remembering and understanding. In J. H. Flavell & E. M. Markman (Eds.), *Carmichael's Manual of Child Psychology (Vol. 1).* New York; Wiley.

Brown, A. L., & DeLoach, J. S. (1978). Skills, plans, and self-regulation. In R. S. Siegler (Ed.), *Children's thinking: What develops?* (pp. 3-55). Hillsdale, NJ: Erlbaum.

Callanan, M. A. (1989). Development of object categories and inclusion relations: Preschoolers' hypotheses about word meanings. *Developmental Psychology, 25,* 207-216.

Carey, S. (1985). *Conceptual change in childhood.* Cambridge, MA: MIT Press.

Chase, W. G., & Simon, H. A. (1973). Perception in chess. *Cognitive Psychology, 4,* 55-81.

Chi, M. T. H. (1978). Knowledge structure and memory development. In R. Siegler (Ed.), *Children's thinking: What develops?* (pp. 73-96). Hillsdale, NJ: Erlbaum.

Chi, M. T. H., Feltovich, P. J., & Glaser, R. (1981). Categorization and representation of physics problems by experts and novices. *Cognitive Science, 5,* 121-152.

Chi, M. T. H., Glaser, R., & Farr, M. J. (1988). *The nature of expertise.* Hillsdale, NJ: Erlbaum.

Chi, M. T. H., Glaser, R., & Rees, E. (1982). Expertise in problem solving. In R. Sternberg (Ed.), *Advances in the psychology of human intelligence, Vol. 1* (pp. 7-75). Hillsdale, NJ: Erlbaum.

Chi, M. T. H., Hutchinson, J. E., & Robin, A. F. (1989). How inferences about novel domain-related concepts can be constrained by structured knowledge. *Merrill-Palmer Quarterly, 35,* 27-62.

Chi, M. T. H., & Koeske, R. D. (1983). Network representation of a child's dinosaur knowledge. *Developmental Psychology, 19,* 29-39.

Coley, J., Shafto, P., Stephanova, O., & Baraff, E. (2005). Knowledge and category-based induction. In W. Ahn, R. L. Goldson, B. C. Love, A. B. Markman (Eds.), *Categorization inside andoutside the laboratory: Essays in honor of Douglas L. Medin. APA Decade of behavior series* (pp. 69-85). Washington, DC: American Psychological Association.

DeCorte, E. (2003). Trasnfer as the productive use of acquired knowledge, skills, and motivations. *Current Directions in Psychological Science, 12,* 142-146.

Ericsson, K. A., & Charness, N. (1995). "Expert performance: Its structure and acquisition": Reply. *American Psychologist, 50*(9), 803-804.

Ericsson, K. A., & Charness, N. (1999). Expert performance: Its structure and acquisition. In S. J. Ceci and W. M. Williams (Eds.), *The nature-nurture debate: the essential readings. Essential readings in developmental psychology* (pp. 199-255). Malden, MA: Blackwell.

Ericsson, K. A., Krampe, R. T., & Tesch-Romer, C. (1993). The role of deliberate practice in the acquisition of expert performance. *Psychological Review, 100,* 363-406.

Ericsson, K. A., & Lehmann, A. C. (1996). Expert and exceptional performance: Evidence of maximal adaptation to task constraints. *Annual Review of Psychology, 47,* 273-305.

Ericsson, K. A., & Smith, J. (1991). *Toward a general theory of expertise: Prospects and limits.* New York: Cambridge.

Flavell, J. H. (1979). Metacognition and cognitive monitoring: A new area of cognitive-developmental inquiry. *American Psychologist, 34,* 906-911.

Gelman, S. A., (2003). *The essential child: Origins of essentialism in everyday thought: Oxford series in cognitive development.* New York: Oxford University Press.

Gentner, D., & Gentner, D. R. (1983). Flowing waters or teeming crowds: Mental models of electricity. In D. Gentner & A. L. Stevens, (Eds.), *Mental Models* (pp. 99-129). Hillsdale, NJ: Erlbaum.

Georghiades, P. (2000). Beyond conceptual change learning in science education: Focusing on transfer, durability, and metacognition. *Educational Research, 42,* 119-139.

Georghiades, P. (2004). Making pupils' conceptions of electricity more durable by means of situated metacognition. *International Journal of Science Education, 26,* 85-99.

Glaser, R. (1987). Thoughts on expertise. In C. Schooler & K. W. Share (Eds.), *Cognitive functioning and social structure over the life course* (pp. 81-94). Norwood, NJ: Ablex.

Gobbo, C., & Chi, M. (1986). How knowledge is structured and used by expert and novice children. *Cognitive Development, 1,* 221-237.

Gopnik, A., & Meltzoff, A. N. (1997). *Words, thoughts, and theories: Learning, development, and conceptual change.* Cambridge, MA: MIT Press.

Hirschfeld, L. A., & Gelman, S. A., (1994). *Mapping the mind: Domain specificity in cognition and culture.* New York: Cambridge University Press.

Hoffman, R. R. (1992). *The psychology of expertise: Cognitive research and empirical AI.* New York: Springer-Verlag.

Inhelder, B. & Piaget, J. (1958). *The growth of logical thinking from childhood to adolescence.* New York: Basic Books.

Johnson, K. E., & Eilers, A. T. (1998). Effects of knowledge and development on subordinate level categorization. *Cognitive Development, 13,* 515-545.

Johnson, K. E., & Mervis, C. B. (1994). Microgenetic analysis of first steps in children's acquisition of expertise on shorebirds. *Developmental Psychology, 30,* 418-435.

Johnson, K. E., & Mervis, C. B. (1997). Effects of varying levels of expertise on the basic level of categorization. *Journal of Experimental Psychology: General, 126,* 248-277.

Johnson, K. E., & Mervis, C. B. (1998). Impact of intuitive theories on feature recruitment throughout the continuum of expertise. *Memory and Cognition, 26,* 382-401.

Johnson, K. E., Scott, P., & Mervis, C. B. (2004). What are theories for? Concept use throughout thye continuum of dinosaur expertise. *Journal of Experimental Child Psychology, 87,* 171-200.

Karmiloff-Smith, A. (1992). *Beyond modularity: A developmental perspective on cognitive science: Learning, development, and conceptual change.* Cambridge, MA: MIT Press.

Kaufman, A. S., & Kaufman, N. L. (1990). *Kaufman Brief Intelligence Test.* Circle Pines, MN: American Guidance Service.

Keil, F. C., & Lockhart, K. L. (1999). Explanatory understanding in conceptual development. In E. K. Scholnick, K. Nelson, S. A. Gelman, & P. H. Miller (Eds.), *Conceptual development: Piaget's legacy: The Jean Piaget symposium series* (pp. 103-130). Mahwah, NJ: Erlbaum.

Lynch, E. B., Coley, J. D., & Medin, D. L. (2000). Tall is typical: Central tendency, ideal dimensions, and graded category structure among tree experts. *Memory and Cognition, 28,* 41-50.

Malt, B. (1995). Category coherence in cross-cultural perspective. *Cognitive Psychology, 29,* 85-148.

Medin, D. L. (1989). Concepts and conceptual structure. *American Psychologist, 44,* 1469-1481.

Medin, D. L., Lynch, E. B., Coley, J. D., & Atran, S. (1997). Categorization and reasoning among tree experts: Do all roads lead to Rome? *Cognitive Psychology, 32,* 49-96.

Medin, D. L., Ross, N. O., Atran, S., Cox, D., Coley, D., Proffitt, J. B., & Blok, S. (2006). Folkbiology of freshwater fish. *Cognition, 99,* 237-273.

Mervis, C. B., & Crisafi, M. A. (1982). Order of acquisition of suborindate-, basic-, and superordinate-level categories. *Child Development, 53,* 258-266.

Mervis, C. B., Johnson, K. E., & Mervis, C. A. (1994). Acquisition of subordinate categories by 3-year-olds: The role of attribute salience, linguistic input, and child characteristics. *Cognitive Development, 9,* 211-234.

Murphy, G. L. (2001). Causes of taxonomic sorting by adults: A test of the thematic-to-taxonomic shift. *Psychonomic Bulletin and Review, 8,* 834-839.

Murphy, G. L. (2002). *The big book of concepts.* Cambridge, MA: MIT Press.

Neisser, U. (1987). *Concepts and conceptual development: Ecological and intellectual factors in categorization: Emory symposia in cognition.* New York: Cambridge University Press.

Neitzel, C., & Stright, A. D. (2003). Mothers' scaffolding of children's problem solving: Establishing a foundation of academic self-regulatory competence. *Journal of Family Psychology, 17,* 147-159.

Perkins, D. N., & Salomon, G. S. (1988). Teaching for transfer. *Educational Leadership, 46,* 22-32.

Proffitt, J. B., Coley, J. D., & Medin, D. L. (2000). Expertise and category-based induction. *Journal of Experimental Psychology: Learning, Memory, and Cognition, 26,* 811-828.

Rakison, D. H. (2003). Parts, motion, and the development of the animate-inanimate distinction in infancy. In D. H. Rakison, & L. M. Oakes (Eds.), *Early category and concept development: Making sense of the blooming, buzzing confusion* (pp. 159-192). New York: Oxford.

Rosch, E., Mervis, C. B., Gray, W. D., Johnson, D. M., & Boyes-Braem, P. (1976). Basic objects in natual categories. *Cognitive Psychology, 8,* 382-439.

Shafto, P., & Coley, J. D. (2003). Development of categorization and reasoning in the natural world: Novices to experts, naïve similarity to ecological knowledge. *Journal of Experimental Psychology: Learning, Memory and Cognition, 29,* 641-649.

Sheya, A., & Smith, L. B. (2006). Perceptual features and the development of conceptual knowledge. *Journal of Cognition and Development, 7,* 455-476.

Shipley, E. F. (1993). Categories, hierarchies, and induction. In D. L. Medin (Ed.), *The psychology of learning and motivation: Advances in research and theory, Vol. 30* (pp. 265-301). San Diego, CA: Academic Press.

Shipley, E. F. (2000). Children's categorization of objects: The relevance of behavior, surface appearance, and insides. In B. Landau, J. Sabini, J. Jonides, & E. L.Newport (Eds.), *Perception, cognition and language: Essays in honor of Henry and Lilsa Gleitman* (pp. 69-85). Cambrdge, MA: MIT Press.

Smeeton, N. J., Ward, P., & Williams, A. M. (2004). Do pattern recognition skills transfer across sports? A preliminary analysis. *Journal of Sports Sciences, 22,* 205-213.

Stright, A. D., Neitzel, C., Sears, K. G., & Hoke-Sinex, L. (2001). Instruction begins in the home: Relations between parental instruction and children's self-regulation in the classroom. *Journal of Educational Psychology, 93,* 456-466.

Tanaka, J. W., & Taylor, M. (1991). Object categories and expertise: Is the basic level in the eye of the beholder? *Cognitive Psychology, 23,* 457-482.

Thorndike, E. L., & Woodward, R. S. (1901). The influence of improvement in one mental function upon the efficacy of other functions. *Psychological Review, 8,* 247-261.

Veenman, M. V. J., Wilhelm, P., & Beishuiszen, J. J. (2004). The relation between intellectual and metacognitive skills from a developmental perspective. *Learning and Instruction, 14,* 89-109.

Waxman, S. B., Lynch, E. B., Casey, K. L., Baer, L. (1997). Setters and samoyeds: The emergence of subordinate level categories as a basis for inductive inference in preschool-age children. *Developmental Psychology, 33,* 1974-1090.

Wellman, H. M. (1990). *The child's theory of mind.* Cambridge, MA: MIT Press.

Whitehurst, G. J., & Sonnenshein, S. (1985). The development of communication: A functional analysis. *Annals of Child Development, 2,* 1-48.

In: Meta-Cognition: A Recent Review of Research...   ISBN: 978-1-60456-011-4
Editors: M.F. Shaughnessy et al. pp. 85-108   © 2008 Nova Science Publishers, Inc.

Chapter 5

TO BE OR NOT 2 BEE:
AN EXAMINATION OF BREAKING SET

Carol L. McGaughey
Houston Baptist University, USA

ABSTRACT

The metacognitive process of breaking set, which involves breaking from a pattern which has been intentionally established through a set of activities or experiences, was examined to ascertain if differences existed between identified gifted children and non-identified children. Using an assessment instrument modeled after the Einstellung Test, which was first used in experiments during the 1920's at the University of Berlin to induce a set for a mathematical solution to volume problems, 102 fifth and sixth grade students were measured in the ability to break set. Findings support the hypothesis that gifted students would break set more frequently than other students. Implications exist in the areas of identification, curriculum, and teacher training.

INTRODUCTION

The Relationship between Breaking Set and Level of Intelligence

What is intelligence? Is it a process or reflected in a product? Is it unchanging throughout one's lifetime? Is it shaped by the environment? Is it mainly a verbal ability? What does it mean to be termed "intellectually gifted?"

These global questions are being examined by researchers such as Howard Gardner and Robert Sternberg, but are also being posed by educators, politicians, and the general public. Is the ubiquitous IQ test valid in an age when multiple intelligences, learning styles, and the triarchic theory are becoming a part of the educational schema (Plucker, Callahan, & Tomchin, 1996)? What effect does the constructivist approach to teaching and learning have on students who are encouraged to set their own goals, explore diverse methods, and create original products (Brooks & Brooks, 1993)? How has research changed ideas about the ability to assess a student's level of intelligence (Lupert & Pyryt, 1996)? How are the gifted distinguished from the average student (Naglieri and Kaufman, 2001)? One research project found that society labels people as gifted to the extent that they meet five criteria: excellence, rarity, productivity, demonstrability, and value (Zhang & Sternberg, 1998).

Historically, individuals who met those contemporary requirements to be termed "gifted" often distinguished themselves by departing from the accepted realm of conventional thought or creation (Filippelli & Walberg, 1997). Galileo, DaVinci, and Martin Luther presented viewpoints that altered their worlds. In retrospect, these individuals sent their societies on different paths affecting the course of history by slightly changing its direction (Boorstin, 1983). In the 20th century, Albert Einstein was an icon of a lone genius who viewed the cosmos differently than his peers (Einstein, 1993). His perceptions opened new realms of investigation that greatly influenced the 20th century.

Even today, one image of a gifted individual is that of the person who doesn't quite fit into everyday life yet has capabilities beyond that considered normal in terms of an area or areas of expertise (Merrell & Gill, 1994). The qualities that cause a gifted person to view the world from a slightly different vantage point are " too often interpreted as weirdness, eccentricity, illogic, and illusionary realities" (Delisle, 2006, p.31). Despite this intuitive concept of a gifted individual as one who breaks with convention or sets a new path, a limited amount of empirical research has been done to examine if a gifted individual has a greater tendency to deviate from a prescribed mode of operation. This need not be restricted to the intellectual realm. It could include the multiple types of intelligence postulated by Gardner (Gardner, 1983). Are the innovative individuals in various areas ones who possess the ability to break set or change cognitive strategies even though they have been patterned to proceed in a set direction or manner?

Breaking Set and its Relationship to Metacognition

In Robert Sternberg's triarchic theory of intelligence," one of the fundamental components are the metacomponents which are "used to plan, monitor, and evaluate problem solving" (Sternberg, 1988, p. 59). The area of metacognition; literally thinking about one's own thinking; appears to be related to the process of breaking set in that it presupposes an analysis of alternatives, a selection or rejection, and a subsequent course of action. However, what distinguishes breaking set from the everyday realm of problem solving is the previous imbedding of a successful pattern which must first be broken before other options can be examined (Dover & Shore, 1991). In terms of metacognition, this may be analogous to first pushing an override switch before other cognitive processes can be utilized.

The link between metacognition and giftedness has been explored by researchers to gain insight into cognitive processing differences between gifted individuals and those whose IQ scores fall in the normal range (Cheng, 1993). Breaking set, which involves changing cognitive strategies after experiencing a set of activities which incline one to a certain type of conscious act, is a relatively unexplored phenomena (Koller, 1992). Most individuals can think of an incident in their own lives where they persisted in an activity, repeating the same set of actions or responses that had led to success previously despite the fact that these actions were now unsuccessful. Sitting in a car and continually grinding the key in the ignition, hitting the same computer commands without a response, and searching places one has already searched for a misplaced item are familiar examples. Individuals are often unable to break set and try something new; their actions, having led to success in the past, thus established a set.

Is there a difference in the ability of gifted individuals to abandon the usual and implement a new approach? Does this apply only to verbal undertakings, or does it encompass spatial conceptualizations as well? Has research into metacognitive abilities discerned any differences?

Research concerning metacognitive abilities of the gifted has revealed distinct differences in their processing abilities (Cheng,1993). Torrance, after years of research with the gifted concluded, "These individuals are able to see problems in ways that others do not, to think divergently about possible solutions, and to use insight processes to solve problems or complete projects" (as cited in Sternberg & Lubart, 1993, p. 8). Breaking set may actually be a factor in successful problem solving that has gone unrecognized in the literature. It may also contribute to the unique perceptions of gifted individuals as they see beyond the conventional set established by their environment and society to a different interpretation (Tucker & Hafenstein, 1997).

Review of Literature on Breaking Set

Numerous research studies have been done on the relationship between metacognitive functioning and gifted individuals. Many deal with the ability to assess processes used for problem solution or the actual ability to use multiple strategies when challenged by hypothetical situations or ill-defined problems (Jausovec, 1994). The number of studies directly related to breaking set, however, is small.

In a study by Kaizer (as cited by Shore, 1986) using a classic concept formation task developed by Bruner, Goodnow and Austin in 1956, cards were used to form a target concept. Subjects were shown cards by the experimenter which depicted one of two large or small triangles or squares of two possible colors, with or without borders. One card was shown, and the subject was informed whether it was an example of the target concept. The subject then chose cards and received information as to whether the concept was represented, or not represented, by the card. Gifted children were asked to do the task when the experimenter alternated random and ordered sets of cards. By recording the number of trials required; the content of the cues used to discover the concept under the two conditions; and the types of errors that were made; the ability to switch strategies was inferred. A structured interview was also part of the study design. A relationship between metacognitive ability and the switching of strategies was noted.

Dover and Shore (1991) identified a task in which processing differences between gifted and average subjects could be quantified and observed. They employed a concept from a classic psychological experiment dealing with "set-breaking" (Dover & Shore, 1991).

This classic experiment employed the Einstellung, or E -Test, designed to examine the development of a set which predisposes an individual to one type of conscious act (Luchins, 1942, as cited by Dover & Shore, 1991). The Einstellung Test was first used in experiments during the 1920's at the University of Berlin to induce a set for a mathematical solution to a series of volume measuring problems. Einstellung translated means habituation and refers to the establishment of an accustomed pattern of response

(Koller, 1992). The original E-Test consists of a series of arithmetic volume-measuring problems involving three jars whose maximum capacities are given. The capacities of these three jars vary with each problem. To solve problems requiring a specified quantity as the final amount in one of the jars without using any other measures, subjects must add water or pour it off from jar to jar. After an initial series of problems requiring the use of all three jars, two problems are presented in which a simpler solution strategy, two jars, will work. However, the problem can also be solved in the same manner as the previous problems by using three jars. Finally, the last problem can only be solved by using just two of the jars, which requires the subject to break the psychological set of successfully using three jars established by the preceding problems.

Dover and Shore (1991) used a test group of 19 11-year-old students classified as gifted due to their scores on an IQ test and 11 average 11-year-old students. The set for successful solution using three water jars was established in problems 1 through 6. The next two problems could be solved using either two or three jars. The critical problem was 9. Only by breaking set and using two jars instead of three, could the task be successfully completed. The last items on the test, problems 10 and 11, could be solved using either the originally established set for successful solution, three jars, or by using two jars. A Metacognitive Knowledge Interview was also conducted to ascertain how the subjects approached the solution to the problem. It posed "structured questions with preplanned probes (as needed) to elicit knowledge about solving the E-Test" (Dover & Shore, 1991, p. 100).

The overall differences between gifted and average subjects scores on the E-Test were statistically significant. In examining further, the researchers found that gifted children who had scored high on flexibility in another instrument solved the problems quickly. The results of the Metacognitive Knowledge Interview indicated that these children also had more metacognitive knowledge than gifted children who solved them slowly. In contrast, average children who were flexible showed more metacognitive knowledge when they took more time, or were slower, on the problems. Regardless of speed, research indicated that inflexible gifted children had less metacognitive knowledge than gifted children who were more flexible. Rigid average children exhibited the least metacognitive knowledge, regardless of speed.

Shore, Koller, and Dover (1994) re-examined results obtained from the water jar study. After further analysis, the data revealed that the alternative solution of two jars was used by gifted subjects when it was available, though not essential to solving the problem, if it was more efficient. Protocol analysis revealed that several gifted subjects hypothesized the existence of other imaginary jars to help them solve the critical ninth problem rather than using two jars. Dover and Shore findings suggested the need for continued research on the metacognitive functioning of gifted students to further investigate their ability to change strategies with greater ease, accuracy, and rapidity than average students.

In a pilot study with 74 sixth grade students, verbal items were used to first establish a set for problem solution in a process similar to that used by the mathematically based E-Test. One verbal item that appeared to resemble the preceding items could only be solved using a different method for solution. In one class of 28 average students, one student broke set and solved the problem in a five minute time period. Using the same problems and procedure, 16 out of 21 students in a class of gifted pupils broke set (McGaughey, 1996).

Research Study on Breaking Set

A research study was designed to examine the degree of difference between identified gifted students and non-identified students in the ability to break set as measured by an assessment instrument which had been devised and field tested (McGaughey, 1996). Additional areas of investigation included verbal, spatial, and gender factors. An assessment instrument which included two sections of verbal items and two sections of spatial items was utilized. Modeled after the set-inducing characteristics of the E-Test, sections were designed to establish a set for successful solution of verbal or spatial problems. A problem which could not be solved using the pattern was introduced. Students had to break set to successfully solve the critical verbal or spatial problem. The following example typifies one type of verbal assessment that was used.

Instructions: Try to find the name for a human body part in the following sentences. The name is in order within the sentence.

Answers indicated for clarity of explanation.

Example: We bought a set of antique *chin*a dishes.
1. The fire al*arm* rang in the morning.
2. It isn't *leg*al to drive without a license.
3. The boy felt extremely afraid *to e*nter the dark room.

The set was established in the first two sentences. Subjects would have internalized the pattern that the body parts are all in the same word. Students would have to "break set" to solve the third sentence and find the name of the body part. The word "toe" spans two words and two lines in this sentence.

There were ten sentences in the first verbal section. Four sentences gave subjects an opportunity to break set. Two of these sentences could only be solved by breaking the established set. The first four sentences in the Assessment Instrument could be solved by finding the one "body part" word that was inside another word. The next two sentences could be solved either by finding a word within a word, or by breaking set and finding a word spanning two words. Sentence number seven could only be solved by breaking set and finding the word "toe." Sentences eight and nine could be solved in either manner, while sentence ten could only be solved by breaking set.

The second verbal section had five items with one involving the ability to break set. The set was established in the first three items. The fourth item required the subject to break set. A re-reading of the directions by subjects, as done during videotaped interviews, revealed that the directions, in essence, revealed the answer, once they were able to break set.

The spatial sections were similarly arranged with five problems in the first section and ten in the second. One item in the first spatial section necessitated breaking set for solution. A second item could also be solved by breaking set or by following the pattern. Two items in the second spatial section could only be solved by breaking set. The following example illustrates one type of spatial assessment that was used.

Instructions: Arrange the following lines to represent the number shown. The lines must remain straight. Draw your answer in the space provided.

Answers indicated for clarity of explanation.

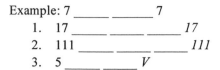

Example: 7 _____ _____ 7
   1. 17 _____ _____ _____ *17*
   2. 111 _____ _____ _____ *111*
   3. 5 _____ _____ *V*

Break set scores were calculated for each section. A subject's total break set score was the sum of break set instances for all four sections. The total number of correct answers, including both set establishment items and break set items, was also calculated for the Assessment Instrument.

Research Hypotheses

Hypothesis One

Research has indicated that there are differences between average students and gifted students in the metacognitive processing of information (Cheng, 1993). The results of a mathematical "set-breaking" experiment using water jars showed a statistically significant difference between subjects of average ability and those who were classified as gifted (Dover & Shore, 1991). A logical hypothesis was that the gifted students would break set more frequently on the assessment instrument than the average students.

Hypothesis Two

The assessment instrument contained both verbal and spatial items. Despite layman's conceptions of gender differences in these areas, as the instrument is assessing the ability to break set, not verbal or spatial abilities, it was hypothesized that there would be no significant differences along gender lines.

Hypothesis Three

Similarly, it was hypothesized that subjects would evidence no difference in their ability to break set in either the verbal or the spatial areas. The items used to establish the set, and even the break set items themselves, were well within the ability level of the average fifth or sixth grader, the population being assessed.

Hypothesis Four

The items on the assessment instrument were intended to be within the ability range of the subjects. For this reason, it was hypothesized that there would be no difference between the gifted subjects' scores and the non-gifted subjects' scores on the items that established set on the assessment instrument.

Hypothesis Five

It was hypothesized that subjects' scores on the assessment instrument and their scores on the Einstellung test would correlate so as to provide another means of evaluating the ability of the assessment instrument to measure breaking set. The Einstellung Test, or E-Test, was first used in experiments during the 1920's at the University of Berlin to induce a set for a mathematical solution to a series of volume measuring problems. A pattern of solution was developed which had to be broken to solve the definitive break set problem.

SIGNIFICANCE OF THE STUDY

The common sense observations that the gifted often follow their own paths, that they may view the word differently from their more "normal" counterparts, and that they are not as restricted by the patterns implicit in society may not have its counterpart in empirical research. Renzulli has devised checklists that include questioning authority as a characteristic of the gifted. However, these checklists do not seem to probe the basis for this behavior (Renzulli, 1977). Could it be that the patterns that often bind peoples' lives for good or for ill are not viewed as inviolate by the gifted but only one of many choices? Could it be that the appellation of evaluation in Bloom's Taxonomy as the highest level of thought and thus indicative of a gifted individual may have its root in the ability to look beyond the obvious and break from ordinary criteria to arrive at a decision (Gowan, Khatena, & Torrance, 1979)? Could it be that the ability to break set, though seemingly a small subset of metacognitive processing, is a characteristic that distinguishes gifted individuals and crosses multiple categories of intelligence?

If so, how could it have been missed all these years? The answer itself is a function of the basic property of breaking set. Most intelligence tests deal with finding patterns in order to solve a problem. Which number comes next in the series? If a triangle is rotated 45 degrees, which picture will show the result? In this analogy, which pair matches the first pair?

The implication is that pattern-finding, or logical solution, reflects intelligence. This has been the core of tests and continues. Even tests, such as the Sternberg Triarchic Abilities Test (STAT), rely on learning from context, reasoning about a hypothetical situation, and solving math problems based on scenarios (Sternberg, Ferrari, Clinkenbeard, & Grigorenko, 1996). The Multiple Intelligence Development Assessment Scales (MIDAS), which has been developed to provide an objective measure of the multiple intelligences, operationalize intelligence as "the ability to solve problems or to create products that are valued within one or more cultures" (Gardner, 1983, p. x).

Both these tests are dependent on content, prior learning, patterns, and tangible products. Despite the fact that current businesses purport to be looking for those who can operate outside of the box, and America defends its educational system as one promoting individual thought instead of the cookie cutter, one right answer curriculum utilized by those nations that outscore the U.S. in math and science, tests are still seeking those who can pattern (James, 1996).

Perhaps it's time to examine those who break the patterns. Isn't this process as valid as finding or creating patterns? Wasn't America founded by those who were able to break patterns? Do some individuals break set more readily? Is this related to their level of intelligence?

By posing these questions and creating an evaluative instrument, a set has been broken. This study examined whether there was a difference between those identified as gifted and those of average ability in the frequency of breaking set on an assessment instrument.

METHOD

Subjects

Subjects in this study were randomly selected from a population of 910 fifth and sixth grade students attending a public school. Fifty-two gifted students and fifty regular education students comprised the study group.

Gifted students were identified through the use of a matrix. To qualify, students scored above 88% on either the Verbal or Non-Verbal section of the Otis-Lennon

School Ability Test and achieved at least a 96% on either the Reading , Mathematics, Social Studies, or Science sections of the Stanford Achievement Test for their respective grade level. Additionally, the Torrance Test of Creative Thinking, a Leadership Measure, a group problem-solving activity, and a Renzulli Teacher survey were also included. However, the determining factors were high scores on the Olsat and the Scholastic Achievement Test.

Subjects in the study were predominantly Caucasian and from the middle to upper middle class range of income. Both regular and gifted subjects were from a similar socio-economic and racial background. The age of the subjects ranged from 9 years 10 months to 12 years 6 months. The average age of the fifth graders was 10 years 7 months while the sixth grade average was 11 years 8 months.

Variables

Intelligence, as determined by the placement or non-placement in a gifted program, was the chief independent variable in this study. Identified gifted students and average students were subjects. Both the gender and the age of the participants, as represented by the average of their respective grade levels, were additional independent variables that were examined in this study.

The dependent variable was the subject's ability to break set as measured by the Assessment Instrument. The effect of the independent variables on the number of instances in which the subject broke set was examined.

Materials and Procedures

The assessment was conducted in a regular classroom. The researcher administered the assessment to each of the groups so as to provide uniformity. The instructions for both Assessment A, the Assessment Instrument, and Assessment B, the E-Test were read aloud to the students.

The ability of the randomly selected participants to break set was measured through the use of the four-part Assessment Instrument. Two parts were verbal and two parts were spatial in character. The examiner distributed the activity and instructed the students to read along as the directions were read aloud. Students were reminded to re-read the directions for each section carefully as they worked through the Assessment Instrument. The directions indicated that subjects could skip a question if they are unable to answer it.

Students were asked if they had any questions on the directions. They were told that the examiner could not answer any questions about the items on the Assessment Instrument. Students would have to make their own decisions after re-reading the directions. Students worked through the Assessment Instrument at their own speed and turned in their papers once they were finished. There was no interaction or talking allowed during the Assessment Instrument.

To assess the subjects' ability to break set, a set of correct responses was established by the Assessment Instrument. A similar problem that could not be solved by the usual method was included. There were two Verbal sections and two Spatial sections. Each section established a set for successful solution in the first three or four problems. Subjects had to break set to solve the definitive problems in each section. Verbal Section One consisted of ten problems. Two could only be solved by breaking set. Verbal Section Two had five problems. One of the problems required the subject to break set. Similarly, Spatial Section One presented five problems with one being a "break set" item. Spatial Section Two gave subjects two opportunities to break from the established set used to solve the other eight problems in the ten-item section.

The total number of break set items successfully solved and the total number of items correctly answered were assessed for each of the four sections. A subject's total break set score for the Assessment Instrument was the sum of break set instances for each section. Each subject also received a score for the total number of correct items on the Assessment Instrument. This included both the break set items and the set establishment items.

Subjects turned in the Assessment Instrument and went to their P.E./ Fine Arts class as they finished. Those who were also taking Assessment B were read the directions, including the two sample problems. Questions about the directions were answered. Subjects then worked through the instrument at their own pace.

Assessment B, the E-Test, was comprised of 11 mathematical problems dealing with measuring volume using water jars. Two problems were illustrated as samples. The problems that followed established a pattern of problem solution that could be expressed by the formula B-A-2C. Problems three through six could be solved using this pattern. Problem seven could be solved either by following the pattern or by breaking set and using the simpler A-C solution. Problem eight could also be solved by using the pattern or by using the formula A + C.

Problem nine could only be solved by breaking set. Problems 10 and 11 could be solved by either using the pattern B-A-2C or by one of the two simpler formulas. Original solutions that used neither the pattern or the simpler solution were also possible for four of the problems.

Subjects completed Assessment B and returned to their scheduled class. Fifth grade subjects who had been randomly selected for the video interview were reminded that it would be held the next day.

During a video interview, subjects were shown the assessment instrument they had completed and asked questions designed to ascertain their reactions to the Assessment Instrument. No checking or coding of the instrument had taken place at that time. The interviews were viewed so as to discern patterns of response and as a reflection of metacognitive knowledge.

Validity and Reliability

The Assessment Activity was developed specifically to measure the ability to break set. With the exception of the Einstellung, or E-Test, which relies on a knowledge of mathematical principles including volume, an instrument does not exist for this express purpose. Construct validity can be inferred through examination of the process involved in the solution of the definitive problems. Professors of statistics and tests and measurement at Baylor University recognized the test items as illustrating the ability to break set. A pilot study conducted with 74 sixth grade students also revealed that the items required the breaking of an established set in order to arrive at a solution (McGaughey, 1996).

The Einstellung Water-Jug test, or E-Test, was first used in the 1920s by Zener and Duncker at the University of Berlin. The psychologist Luchins conducted the first set breaking experiments with the E-test in North America in 1942 (Dover & Shore, 1991). Since then it has been used to illustrate the development, or non-development, of set in subjects, as well as the subject's ability to break set to solve problems that do not follow a pattern.

In this study, 27 subjects took both Assessment A and the E-Test, known as Assessment B. The scores of the subjects were compared to assess the validity of Assessment A in measuring a subject's ability to break set.

Research Design

Due to the necessity of having two distinct groups of subjects differing in IQ, a causal comparative design was used (Gay, 1996). This study attempted to ascertain the degree of difference in the ability to break set between those of high IQ, as determined by their placement in a gifted program, and those of average ability. As high IQ was a characteristic already possessed by one group of subjects, an ex post facto study was the most appropriate design.

The null hypothesis was that there would be no difference in performance on the assessment instrument between gifted students and non-gifted students in their ability to break set.

Additionally, there would be no differences shown between males and females in respect to breaking set.

RESULTS OF THE RESEARCH STUDY

In this study of the relative differences between the gifted and the non-gifted in the ability to break set, five hypotheses were generated.

1. The primary hypothesis was that the gifted would break set on the Assessment Instrument more frequently than the non-gifted.
2. Gender would not have an effect on either the verbal or spatial items on the Assessment Instrument.

3. There would be no differences shown by the subjects themselves in their abilities to break set in either the verbal or spatial areas.
4. Gifted and non-gifted subjects' scores on the items used to establish set should be similar indicating that it was the process of breaking set that distinguished the scores.
5. The Assessment Instrument would correlate with the E-Test, an instrument previously used in research to ascertain the ability to break set.

Each of these hypotheses was analyzed separately so as to ascertain the corresponding support or non-support in the data. Since the results of the primary hypothesis are impacted by the findings of hypotheses two, three, and four, these results will be presented first, beginning with hypothesis four and ending with hypothesis one. Hypothesis five, which deals with comparisons between the E-Test and the Assessment Instrument, will be presented last. Type I error was controlled for the entire research study by using the Bonferoni method (i.e., dividing the level of significance, .05, by the number of planned comparisons, 15). The resulting significance level was set at .003.

Research Hypothesis Four

Although this research study involved two separate groups, one of identified gifted students and one of non-gifted students, the purpose was not to assess levels of knowledge or replicate the traditional IQ test. For this reason, the Assessment Instrument was designed to be understandable by students of varying ability levels within the framework of an age range from approximately nine years upward. Due to this design, hypothesis four was that there would be no significant differences in the ability of the two groups to complete the non-break set items.

In order to test this hypothesis, subjects' break set scores were subtracted from their total scores on the Assessment Instrument. Total scores included all the correct answers to set formation items, items that did not necessitate breaking set to be solved, as well as the definitive break set items. This calculation would control for the hypothesized greater ability of the gifted to correctly answer the break set items, thus giving them a higher total score. It would also assess if the items on the Assessment Instrument were of a difficulty level that necessitated superior intellect for success. Once this revised total was computed, the mean of group one, the identified gifted students, was compared to the mean of group two, the non-gifted (See Table 1).

Although the means for the two groups did show a variation with the gifted scoring a higher number of total correct non-break set items on the Assessment Instrument, the difference was not statistically significant. The non-gifted group did contain a greater variance due to a few of the participants' inability to correctly complete the non-break set items on the Assessment Instrument. However, the data supported the hypothesis that there would be no significant difference between the gifted and the non-gifted in their ability to complete the non-break set items.

Table 1. A Comparison of the Revised Total Means on the Assessment Instrument

Group	*n*	Total Revised Mean	SD	t(100)
Gifted	52	22.35	1.58	1.8
Non-Gifted	50	21.44		3.23

Research Hypothesis Three

Hypothesis three proposed that there would be no differences between a subject's break set scores in either the verbal or the spatial areas as the Assessment Instrument was designed to determine whether subjects can break set, not their strengths in one particular area.

The total number of break set items successfully completed for each section was computed during the initial scoring of the Assessment Instrument. A combination score was then calculated by adding the number of break set items completed in the two verbal sections together to arrive at a total verbal score. A similar calculation was done with the two spatial sections resulting in a total spatial break set score. In a comparison, the total verbal and total spatial break set scores were similar (See Table 2).

The mean for the total verbal was .755 with a standard deviation of 1.16, while the total spatial mean was .833 with a standard deviation of 1.10. The similarity in the means and standard deviations supported the hypothesis that there would be no significant differences between scores on the verbal sections and scores on the spatial sections in the ability to break set.

A further examination of differences was obtained by subtracting the total spatial break set score from the total verbal break set score to ascertain differences between individual scores on the two types of sections. The results approach a normal curve for this sample population (See Figure 1).

A paired t-test revealed that the probability of the mean difference of -.078 was .59. With a level of .003 necessary for significance, this showed that the difference between the total verbal and the total spatial break set scores did not fall in the significant range.

The data supported the research hypothesis that there would be no significant difference between subjects' break set scores on the verbal and the spatial sections.

Table 2. Total Verbal and Total Spatial Break Set Scores

Break	Set	Answers*n*	Mean SD
Verbal	7	.755	1.16
Spatial	4	.833	1.10

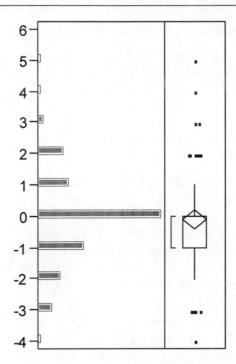

Figure 1. Differences Between the Total Spatial and the Total Verbal Break Set Scores.

Research Hypothesis Two

The Assessment Instrument contained two sections of verbal items and two sections of spatial items. Hypothesis two proposed that there would be no significant differences in subjects' break set scores on these sections related to gender. Since the process of breaking set was the focus, not inherent ability in verbal or spatial problem solving, it was hypothesized that the break set scores of males and females would not reflect significant score differences. The results supported this hypothesis (See Table 3).

Table 3. Mean Scores on Verbal and Spatial Sections by Gender

Group	n	Verbal 1	Verbal 2	Spatial 1	Spatial 2
1. Male	48	.			
Mean	.729	.02	.031	.58	
SD	1.14	.14	.59	.71	
2. Female	54				
Mean	.759	.00	.203	.57	
SD	1.13	.00	.49	.79	

Note: No significant differences across Verbal 1, Verbal 2, Spatial 1, or Spatial 2.
All numbers represent frequencies.

Table 4. Mean Scores on Verbal and Spatial Totals by Gender

Group	n	Verbal Totals	Spatial Totals
1. Male	48	.	
Mean	.75		.90
SD		1.19	.99
2. Female	54		
Mean		.76	.78
SD		1.13	1.19

Note: No significant differences across Verbal Totals and Spatial Totals.
All numbers represent frequencies.

The number of break set items successfully completed in the two verbal sections was added together to arrive at a break set total for the verbal sections. The same procedure was used with the two spatial sections resulting in a break set total for the spatial items. A display of the gender data by break set totals for the verbal and spatial sections reaffirmed the lack of gender difference (See Table 4).

An examination of the means of the subsections by gender did not reflect statistically significant score differences. A comparison of the verbal and the spatial totals by gender supported the same hypothesis of no difference. Hypothesis two, which proposed that there would be no significant gender differences, was supported by the data.

Research Hypothesis One

Hypothesis one dealt with the core issue of differences between gifted individuals and the non-gifted population in their metacognitive processing resulting in an increased ability to break set. It was hypothesized that the gifted group would break set on the Assessment Instrument more frequently than the non-gifted group. Since no significant differences were shown on the Assessment Instrument as a result of knowledge, verbal or spatial ability, or gender, any differences in the break set scores could be as a result of differences in the metacognitive processing of the two groups.

The resulting data from this study confirmed this hypothesis. An examination of the means of the two groups revealed statistically significant differences, $t(100) = 4.42$; $p < .003$, between gifted and non-gifted groups.

As shown in Table 5, the mean number of break set items correctly completed was 2.84 with a SD of 1.86 for the gifted students. The mean for the non-gifted was .88 with a SD of 1.27. Thus, the null hypothesis that there would be no difference between the ability of the two groups to break set was rejected.

As Figure 2 illustrates, the gifted group broke set significantly more frequently than the non-gifted group.

The data supported the first hypothesis that gifted students would break set more frequently on the Assessment Instrument than the non-gifted students. Since other factors, such as knowledge, ability in verbal or spatial areas, and gender had already been examined with no significant differences found between the two groups, the results from the statistically significant differences on the break set items point to metacognitive processing differences.

Table 5. Comparison of Breaking Set Means on the Assessment Instrument

Group	*n*	Break set mean	SD	t (100)
Gifted	52	2.25	1.86	4.42[*]
Non-Gifted	50	.88	1.27	

[*] $p \leq .003$

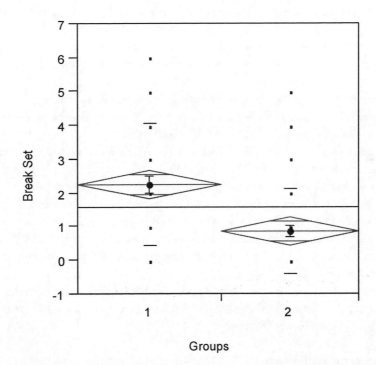

Figure 2. A Comparison of Break Set Means by the Gifted (1) and Non-Gifted (2).

Research Hypothesis Five

Breaking set is a relatively unexamined area in research dealing with cognitive processing differences between the gifted and the general population. Only one other instrument, the E-test, which was originally designed to illustrate the formation of a mental set mathematically, has been used for that purpose (Dover & Shore, 1991). Hypothesis five postulated that there would be correlations between the E-test and the Assessment Instrument that was devised specifically to measure the ability to break set. Both instruments use a pattern of response in the initial items to establish a set for successful solution of the problems presented. To solve the definitive problem or problems on both instruments, the set must be broken. For the E-test, a specific formula, or pattern of solution, could be used to solve all but one of the mathematical problems presented to the subjects. Two of the problems could also be solved either by using the pattern or by a more direct solution that broke the pattern.

Table 6. Comparison of Breaking Set Means on the E-Test

Group	n	Break set	meanSD
Gifted	14	1.79	1.72
Non-Gifted	13	.61	1.44

A random sub sample (n = 27) of the study participants took the E-test as well as the Assessment Instrument. There were 14 gifted subjects and 13 non-gifted subjects in this sub sample. Once again, the gifted population, group one, broke set more frequently than the non-gifted population . A comparison of the means revealed that the differences were not statistically significant (See Table 6).

After converting break set scores on both instruments to percentages , a paired t-test analysis showed that the mean difference between the break set scores on the E-Test and on the Assessment Instrument was not statistically significant.

The patterns found by both the E-Test and the Assessment Instrument were similar in relation to the break set items. The gifted group broke set more frequently than the non-gifted on both instruments. A t-test analysis showed there were no significant differences between subjects' break set scores on the Assessment Instrument and their scores on the E-test. The correlation between scores on the two instruments was .08. Further examination of the data concerning subjects' scores on the E-test revealed that gender factors and mathematical knowledge seemed to have an effect as reflected by the data. Gifted males surpassed the other groups in breaking set.

On the Assessment Instrument , there was no significant difference between the break set scores by gender. Nor were there significant differences between the subjects in their ability to complete the set establishment items.

Quantitative Results Summary

Five research hypotheses were presented in this study of the relative strength of breaking set in a gifted population in comparison to a non-gifted population. The primary hypothesis that the gifted would break set on the Assessment Instrument more frequently than the non-gifted was supported at the established .003 level of significance.

The second hypothesis was that gender would not have an effect on either group's ability to break set in the verbal or spatial sections of the Assessment Instrument. This was supported as the differences between the gender means for breaking set were not statistically significant.

The third hypothesis proposed that there would be no differences shown by the subjects themselves in their abilities to break set in either the verbal or spatial areas as what was being assessed was their processing, not specific content knowledge. Once again, this hypothesis was supported as a paired t-test revealed that the differences between the means for the subjects' verbal and spatial scores were not statistically significant.

The fourth hypothesis was that the subjects' revised total scores on the Assessment Instrument: the number correct on the set-establishment items: would not reflect high-IQ or advanced knowledge, but be similar for both gifted and non-gifted groups. This hypothesis was supported, as both gifted and non-gifted subjects' scores on the items used to establish set were similar with a t-test indicating no significance to the difference between the means.

The fifth hypothesis was that the Assessment Instrument would correlate with the E-Test, an instrument previously used in research to ascertain the ability to break set. This hypothesis was not supported by the research data as the correlation coefficient was .08. The differences between the subjects' scores on the two instruments was shown to be non-significant in a paired t-test analysis. Other factors, such as gender and mathematical ability, were examined to ascertain if these, or the sample size (n= 27) , had an effect. More variability was shown between genders and grade level groups on the E-test, however the difference in sample size, (n=102 for the Assessment Instrument), was also a factor.

Qualitative Results Summary

Video interviews were conducted to gain insight into the subjects' experiences with the Assessment Instrument. Participants had been randomly selected during the initial selection process. Twenty-four video interviews were conducted by the researcher with 12 fifth graders being interviewed and 12 sixth graders.

The interview for the fifth grade subjects was conducted the day after taking the Assessment Instrument while the sixth grade interviews were conducted three days later. Students were given their assessments to look at during the interview. None of the assessments had been checked or coded at that time. Each participant was asked the same questions in the same order by the researcher.

1. How did you feel about taking this Assessment Instrument?
2. Did you get stuck on any part?
3. How did you handle the difficult questions?
4. Which part did you feel that you were best at, the written part or the drawing part?
5. Is there any question that you really want to know the answer to at this time?
6. Now that you see the correct answer, what do you think?
7. What comments do you have about your participation in this research or the Assessment Instrument(s) that you took?

An examination of the subjects' answers was conducted to establish patterns of response and to investigate if there were variations in response by the two groups studied, the gifted and the non-gifted.

The Assessment Instrument was viewed positively by both groups due to the ease of completion of most of the non-break set items on the assessment. Twenty-four correct responses out of 30 could be made by completing these items. Altogether, there were 11 opportunities to break set, however only three verbal problems and three spatial problems could be completed only by breaking set. One theme that was a noticeable thread through the interviews was the concentration on these correct responses by the non-gifted group. They were pleased with their performance and showed their favorite part of the assessment with pride. They realized that there were some hard items, however they didn't dwell too long on these. Some just guessed while others skipped them.

In contrast, the gifted group noted that the assessment was easy for the most part, but they did dwell on the items they had been unable to solve. This may have been due to the "Ziegarnik Effect," which deals with the tendency to recall failures longer than successful experiences (Wood, 2001). Some students correctly solved these missed items during the interview reporting that they had been thinking about them. Others, with minimal prompting, solved them after looking at a break set item they had successfully completed and transferring the concept to the item they had been unable to solve. The gifted subjects had a desire to know all the correct answers to the problems they had been unable to solve, perhaps indicating a higher degree of motivation.

The greatest difference in response was observed when students were asked if they would like to see the answer to a question that they had been unable to answer. A break set answer was then revealed to the subject. The non-gifted often found it difficult to accept the answer and questioned it. Even days after taking the assessment instrument, they were unable to break set. Several of the non-gifted group were unable to understand the break set answer until it was explained.

The gifted group found the break set answer a source for exclamation and amusement. It seemed to satisfy them. They appeared to recognize it as the correct answer immediately. Many began negotiating to know the answer to another break set item. Some asked friends who participated in the interviews which item they had been told the answer to so as to complete their solution to the break set items they had been unable to solve. This quest to identify the correct answer may be a reflection of their metacognitive processing . They desire to know the correct way to process this information so they will be able to proceed in a successful manner if confronted with a similar situation.

This difference in the perception of the break set items corresponded to the statistical findings of a significant difference between the mean break set scores of the gifted group and the non-gifted group on the Assessment Instrument. The gifted group focused on the break set items. They continued to process the items well after the assessment was over. They were stimulated by the solution to the items as evidenced by their reactions. They had a desire to know how to solve, or successfully process, the remaining break set items. Finally, they reflected positively on an experience which one summed up as "people wanting to know how you think."

Discussion

Questions about the nature of intelligence and the characteristics of those individuals designated as gifted have led researchers to examine the processing ability of gifted individuals in an attempt to assess differences (Sternberg, 1985). Metacognitive processing differences have been ascertained between gifted individuals and the non-gifted (Cheng, 1993). Yet most instruments currently used for the study and identification of the gifted deal mainly with one aspect of intellectual processing, the ability to find patterns. This belies the populist identification of an individual who is gifted as one who doesn't always fit the pattern, who may be a maverick, or who goes against the grain to discover a breakthrough in a field of study (Gillis, 1999). This researcher noted the discrepancy and authored an Assessment Instrument designed to identify the ability to break set, or to break an established pattern rather than to identify or continue one (McGaughey, 1996).

The focus of this study was to examine the metacognitive process of breaking set. Research hypothesis one, which proposed that the gifted individuals would break set more frequently than the non-gifted group, was the core of the research study. This hypothesis was supported by the statistically significant break set scores of the gifted group on the Assessment Instrument. This statistical finding represented the culmination of over twenty years of observation, curriculum writing, journal reading, and action research by this investigator (McGaughey, 1996).

Theorists have proposed the existence of metacognitive differences between gifted individuals and non-gifted, yet objective measurement of these characteristics has not been a focus of extensive research (Cheng, 1993). Various research studies have dealt with problem solving, attitudes toward knowledge, and the teaching of cognitive processes (Mobley, Doares, and Mumford, 1992). The difficulty inherent in many of these studies was the subjective nature of the assessment utilized (Schwanflugel, Stevens, and Carr, 1997). Observation, surveys, and judgment by criteria were affected by the subjective nature of the scores that resulted from such a design (Anderson, 1986). Yet any quantification of intellectual processing seemed to lead to a focus on one aspect of intellectual processing, that of patterning. An examination of existing tests that seek to determine intellectual functioning revealed that the identification or continuation of a pattern was the underlying process being tested. Gifted individuals surpassed non-gifted individuals in their ability to recognize, complete, or continue patterns (Gowan, Khatena, & Torrance, 1979). Thus, this process has been the signature core of tests determining entrance into special programs for the gifted.

Those individuals who have worked extensively with gifted individuals who have been placed into special programs by their ability to excel at tests requiring superior processing ability of patterns have noted that this characteristic does not seem to be as evident in their day-to-day behavior. A more consistent pattern of the gifted student might be that they thrive on challenge, the unusual, the novel, the questioning of the accepted method of procedure, the "what ifs" of a certain case taken beyond any intended analysis, the unique perspective, the bending of parameters (LaFrance, 1994). It was this obvious overt let's-go-beyond-the-pattern behavior expressed in the lives of the gifted that did not seem to be accurately portrayed in IQ tests or even in the instruments searching to identify multiple types of intelligence (Gardner,1983). Intelligence tests deal with correct answers in a certain amount of time, but they aren't intended to measure how much a person desires to know the correct answer or the quality of thought generated by the question (Bouchard, 2004).

Teachers of the gifted recognize that the gifted break patterns, not just follow them (Merrell and Gill, 1994). In any school, there are as many teachers, or more, who will refuse to teach the gifted students due to this propensity to not see rules as inviolate. "Moreover, attempts to maintain classroom order by discouraging gifted students' enthusiastic, but sometimes inappropriate behavior, may lead to a suppression of their desire to learn" (Ashman, Wright, and Conway, 1994, p. 198). Despite this, research into this common sense distinguishing characteristic of gifted individuals was not extensive. The quantification of such intellectual processing was practically non-existent.

This study was an indication that breaking set; a metacognitive process; could be quantified. A series of sentences that established a set, followed by a sentence that necessitated the breaking of the set for successful solution, had already been developed by this researcher and was used in action research with classes of both gifted and non-gifted students over the course of several years. The results consistently revealed that the gifted were able to break set and solve the definitive problem with greater success than the non-gifted.

Limitations

The generalizability of the findings of this study are limited by several factors. First, only students who were 5th or 6th graders were assessed. Their ages ranged from nine to twelve years. Second, all the subjects were from one school which is located in a middle to high socio-economic area. Third, only a small subset (n=27) also took the E-test, leading to questions about the comparability with the results from the Assessment Instrument (n=102).

An additional limitation is the Assessment Instrument itself. Although items had been used in action research and a more formalized pilot study (McGaughey, 1996), the instrument as a whole had not been utilized to ascertain the ability to break set. The results from this study indicate the strength of the instrument to discern a difference between the gifted and the non-gifted in their ability to complete the break set items on the Assessment Instrument. However, sections one and four of the instrument , the first verbal section and the second spatial section, were more effective determiners than sections two and three, the second verbal section and the first spatial section. An item difficulty analysis in these two sections could be conducted to ascertain what caused subjects difficulty in the break set items.

There are instruments available for measuring metacognition, however, the instrument' validity and psychometric soundness have not always been subject to extensive evaluation (Sigler & Tallent-Runnels, 2006). It is important that rigor be exercised in the evaluation and use of the Assessment instrument.

Implications

The purpose of this research study was to determine the relative strength of the metacognitive process of breaking set in a group of gifted students. It arose out of the observation that conventional assessments of the gifted are based on patterns, yet the gifted tend to break patterns. With the Assessment Instrument illustrating a statistically significant difference between the gifted subjects and the non-gifted in their ability to break set, a metacognitive characteristic begins to emerge.

The practical implications for the use of a process that appears to be utilized to a greater degree by gifted individuals than by the non-gifted are widespread. The first lies in the realm of identification. If this is a distinguishing process, it could be incorporated into assessments designed to identify the gifted. Since the Assessment Instrument seems to be within the range of the average nine to twelve year old student, appears free of gender bias, and allows a student to succeed in both verbal and spatial areas, it could be a relatively content free means of identification. Just as nonverbal reasoning tests are being included to assist in identification of underachieving or culturally deprived gifted students, perhaps a child's ability to break set could serve this purpose as well (Lohman, 2005). A modification could be made to be used in the various areas of giftedness as postulated by Gardner (Gardner, 1983). As a process, breaking set is not content specific, but relies on the establishment of a set, and then the required breaking of that set in order to successfully solve a definitive problem. This could be applied to areas as diverse as dance and art.

Curriculum for the gifted is another area of application. With the knowledge that this is a processing difference of the gifted, this propensity could be used, encouraged, and developed so as to recognize and appreciate the process that so often isolates or sets the gifted apart from the regular population. If it is this innate processing difference that has led gifted individuals in various disciplines throughout the centuries to make breakthrough discoveries, then it should be strengthened, not discouraged. Even a small amount of exposure to such exercises as are contained in the Assessment Instrument has led to gifted students looking more carefully at other activities to examine the possibilities for alternate solutions. Training activities with the non-gifted could also be implemented to encourage them to develop alternate processing methods.

A curious, but not statistically significant difference, was discovered during the course of this research. When examining to see if there were any significant differences between the scores of fifth and sixth graders on the Assessment Instrument, it was noted that the break set scores of the gifted improved from fifth to sixth grade while the non-gifted break set scores declined. This was not part of the original study, and did not meet the level of significance required by this study, however it might indicate a trend. The metacognitive process of breaking set could grow in strength as the gifted individual matures, yet diminish as the non-gifted internalize the conforming rules of society. If this is the case, the non-gifted need to be exposed to opportunities to break set so as to develop their processing capability.

In an age of computers, when technological creations contain more factual information than the most knowledgeable human, can complete complex patterns faster than their creators, and can even beat the best chess player, the process of breaking set is beyond the capability of the most advanced machine. Breaking set is a processing difference that seems to lead to new knowledge. It is a discovery, an "Ah, Ha!" with its own logic. Just as the gifted subjects in the video interviews reacted with amusement at the break set answer, so are they entertained and energized when this processing difference is imbedded in their curriculum (McGaughey, 1996).

Teacher training is another area which could be affected by the recognition of differential metacognitive processing by the gifted. Training programs for the teachers of the gifted vary widely. However, most include seminars about the nature and needs of the gifted. The inclusion of metacognitive processing differences could help teachers understand the importance of varying the curriculum for the gifted to allow for and encourage these processing differences. The emergence of new technologies in the classroom and the constructivist approach lend themselves to the gifted student's exploration of the diverse interests that may be beyond the mainstream of academic content for the student's grade level (Mann, 1994). Teacher training that includes an awareness of breaking set as a metacognitive processing difference could assist teachers with planning learning opportunities that provide for gifted students to utilize this ability in academically and socially acceptable ways. Designing better learning situations for gifted students is an area of constant concern (Shore, 2006). Contemporary American schools, by design and often by ideology, are "unable to nurture children who cannot think inside the box" (Davidson & Davidson, 2004, p. 22).

Finally, a modification in society's perception of the gifted may occur with greater awareness; that there are quantifiable reasons why the gifted seem to deviate from the norm, not just academically, but in other areas as well. Unlike other special populations, their differences are not as readily observable. "But their unusual interests, independence of thought, and nonconforming behavior may give them some uncomfortable moments" (Walker, 2002, p. 68). It is easier to overlook their needs since they are not as obvious. The U.S. Department of Education's assessment of program's and services for the gifted, *Excellence: A Case for Developing America's Talent*, reported that the nation's most talented students were performing far below their potential ."Fueled by the indifference of the American people to the needs of children with special talents and buffeted by a failure of our schools to meet, much less, exceed international academic standards, a rising tide of mediocrity has begun to swamp our nation and extinguish the sparks of genius that have made America great "(Desmond, 1994, p.224).

With the emergence of metacognitive processing differences, the recognition of innate attributes that may be causative factors for behavioral and academic variations between the gifted and the non-gifted may lead to a greater acceptance. The often negative social climate in which gifted individuals find themselves may be modified, allowing them to reach their potential.

Future Research

Continued research is needed to further delineate the relationship between giftedness and breaking set. The Assessment Instrument that was used in this study can be modified using the knowledge gained from this study. It can also be adapted to be applied in other areas such as kinesthetic or artistic to see if the process crosses disciplines.

The possibility of subjects taking the Assessment Instrument while an MRI brain scan is being conducted would fuse new developments in brain research with the exploration of a processing difference in individuals that could be physiologically manifested and measured (Robinson, 2006). Quantification of differences between gifted individuals and the non-gifted could alleviate the riddle of identification. If a gifted individual could be identified as easily as blood pressure is measured or a temperature is taken, the disparity of identification for the various programs around the nation and the world might improve.

This does not eliminate the need for studies that use methods besides an objective assessment. Qualitative studies using one-on-one protocol analysis would provide insight into the mental processes at work as subjects are confronted with a problem requiring them to break set. Additional descriptive studies can be conducted to continue to try to ascertain the strength of this characteristic in the gifted population. Experimental studies could be done to see if this ability could be taught through intervention strategies. The scores on a pre-test and a post-test could be compared for two groups. In order to obviate the possibility of sensitization of the control group, a posttest-only control group design study may need to be conducted to assess the effectiveness of any training activities in breaking set.

The search for other distinguishing quantifiable processing differences beyond logical patterning and breaking set could open up possibilities of identification that do not appear as content or knowledge related as the current instruments that are pattern dependent. An initial break with the use of logical patterning for assessment may lead to the discovery of other processing areas that have been touched upon in research; possibly as subsets of other broader areas; but have not yet been fully explored.

Although breaking set may initially appear to be a subset of problem solving, it may also be a distinct metacognitive ability whose strength may be indicative of giftedness. Perhaps those who hear a different drummer or take the path less traveled are those with the ability to break set.

REFERENCES

Anderson, M. A. (1986). Protocol analysis: A methodology for exploring the information processing of gifted students. *Gifted Child Quarterly, 30*, 28-33.

Ashman, A. F.,Wright, S. K., Conway, R. N. (1994). Developing the metacognitive skills of academically gifted students in mainstream classrooms. *Roeper Review,16*, 198-204.

Boorstin, D .J. (1983*). The discoverers: A history of man's search to know his world and himself.* New York, N.Y.: Random House.

Bouchard, L.L.(2004). An instrument for the measure of Dabrowskian overexcitabilities to identify gifted elementary students. *Gifted Child Quarterly, 48*, 339-351.

Brooks, J. G. & Brooks, M. G. (1993). *The case for constructivist classrooms.* Virginia: Association for Supervision and Curriculum Development.

Bruner, J. S.,Goodnow, J. J., Austin, G. A. (1956). *A study of thinking.* New York: Wiley.

Cheng, P. (1993). Metacognition and giftedness: The state of the relationship. *Gifted Child Quarterly, 37*, 105-112.

Davidson, J. & Davidson, B. (2004). *Genius denied.* New York : Simon & Schuster.

Delisle, J.R. (2006). *Parenting gifted kids.* Waco, TX: Prufrock Press.

Desmond, C. F. (1994). A national tragedy: The retreat from excellence in America. *Roeper Review, 16*, 224-225.

Dover, A., & Shore, B. (1991). Giftedness and flexibility on a mathematical set- breaking task. *Gifted Child Quarterly, 35,* 99-107.

Einstein, A. (1993). *Out of my later years.* New York, N.Y.: Wings Books.

Filipelli, L. A. & Walberg, H.J. (1997) *Childhood traits and conditions of eminent women scientists. Gifted Child Quarterly, 41*(2), 95-103.

Gardner, H. (1983). *Frames of mind: the theory of multiple intelligence.* New York, N.Y.: Basic Books.

Gay, L. R. (1996). *Educational research: Competencies for analysis and application* (5th ed.). Upper Saddle River, NJ: Prentice-Hall.

Gillis, J. (1993, January 29-31). Will kids in the next millennium study the discoveries of Copernicus, Newton, Einstein, and Venter? *USA Weekend*, 4-5.

Gowan, J. C., Khatena, J. , & Torrance, E. P. (Eds.) . (1979). *Educating the ablest.* Washington: F. E. Peacock Publishers, Inc.

James, J. (1996). *Thinking in the future tense: leadership skills for a new age.* New York, N.Y.: Simon and Schuster.

Jausovec, N. (1994). Can giftedness be taught? *Roeper Review, 16*, 210-214.

Koller, M. (1992). *More from the water jars.* Unpublished master's thesis, McGill University, Montreal, Canada.

LaFrance, E.B. (1994) An insider's perspective: Teacher's observations of creative thinking in exceptional children. *Roeper Review, 16*, 256-257.

Lohman, D.F. (2005). The role of nonverbal ability tests in identifying academically gifted students: An aptitude perspective. *Gifted Child Quarterly, 49*,111-140.

Lupert, J. L. & Pyryt, M.C. (1996)."Hidden gifted" students: Underachiever prevalence and profile. *Journal for the Education of the Gifted, 20*, 36-53.

Mann, C. (1994). New technologies and gifted education. *Roeper Review, 16*, 172-176.

Merrell, K.W. &Gill,S.J. (1994). Using Teacher Ratings of Social Behavior to Differentiate Gifted from Non-Gifted Students. *Roeper Review,16*, 286-289.

McGaughey, C. L. (1996). Is breaking set a metacognitive characteristic of the gifted? *Teacher Education and Practice,12*, 85-96.

Mobley, M. I., Doares, L. M. , & Mumford, M. D. (1992). Process analytic models of creative capacities: Evidence for the combination and reorganization process. *Creativity Research Journal,5 ,* 125-155.

Naglieri, J.A. & Kaufman, J. C. (2001). Understanding intelligence, giftedness and Creativity using the PASS theory. *Roeper Review, 23*, 151-156.

Plucker, A. P., Callahan, C.M., &Tomchin, E.M. (1996). Wherefore art thou, multiple intelligences? Alternative assessments for identifying talent in ethnically diverse and low income students. *Gifted Child Quarterly,17*, 81-92.

Renzulli, J. S. (1977). *The enrichment triad model: A guide for development of defensible programs for the gifted.* Mansfield Center, CT: Creative Learning Press.

Robinson, N. M. (2006). A report card on the state of research in the field of gifted education. *Gifted Child Quarterly, 50*, 342-347.

Schwanenflugel, P.J., Stevens, T. P., & Carr, M. (1997) Metacognitive knowledge of Gifted children and nonidentified children in early elementary school. *Gifted Child Quarterly, 41*, 25-36.

Shore, B. M. (1986). Cognition and giftedness: New research directions. *Gifted Child Quarterly, 30*, 24-29.

Shore, B. M. (2006). Yogi Berra's Chevy truck: A report card on the state of research in the field of gifted education. *Gifted Child Quarterly, 50*, 351-354.

Shore, B. M., Koller, M., & Dover, A. (1994). More from the water jars: A reanalysis of problem-solving performance among gifted and nongifted children. *Gifted Child Quarterly, 38*(4), 179-183.

Sigler, E. A. & Tallent-Runnels, M. K. (2006). Examining the validity of scores from an instrument designed to measure metacognition of problem solving. *Journal of General Psychology, 133*, 257-276.

Sternberg, R.J. (1985). *Beyond IQ.* New York: Cambridge University Press.

Sternberg, R.J. (1988). *The Triarchic Mind.* New York: Penguin Books.

Sternberg, R.J., Ferrari, M., Clinkenbeard, P. R., & Grigorenko, E. L. (1996). Identification, instruction, and assessment of gifted children: A construct validation of a triarchic model. *Gifted Child Quarterly, 40*(3), 120-137.

Sternberg, R. J. & Lubart, T. I. (1993). Creative giftedness: A multivariate investment approach. *Gifted Child Quarterly, 37*(1), 7-8.

Tucker, B. & Hafenstein, N. L. (1997). Psychological intensities in young gifted children. *Gifted Child Quarterly, 41*(3), 66-75.

Walker, S. Y. (2002). *The survival guide for parents of gifted kids.* Minneapolis, MN: Free Spirit Publishing, Inc.

Wood, F. H. (2001). Looking back-looking ahead: Programs for students with emotional and behavioral problems at the millennium. *Preventing School Failure, 45*(2), p. 58-64.

Zhang, L. & Sternberg, R.J. (1998). The pentagonal implicit theory of giftedness revisited: A cross-validation in Hong Kong. *Roeper Review, 21*(2), 149-153.

In: Meta-Cognition: A Recent Review of Research...   ISBN: 978-1-60456-011-4
Editors: M.F. Shaughnessy et al. pp. 109-125   © 2008 Nova Science Publishers, Inc.

Chapter 6

METACOGNITION IN THE GIFTED:
CONNECTIONS TO EXPERTISE

Marty Carr and Gita Taasoobshirazi
University of Georgia, Athens, Georgia, USA

ABSTRACT

Gifted children are assumed to show better performance in all areas, but this is not the case for metacognition. In some cases gifted children show the expected advanced metacognitive performance but in other cases their metacognitive performance differs little from average children. By considering the development of gifted performance from the perspective of expertise we can better understand why this discrepancy occurs. In this chapter we discussed how metacognition supports the emergence of expertise and gifted performance and how the more expert knowledge and skills of gifted children supports more advanced metacognitive skills.

Gifted students have often been described as being unique and qualitatively different from average students (e.g. Kanevsky & Geake, 2004), but there is little evidence for this (Perleth, Sierwald, & Heller, 1993). To be qualitatively different would require evidence that gifted students possess cognitive processes that average students do not possess. The research to date indicates that while gifted students score on the upper end of the continuum of ability tests typically used to identify them, they do not possess cognitive resources that would separate them from average functioning students. This is also the case when metacognition is examined. Gifted students possess more knowledge about their memory systems and seem to be better at transfer, but typically do about as well as average children when monitoring. There is little evidence that gifted children's metacognitive knowledge is qualitatively different from that of average children.

Why is it that gifted children are often perceived as being qualitatively different from average children? We argue that gifted children appear to be qualitatively different from average children because their performance is more expert than that of average children.

Expert performance is qualitatively different from novice performance because experts differ from novices in the depth, breadth, and organization of their knowledge. Experts and novices also differ in the types of strategies they use to solve problems, and in their use of metacognition to reflect on and guide their problem solving. Metacognitive knowledge and skills, in particular, are thought to be critical for conceptual change and the emergence of expert performance. If gifted children's performance is more expert performance then they should show higher levels of metacognition as it relates to specific domains of expertise. Unfortunately, little research examining metacognition in gifted students has examined the development of metacognition within the context of emerging domain specific expertise.

The idea that giftedness should be viewed from the perspective of expertise is not a new one. Schneider (1993, 1997) discussed the connection between giftedness and expertise noting that gifted performance in adulthood had much more to do with the willingness to put the time and effort into becoming expert than innate talent. Schneider suggested that a certain level of talent, as measured by IQ, was necessary, but that other factors come into play once that level is reached. In line with this, Lohman (2005) proposed that gifted individuals be identified based on their aptitudes for performance in specific domains as opposed to more general intelligence. This aptitude could take the form of emerging expertise in the form of fluent basic skills or personality characteristics that facilitate the acquisition of expertise. Ericsson, Nandagopal, and Roring (2005) go further to argue that giftedness is not the result of innate differences or talents, but the early acquisition of expertise. They argue that the disconnect between giftedness in childhood and achievement in adulthood is due to the failure to define giftedness as the early emergence of expertise. Recent longitudinal research supports the need to define giftedness within domains of emerging expertise as opposed to a more domain general construct (Perleth, Sierwald, & Heller, 1993).

For the purposes of this chapter, we propose that gifted children begin with some advantages that are likely innate, but that it is the early emergence of expertise, and the metacognitive knowledge that supports expertise, that qualitatively discriminates between gifted and average children. There is substantial evidence that gifted children differ from average children in basic skills. Some infants, for instance, have better memories than others in that they more quickly habituate to tasks, and this tendency to habituate correlates with IQ test scores given several years later (Fagan & Haiken-Vasen, 1997). Gifted children are also more efficient in their cognitive processing in that they have higher speed of processing (Jensen, 1982). Gifted and creative children also differ from their average peers in that they are temperamentally more persistent (Newell, Shawn, & Simon, 1962; Roe, 1952) and this persistent temperament predicts better school performance (Martin & Holbrook, 1985) and creative accomplishments (Simonton, 2004). Gifted children, however, differ primarily from average children in that they possess a number of characteristics typical of expertise. Gifted children have greater automaticity, which is a characteristic of experts (Sternberg & Hovarth, 1998), and are characterized by their superior higher order processing, including metacognition and executive control (Brewer, 1987). It is suspected that early emerging advantages in basic processes support the emergence of higher order processing characteristic of gifted and expert performance, but this has not been tested using longitudinal study designs (Perleth, 1993).

In this chapter, we will briefly review the work on expertise, and use this work as a basis for the interpretation of the work on metacognition in gifted populations. Our approach is in line with the work of Sternberg (2001) who proposed that the development of expertise is linked to the development of metacognitive skills, knowledge, strategies, and motivation learn. Thus, metacognition is linked to the emergence of expert performance. We will argue that its existence in higher levels in gifted children promotes the emergence of expertise and that emerging expertise supports the further development of metacognition. Below we briefly review the characteristics of expertise with a particular focus on the role of metacognition in the development of expertise. We then review the literature on metacognition in the gifted to determine whether the evidence supports the connection between giftedness, metacognition and emerging expertise.

CHARACTERISTICS OF EXPERTISE

What we know about expertise suggests that experts differ from novices in the depth, extent, and organization of their knowledge, the strategies they use to solve problems, and the way they categorize problems. Experts in all subject domains have greater domain knowledge, and this knowledge is more conceptual and better organized from that of novices (Bruning, Schraw, Norby, & Ronning, 2004). Evidence of the difference between experts and novices in their conceptual knowledge, and how they store, relate, and use this domain knowledge can be found in how they categorize problems (Chi, Feltovich, & Glaser, 1981). Studies of problem categorization indicate that expert problem solvers tend to categorize two problems as similar when the same law or principle can be applied to solve the problems. Novice problem solvers, in contrast, tend to categorize two problems as similar when the problems share the same surface features such as terminology or objects (Chi et al., 1981). These differences appear in child experts as well as adult experts (e.g. Chi & Koeske, 1983) suggesting that it is the development of domain specific expertise and not maturation that influences how knowledge is organized.

Strategy use discriminates between novices and experts because it is linked to differences in conceptual knowledge. For example, in physics, the expert uses the working forward strategy involving the identification of a major principle or law when solving physics problems (Anzai, 1991). This strategy requires sufficient knowledge of the domain needed for meaningful problem solving (Schneider, 1993). In contrast, novices use the working backward strategy that is driven by the givens of the problem, not by an awareness of the underlying principles or laws (e.g. Anzai, 1991).

Experts are faster than novices in processing information because they search and represent problems much more efficiently (Charness, 1991). Experts are better at identifying what is important and when it is important, and this assists their processing by minimizing irrelevant information (Dryfus & Dryfus, 1986, 1996). This has implications for the ability of the individual to use metacognitive knowledge and skills. Speeded retrieval of knowledge releases cognitive resources allowing the expert to reflect on what he or she is doing and what needs to be done (Garofalo, 1986), and to plan further out (Dunphy & Williamson, 2004).

Expert problem solvers possess high levels of metacognitive declarative knowledge in that they can describe the strategies they are using, know why they are using them, and can select alternative strategies if the one they are using is not working. In contrast, novice problem solvers are unable to explain and monitor their choice and use of strategies very well, and will continue to use a strategy even after it has failed to work (National Research Council

NRC], 2001). Expert musicians, for instance, metacognitively reflect on what they are doing and what they need to do during practice and performance (Hallam, 2001). In general, one can expect metacognitive knowledge and regulation to improve as knowledge (and expertise) within a particular domain increases (Flavell, 1992). For example, metacognition in the form of self-explanations has been associated with an increase in understanding and better problem solving (Koch, 2001).

How Important is Metacognition for Expertise?

Metacognition increases as an individual gains more knowledge and moves towards expertise. At the same time, metacognition supports the emergence of expertise. When working in a new domain, the ability to reflect on inconsistencies between what one currently holds to be true and what the evidence suggests to be true promotes better learning (Kuhn, 2006). Novices who possess better metacognitive skills, therefore, will move more quickly towards expertise.

High levels of metacognition have been found to compensate for low problem solving ability and support the emergence of better problem solving (Howard, McGee, Shia, & Hong, 2001). Swanson (1990) found when examining high school students' verbal responses to a questionnaire, that low-aptitude, highly metacognitive students outperformed high-aptitude, low metacognitive students in determining the number of steps needed to solve pendulum and fluid problems. This study is important because it indicates that metacognitive knowledge contributes to achievement above and beyond the contributions of knowledge and general ability, making it critical for the move from novice to expert.

Adults are more likely than children to use metacognition when solving problems, even in a new domain for which they have no knowledge. As a result, they are more able than children to reflect on a mismatch between what they expect to occur and what actually occurs during problem solving, allowing them to make appropriate changes to their conceptual knowledge (Kuhn, Katz, & Dean, 2004; Kuhn & Pease, 2006). This ability is independent of domain specific expertise, so it is likely that higher levels of metacognitive reflection in adults is the result of a more efficient working memory. One question regarding the role of metacognition in the early emergence of expertise in gifted children is whether the more efficient working memory of gifted students allows them to metacognitively reflect during learning in a way similar to that of adults. If this is found to be the case, then the emergence of expertise may be accelerated as gifted children metacognitively reflect on their knowledge and make changes in their own beliefs at higher levels than average children.

Another way that metacognition promotes expertise is by enabling individuals to deal with novel problems that cannot be automatically solved through rote application of well-learned procedures. Crowley, Shrager and Siegler (1997) propose that associative and metacognitive systems work together during problem solving. When a problem is highly familiar and easy there is no need to bring metacognitive processing on line. Instead, the individual simply pulls the solution from memory. This happens when individuals are solving a very familiar problem that has been solved many times in the past. Alexander and Schwanenflugel (1994), for instance, found that when a child has substantial knowledge in a domain, strategy use was predicted by knowledge, not declarative metacognitive knowledge about strategies. The metacognitive system comes on line if a problem should develop during problem solving, or if the problem is new and unfamiliar. When this happens metacognitive processing is used to evaluate the problem and select the best course of action. Shin, Jonassen, and McGee (2003), for instance, found that high school astronomy students with good metacognitive skills were more likely to do well on problems requiring conceptual understanding and that were presented in an unfamiliar context. In contrast, they found that metacognition was not a strong predictor of performance on problems that could be solved in a familiar context. If Crowley et al. (1996) are correct that metacognitive processing is used only for novel and difficult tasks, then we would not expect to see consistently higher use of metacognitive knowledge and skills in gifted children. Instead, gifted children would utilize metacognitive processing when attempting an unfamiliar or challenging task in a domain of emerging expertise.

This maintenance of high levels of metacognitive processing takes place during deliberate practice which is the means by which expertise emerges and discriminates between average and elite performers (Ericsson, 1996). Deliberate practice in emerging experts involves a considerable amount of practice that is distinguished by its high quality. During deliberate practice, experts set goals for improving performance, attempt to achieve those goals, evaluate their progress toward the goals, and change performance to better meet the goals. This practice is highly thoughtful and reflective. Expert performers appear to possess and use several forms of metacognition including the possession of a variety of strategies, knowledge about how and when these strategies are used, and the ability to monitor whether the strategy allows the individual to meet his or her goals (Flavell, 1992). If gifted children are emerging experts they should not only practice more, but should practice *deliberately* including setting goals for learning, reflecting on whether they have achieved those goals, and altering their performance to achieve goals.

Gifted children may differ in the point at which they shift from metacognitive to associative processing as a function of the amount of deliberate practice. Ericsson, Nandogopal and Roring (2005) argue that experts suppress the associative system in favor of metacognitive processing during deliberate practice. Instead of leveling out at an acceptable, but not high level of performance, the emerging expert continues to actively reflect on what he or she is doing with the goal of improving performance. If giftedness is emerging expertise, then we should see a tendency to suppress the associative system and activate the metacognitive system during deliberate practice and when the gifted child is faced with a novel or difficult task. We should see more metacognitive processing only as a part of goal-driven performance, rather than across all tasks.

The maintenance of high levels of deliberate practice requires that the individual be highly motivated and persistent, two characteristics of gifted children. The more an individual practices, the more expert he or she becomes regardless of initial talent and ability (Ericsson, 1996). Roe (1952), for example, showed that scientists who excel in their field differ from their less eminent colleagues not in intellectual ability, but rather in capacity for concentration and hard work. Gifted children are often characterized as being fascinated by specific topics or hobbies. It is within these domains that gifted children should show high levels of deliberate practice comprised of substantially higher levels of reflective, goal oriented practice.

Expertise, in turn, supports metacognitive processing in that experts are more aware of what they do and do not know. Novices and unskilled individuals are less able than experts to assess their lack of knowledge (Dunning, Johnson, Ehrlinger, & Kruger, 2003), which makes it less likely that they will be able to be correct their performance. Expert knowledge also provides a basis from which individuals can metacognitively reflect on the difficulty level of a task (Efklides, Papadaki, Papantoniou, & Kiosseoglou, 1998). As gifted children become more expert, their knowledge will support metacognitive reflection and monitoring. As expertise emerges with deliberate practice, the ability to metacognitively reflect and make correct decisions increases as a function of that expertise.

METACOGNITION, GIFTEDNESS, AND EXPERTISE

Metacognition may promote expertise in gifted children in several ways. First, if the more efficient working memory of gifted children allows them the resources to metacognitively reflect even in a new domain, then gifted children should progress through the initial stages of expertise faster than average children. Second, as expertise emerges in gifted children, an increase in domain specific knowledge should include declarative metacognitive knowledge that would support better strategy use. Third, emerging expert knowledge should support monitoring with gifted children using their knowledge base to make correct decisions about their accuracy and the need to alter problem solving. Fourth, the emerging expert knowledge base should support far transfer because gifted children will be more aware of common underlying features of the problems. Fifth, metacognitive monitoring should be most evident during periods of deliberate practice and when gifted children are faced with novel or difficult tasks.

One of the problems that you will see below is that it is difficult to assess these claims because most of the work on metacognition in gifted children has dealt with basic memory or reading skills. What little work that has been done within domains of emerging expertise, however, supports the connection between metacognition and the early emergence of expertise in the gifted.

Metacognition is multifaceted, typically including declarative knowledge about strategies (specific strategy knowledge), task characteristics, and person characteristics, as well as procedural knowledge for monitoring, strategy regulation, and control. There has been considerable research done examining both declarative and procedural metacognition in gifted students. Some of this research supports the view that metacognition is linked to emerging expertise in gifted children. Other research, however, suggests that gifted children do not show these characteristics.

DECLARATIVE METACOGNITION

The work on expertise tends to focus less on declarative metacognitive knowledge and more on monitoring and other procedural metacognitive skills. It would be expected, however, that if gifted children are displaying more expert knowledge, they should have more declarative knowledge about the more advanced strategies that they use. They would be better able to describe when, why, and how to use strategies. They would also know more about their own and others limitations as learners and about task characteristics that influence strategy choice. This would be evident during deliberate practice when they must select and apply the best strategy to maximize performance.

The bulk of the research examining declarative knowledge about strategies indicates that gifted students possess more metacognitive knowledge about strategies. In a review of the research, Alexander, Carr, and Schwanenflugel (1995) found that gifted children show superior ability in their declarative metacognitive knowledge and that this advantage was apparent during early elementary school, late elementary school, and junior high and high school. For example, gifted children in early and late elementary school had better knowledge of the variables that affect memory (Borkowski & Peck, 1986; Kurtz & Weinert, 1989). Other work by Schofield and Ashman (1987) and Swanson (1992) found that gifted middle school age students scored higher on measures of metacognitive knowledge than non-gifted students. Gifted high school students have been found to have higher declarative metacognition about decision making (Ball, Mann & Stamm, 1994). Interestingly, declarative metacognitive knowledge even discriminates learning disabled gifted children from learning disabled children (Hannah & Shore, 1995).

Some studies found no ability group differences in declarative metacognition. For example, Kontos, Swanson, and Frazer (1984) found no differences in junior high school age students' knowledge of variables that influence memory and effort. Chan (1996) only found a significant difference in knowledge about reading strategies for gifted girls, but not boys. Perleth, Heller and Hany (1994) also found little evidence for the superiority of gifted second and fourth grade children in metamemory and strategy use. When no differences have been found it is typically the result of problems with the study including tasks that were too easy or a median split was used to create ability categories (Alexander et al., 1995). For example, Chan asked middle school students about the effectiveness of different reading strategies, such as the use of a topic sentence, that were likely known by most students that age.

The results of these studies suggest that gifted children know more about the strategies that they use to remember information, and are more aware of variables that will limit their ability to learn, including limitations of their own abilities. Although the bulk of the research to date suggests a monotonic relationship between ability level and metacognition with gifted children possessing better declarative metacognition at every age, longitudinal work by Alexander, Fabricius and Fleming (2001) indicates that declarative metacognitive knowledge increases with time as a function of ability. This means that gifted children's advantage in strategy knowledge increases over time, and possibly with increasing expertise

Much more work, however, needs to be done to determine whether metacognitive declarative knowledge is an outcome of the early and faster acquisition of domain specific expertise by gifted children, and the role of expertise in increasing metacognitive knowledge. The limited nature of the questions used to assess metacognition and the focus on declarative metacognition for memory may conceal accelerating group differences in declarative metacognition with declarative metacognitive knowledge increasing as a function of more sophisticated strategy use within domains of knowledge. We need to know more about domain specific strategies that are related to more advanced skills. Work also needs to be done examining the role of declarative metacognitive knowledge during deliberate practice as expertise is emerging.

METACOGNITIVE MONITORING

If giftedness is a form of accelerated expertise, metacognitive monitoring should discriminate between gifted and average students during deliberate practice and when the gifted child is faced with a novel or difficult task that cannot be easily solved using associative processing. Gifted children will reflect more on the outcomes of their practice and take these outcomes into consideration for future practice. When faced with a challenging task, gifted children will be better able to reflect on the problem and develop more effective strategies to solve that problem.

Monitoring might also promote learning as gifted children reflect on inconsistencies between what they know and new information that contradicts their beliefs. This type of metacognitive monitoring is difficult at any age including adulthood (Johnson, Taylor & Raye, 1977), in part because it requires individuals to override the tendency to ignore inconsistencies or to fill in inconsistent or missing information with existing prior knowledge. Even in individuals with substantial domain specific knowledge, monitoring requires effort and focused attention. If giftedness is early and accelerated expertise, then gifted children should be better able to suppress the tendency to ignore inconsistencies. Conceptual change should be faster in gifted children as they become aware of inconsistencies and accommodate to new information.

As with the work on declarative metacognitive knowledge, much of the work on metacognitive monitoring has been domain general, typically involving memory monitoring and text comprehension. In a review of nine studies, Alexander, et al. (1995) found only a slight advantage for gifted children over non-gifted children in cognitive monitoring, and that gifted children frequently performed at the same level as average children. Work by Schneider and his colleagues (Schneider & Bjorklund, 1992; Schneider & Korkel, 1989), for instance, indicated no differences in feeling of knowing judgments and prediction accuracy.

There is little evidence that gifted children are better at monitoring their strategy use. Bjorklund et al, (1992), for instance, found no difference in the ability of early elementary gifted and average students' ability to recall a strategy just used. Work by Bouffard-Bouchard, Parent and LeFebre (1993) is in line with this finding with average and gifted eighth grade students being similar in their monitoring of processing and planning while doing a verbal concept identification task in which they had to find a word that best fit into a sentence frame. Gifted students, however, were more likely to monitor the amount of time they were taking to solve problems and were more accurate in estimating the number of correct responses they found, whereas the average students tended to overestimate their successes (Bouffard-Bouchard et al., 1993).

These results suggest that gifted children are not suppressing the associative system in favor of the metacognitive system. The failure to find ability group differences in monitoring cannot be interpreted to mean that gifted children are not emerging experts. None of the research on metacognitive monitoring examined this process within specific domains of expertise or during deliberate practice. Much of the work reviewed by Alexander and Schwanenflugel (1994) on metacognitive monitoring involved median splits resulting in less than clear grouping of students into high and average ability groups (e.g. Schneider, Korkel, & Weinert, 1989). In several cases, the tasks were quite simple and required little thought to solve (e.g. Bjorklund et al., 1992) and for which there would be no reason to use more effortful metacognitive processing instead of associative processing. To test the hypothesis that gifted children are more likely to monitor their problem solving and their progress toward goals within emerging domains of expertise, research needs to compare gifted to average performance during practice and during problem solving in a specific domain. A microgenetic research design in which students are observed practicing or solving domain specific problems repeatedly over a relatively short period of time would provide insight into the role of monitoring on expertise. Of particular interest is whether gifted students suppress the emergence of the associative system to maintain high levels of metacognitive processing during deliberate, focused practice as hypothesized by Ericsson et. al (2005). It is the existence of this tendency that might best discriminate children who go on to become elite performers in adulthood from those children who go on to become good, but not excellent performers.

When more difficult tasks have been presented to gifted children monitoring was more likely to be activated. Research by Swanson (1989) indicated no differences in sixth grade students' responses to low effort tasks, but found differences in favor of gifted students for high effort tasks. Specifically, gifted students were more likely to be aware of interference from a secondary task and to selectively attend to certain aspects of the task when the task was more difficult. These results suggest that metacognitive monitoring is activated when students are faced with more difficult tasks that require them to use their conceptual knowledge to set up and solve problems.

STRATEGY USE AND TRANSFER

If gifted students are emerging experts and moving toward expertise at a faster pace than average children, they should show the early emergence of domain specific strategies characteristic of more expert performance. Although they may possess a range of problem solving strategies, they may not necessarily use more strategies than average children because strategy use would be limited to the most effective or efficient strategies. Furthermore, the emerging expert should be better able to transfer strategies because he or she possesses an deeper understanding of the domain and can see the underlying commonalities between the task from which a strategy is transferred and a new task. Average children, in contrast, should be more influenced by the surface features of the tasks and be less able to transfer strategies, even if the tasks differ superficially.

The research to date is inconsistent, with some studies indicating an advantage for gifted students in terms of outcomes of strategy use and diversity of strategies used and other studies showing no difference, or even an advantage for average students (Alexander & Schwanenflugel. 1994; Carr, Alexander, Schwanenflugel, 1996). For example, Schraw, Horn, Thorndike-Christ, and Bruning (1995) found that high self-knowledge college students used more cognitive strategies and used those strategies more flexibly in a way that was linked directly to higher academic achievement. Shore, Koller and Dover (1994), in contrast, found that gifted children did not always outperform average children on a water jar problem. It was the existence of metacognition that increased the likelihood that the children would successfully detect a correct response pattern. In regard to strategy regulation, Schofield &

Ashman (1987) found that gifted fifth and sixth graders were more likely than above average and average peers to plan ahead during problem solving.

Giftedness effects tend to occur when more complex strategies were examined (e.g. Anderson, 1985; Muir, Masterson, Winer, Lyon, & White, 1989; Swanson, 1992). When gifted children were given a relatively simple task, such as the use of a clustering strategy, no ability differences were found (e.g. Harnishfeger & Bjorklund 1990). This lends support to the claim that giftedness effects should be evident in the emergence of complex strategies linked to expert knowledge. For more familiar tasks, no group differences would be expected because associative processing would dominate.

A number of studies point to the need to link superior strategy use to related domain specific knowledge as opposed to a general measure of intelligence. Alexander and Schwanenfugel (1994) found that domain specific knowledge was a much stronger predictor of memory strategy use than general intelligence. Similarly, Swanson, O'Connor, and Carter (1991) found no ability group differences in the types of strategies gifted and average children used. Instead, the strategies used were linked to expertise with both average and gifted students having expertise related to the strategies used. If strategy use is linked to domain specific knowledge more than general ability, then ability group differences in strategy use should be most evident within specific domains of emerging expertise.

When domain specific strategies were investigated, gifted students show more expert and advanced strategy use. Geary and Brown (1991) found that gifted eight and nine year olds were more likely to use a more advanced mathematical strategy. In addition, Span & Overtoom-Corsmit (1986) found that gifted high school students were more likely than less gifted students to use complex strategies to solve difficult mathematics problems. The highly gifted group used estimation, comparing, and formula searching strategies more often than their less gifted counterparts. These strategies, particularly estimation, require more expert knowledge of the domain in order to be effective.

A number of studies including work by Peck and Borkowski (1983) and Perleth, Heller and Hany (1994) found that gifted students were significantly better at transferring trained strategies to new and different tasks (far transfer). This ability was evident throughout childhood and adolescence. Borkowski and Peck (1986) found that gifted eight-year-olds were more likely to transfer a trained elaboration strategy to a very different task. When comparing gifted and regular high school students, gifted students were found to transfer newly acquired strategies more successfully to a new domain compared to average students (Scruggs, Mastropieri, Jorgensen, & Monson, 1986). Far transfer involves the ability to recognize similarities between tasks and to understand how a strategy can be modified to fit the new task. The research to date indicates that gifted children either possess or quickly acquire that knowledge. In a longitudinal study of ninth grade students' mathematical problem solving, Sriraman (2003) found that mathematically gifted students were more able than average students to uncover the underlying principle to the problems and transfer that principle to new problems that utilized the same principle. This is the type of situation that one would expect metacognitive processes to come on line in place of associative processing, and likely explains the difference between gifted and average children's ability to far transfer. Unfortunately, no research has examined the role of metacognition on transfer within a domain of expertise. If gifted children are emerging experts then the ability to far transfer should be most evident when there is a strong conceptual knowledge base to support that transfer. One study by Span and Overtoom-Corsmit (1986) indicates that far transfer is more likely to occur for gifted children within the domain of mathematics, but did not test whether far transfer was supported by conceptual knowledge.

In sum, an explanation of how metacognition influences learning in gifted children is limited by the tendency to work with memory strategies and not within specific content domains. If giftedness is emerging expertise then metacognition should support the emergence of expertise and, over time, become strongly linked to performance in domains of higher expertise. As domain specific knowledge increases, metacognition should also increase. Much more work needs to be done on the role of metacognition in the learning of gifted children.

CONCLUSION

Gifted children share many commonalities with experts (Bruning et al., 2004). They tend to have a broader knowledge base (Muir-Broaddus & Bjorklund, 1990) which allows them to process information in a way similar to that of experts (Davidson, 1986). They are able to combine concepts in ways not available to average students because they can see connections between concepts not evident at a surface level. Gorodetsky and Klavir (2003) for instance, found ability group differences in the subprocesses used during problem solving with gifted children taking advantage of the ability to see connections on a deeper level and constructing solutions based on those connections. Average students were less able to do this because they did not see the connection between the problem they were solving and previous problems that they had solved. Other work by Bransford, et al. (1982), indicates that successful fifth-graders are able to detect and fix problems even when information is presented in an arbitrary manner. The successful fifth graders were able to go beyond the surface features of the problem to determine what was important to attend to and what needed to be done in what order to solve the problem. As such, the rich, deep knowledge of the gifted child substantially supports goal-directed problem solving. Further, like experts, gifted students possess more knowledge about their memory systems, have more strategies at hand to work with, and are better at transferring those strategies across different problem solving contexts. However, these differences do not explain why some gifted children go on to become elite performers and others do not.

This disconnect may occur because criteria used to identify gifted children tend to focus less on the processes that promote expertise and more on states, primarily knowledge states, that characterize above average performance. In particular, the failure to focus on deliberate practice and the metacognitive skills and processes that are a part of that practice are reasons for this disconnect. While some gifted students who go on to become eminent adults may continue to improve in their chosen field of expertise through deliberate practice, many gifted children may level out at an acceptable, but not high level of performance, because they fail to actively reflect on what they are doing and on the goal of improving performance. They will have some expertise in an area, but will not be capable of the highest levels of performance. The opportunity for elite performance is cut short by quick learning and a willingness to settle for less than the best performance (Ericsson et al., 2005).

The willingness to put in the time to fine tune performance may be a pivotal factor in determining which path gifted children take in adulthood. Gifted children are characterized by the tendency to spend substantial time mastering a domain of interest and the skills used in that domain (Winner, 2003). For example, parents of gifted children have reported that they spend considerable amounts of time working on artwork (Hyllegard, 2000) and reworking word problems (Bouffard-Bouchard, Parent, & Larivee, 1993). This effort is directed in that gifted students put in more effort in the selection of appropriate strategies and setting of specific goals (Bouffard-Bouchard et al., 1993). As such, the metacognitive skills and knowledge necessary to fine tune performance are supported by high levels of motivation and commitment typical of self-regulated learning (Zimmerman, 2000).

According to Bloom (1985) the role of social support in influencing the development of expertise is critical. This support provides the gifted child with both a model of the skills and motivations needed to become an elite performer. In the first few years of practice, there is a highly supportive home environment in which motivation and deliberate practice are stressed. Parents support the development of metacognitive skills that support deliberate practice. For example, Moss and Strayer (1990) Moss (1990) and found that mothers of gifted preschoolers scaffolded metacognitive activities by directing their children to use metacognitive strategies. During the middle years, the first signs of expertise emerge, and the student becomes increasingly dependent on skilled mentors. In the later years, as an individual becomes more advanced, social support is obtained through a single master teacher alongside steady practice and feedback. The master teacher likely directs the emergence of higher level skills including the metacognitive skills needed to achieve elite status. Work by Bloom and others indicates that it is the combination of the need by the gifted child to achieve elite status and their involvement with an expert performer who can teach and model the skills needed for expertise that accounts for why some children go on to become elite performers and others do not.

In sum, metacognitive skills and knowledge help jump start the early emergence of expertise and accelerate the process. As expertise emerges, metacognitive skills and knowledge become increasingly intertwined with the emerging expert knowledge base as gifted students engage in deliberate practice, reflect on what they know and can do, and what their goals are for performance. The lack of longitudinal work examining the development of expertise within domains makes it difficult to determine exactly how metacognition supports and is supported by emerging expertise. Such research would provide insight on specific strategies (e.g. the working forward and working backward strategy) used in specific domains. This is an area that future research needs to focus on in order to better understand the relationship between giftedness, metacognition, and expertise.

REFERENCES

Anzai, Y. (1991). Learning and use of representations for physics expertise. In K.A. Anders & J. Smith (Eds.), *Toward a general theory of expertise* (pp. 64-92). New York: Cambridge University Press.

Alexander, J.M., Carr, M., & Schwanenflugel, P.J. (1995). Development of metacognition in gifted children: Directions for future research. *Developmental Review, 15*, 1-37.

Alexander, J.M., Fabricius, W.V., Fleming, V.M., Zwahr, M., & Brown, S.A. (2001). The development of metacognitive causal explanations. *Learning and Individual Differences, 13,* 227-238.

Alexander, J.M., & Schwanenflugel, P.J. (1994). Strategy regulation: The role of intelligence, metacognitive attributions, and knowledge base. *Developmental Psychology, 30,* 709-723.

Anderson, M.A. (1985). *Information processes used by gifted and average elementary students when solving written discourse problems.* Paper presented at the annual meeting of the American Educational Research Association, Chicago, IL.

Ball, C., Mann, L., & Stamm, C. (1994). Decision-making abilities of intellectually gifted and non-gifted children. *Australian Journal of Psychology, 46,* 13-20.

Bjorklund, D.F., Schneider, W., Harnishfeger, K.K., Cassel, W., Bjorklund, B.R., & Bernholtz, J.E. (1992). The role of IQ, expertise, and motivation in the recall of familiar information. *Contemporary Educational Psychology, 17,* 340-355.

Bloom, B.S. (1985). *Developing talent in young people.* New York: Ballantine Books.

Borkowski, J.G., & Peck, V.A. (1986). Causes and consequences of metamemory in gifted children. In R. J. Sternberg & J. E. Davidson (Eds.), *Conceptions of giftedness* (pp. 182 - 200). Cambridge: Cambridge University Press.

Bouffard-Bouchard, T., Parent, S., & Larivee S. (1993). Self-regulation on a concept-formation task among average and gifted students. *Journal of Experimental Child Psychology, 56,* 115-134.

Bransford, J., Stein, B., Vye, N., Franks, J., Auble, P., Mezynski, K., & Perfetto, G. (1982). Differences in approaches to learning: An overview. *Journal of Experimental Psychology: General, 111,* 390-398.

Brewer, N. (1987). Processing speed, efficiency and intelligence. In J.G. Borkowski & J.D. Day (Eds.), *Cognition in special children: Comparative approaches to retardation, learning disabilities, and giftedness* (pp. 15-48). Norwood, NJ: Ablex publishing.

Bruning, R.H., Schraw, G.J., Norby, M.N., & Ronning, R.R. (2004). *Cognitive psychology and instruction (4th ed.).* Upper Saddle River, NJ: Pearson.

Carr, M., Alexander, J., & Schwanenflugel, P. (1996). Where gifted children do and do not excel on metacognitive tasks. *Roeper Review, 18,* 212-217.

Chan, L.K.S. (1996). Motivational orientations and metacognitive abilities of intellectually gifted students. *Gifted Child Quarterly, 40,* 184-193.

Charness, N. (1991). Expertise in chess: The balance between knowledge and search. In K.A. Ericsson & J. Smith (Eds.), *Towards a general theory of expertise: Prospects and limits* (pp. 39-63). Cambridge, England: Cambridge University Press.

Chi, M.T.H., Feltovich, P.J., & Glaser, R. (1981). Categorization and representation of physics problems by experts and novices. *Cognitive Science, 5,* 121-152.

Chi, M., & Koeske, R. (1983). Network representation of a child's dinosaur knowledge. *Developmental Psychology, 19,* 29-39.

Crowley, K., Shrager, J., & Siegler, R. S. (1997). Strategy discovery as a competitive negotiation between metacognitive and associative mechanisms. *Developmental Review, 17,* 462-489.

Davidson, J.E. (1986). Insight and giftedness. In J.R. Sternber, & J.E. Davidson (Eds.), *Conceptions of giftedness* (pp. 201-222). Cambridge, MA: Cambridge University Press.

Dreyfus, H.L., & Dreyfus, S.E. (1986). *Mind over machine: The power of human intuition and expertise in the era of the computer*. New York: MacMillan.

Dreyfus, H.L., & Dreyfus, S.E. (1996). The relationship of theory and practice in the acquisition of skill. In P.A. Benner, C.A. Tanner & C.A. Chesla (Eds.), *Expertise in Nursing Practice* (pp. 29–47). New York: Springer Publishing Company, Inc.

Dunphy, B.C., & Williamson, S.L. (2004). In pursuit of expertise: Toward an educational model for expertise development. *Advances in Health Sciences Education, 9*, 107-127.

Dunning, D., Johnson, K. L., Ehrlinger, J., & Kruger, J. (2003). Why people fail to recognize their own incompetence. *Current Directions in Psychological Science, 12*, 83-87.

Efklides, A., Papadaki, M., Papantoniou, G., & Kiosseoglou, G. (1998). Individual differences in feelings of difficulty: The case of school mathematics. *European Journal of Psychology of Education, 13*(2), 207-226.

Ericsson, K.A. (1996). The acquisition of expert performance. In K.A. Ericsson (Ed.), *The road to excellence: The acquisition of expert performance in the arts, sciences, sports, and games* (pp. 1-50). Mahwah, NJ: Erlbaum.

Ericsson, K.A., Nandagopal, K., & Roring, R.W. (2005). Giftedness viewed from the expert performance perspective. *Journal for the Education of the Gifted, 28*, 287- 311.

Fagan, J.F. III, & Haiken-Vasen, J. (1997). Selective attention to novelty as a measure of information processing across the lifespan. In J.A. Burack & J.T. Enns (Eds.) *Attention, development, and psychopathology* (pp. 55-73). New York: Guilford Press.

Flavell, J. H. (1992). Cognitive development: Past, present, and future. *Developmental Psychology, 28*, 998-1005.

Garofalo, J. (1986). Metacognitive. Knowledge and metacognitive process: Important influences on mathematical performance. *Research & Training in Developmental Education, 2*, 34–39.

Geary, D.C., & Brown, S. C. (1991). Cognitive addition: Strategy choice and speed of processing differences in gifted, normal, and mathematically disabled children. *Developmental Psychology, 27*, 398–406.

Gorodetsky, M., & Klavir, R. (2003). What can we learn from how gifted/average pupils describe their process of problem solving? *Learning and Instruction, 13*, 305-325

Hallam, P. J. (2001). *Report on Learning Record 2001 moderations: Reliability and validity findings*. San Diego, CA: Center for Language in Learning.

Hannah, C. L., & Shore, B. M. (1995). Metacognition and high intellectual ability: Insights from the study of learning-disabled gifted students. *Gifted Child Quarterly, 39*, 95-109.

Harnishfeger, K.K., & Bjorklund, D.F. (1990). Memory functioning of gifted and nongifted middle school children. *Contemporary Educational Psychology, 15*, 346-363.

Howard, B.C., McGee, S., Shia, R., & Hong, N. (2001, April). *Computer-based science inquiry: How components of metacognitive self-regulation affect problem- solving.* Paper presented at the American Educational Research Association Meeting, Seattle, WA.

Hyllegard, R. (2000). Parental attribution of artistic ability in talented children. *Perceptual and Motor Skills, 91*, 1134-1144.

Jensen, A.R. (1982). The chronometry of intelligence. In R. J. Sternberg (Ed.), *Advances in the psychology of human intelligence* (pp 255-310). Hillsdale, NJ: Erlbaum.

Johnson, M.K., Taylor, T.B., & Raye, C.L. (1977). Fact and fantasy: The effects of internally generated events on the apparent frequency of externally generated events. *Memory & Cognition, 5*, 116-122.

Kanevsky, L., & Geake, J. (2004). Inside the zone of proximal development: Validating a multifactor model of learning potential with gifted students and their peers. *Journal for the Education of the Gifted, 28*, 182-217.

Koch, A. (2001). Training in metacognition and comprehension of physics texts. *Science Education, 85,* 758-768.

Kontos, S., Swanson, H.L., & Frazer, C.T. (1984). Memory metamemory connection in intellectually gifted and normal children. *Psychological Reports, 54*, 930-933.

Kuhn, D. (2006). The Development of Learning. *Journal of Cognition and Development, 7,* 309-312.

Kuhn, D., Katz, J. B., & Dean, D., Jr. (2004). Developing reason. *Thinking & Reasoning, 10,* 197-219.

Kuhn, D., & Pease, M. (2006). Do Children and Adults Learn Differently? *Journal of Cognition and Development, 7,* 279-293.

Kurtz, B.E., & Weinert, F.E. (1989). Metamemory, Memory Performance, and Causal Attributions in Gifted and Average Children. *Journal of Experimental Child Psychology, 48,* 45-61.

Lohman, D.F. (2005). An aptitude perspective on talent: Implications for identification of academically gifted minority students. *Journal for the Education of the Gifted, 28,* 333-360.

Martin, R P., & Holbrook, J. (1985). Relationship of temperament characteristics to the academic achievement of first-grade children. *Journal Psychoeducational Assessment, 3,* 377–386.

Moss, E. (1990). Social interaction and metacognitive development in gifted preschoolers. *Gifted Child Quarterly, 34*, 16-20.

Moss, E., & Strayer, F.F. (1990). Interactive problem-solving of gifted and non-gifted preschoolers with their mothers. *International Journal of Behavioral Development, 13,* 177-197.

Muir, J. Masterson, D.,Winer, Lyon, K., & White, K. (1989). *Training and transfer of an organizational strategy in gifted and high-average children.* Presentation at the Society for Research in Child Development. Kansas City, MO.

Muir-Broaddus, J. E., & Bjorklund, D. F. (1990). Developmental and individual differences in children's memory strategies: The role of knowledge. In W. Schneider & F.E. Weinert (Eds.), *Interactions among aptitudes, strategies, and knowledge in cognitive performance.* New York: Springer-Verlag.

National Research Council. (2001). Assessment in practice. Knowing what students know: The science and design of educational assessment. Washington DC: National Academy Press.

Newell, A., Shawn, J.C. & Simon, H.A. (1962). The process of creative thinking. In H. Gruber, G. Terrell, & M. Wertheimer (Eds.), *Contemporary approaches to creative thinking* (pp. 43-62). New York: Atherton.

Peck, V., & Borkowski, J.G. (1983, April). *The emergence of strategic behavior and metamemory in gifted children.* Paper presented at the biennial meeting of the Society for Research in Child Development, Detroit.

Perleth, C. (1993) Indicators of high ability in young children, in K.A. Heller, F.J. Monks & A.H. Passow (Eds.), *International handbook of research and development of giftedness and talent* (pp. 283-310). Oxford: Pergamon Press.

Perleth, C., Heller, K. A., & Hany, E. A. (1994). Strategy use and metamemory in gifted and average primary school children. In *Competence and responsibility, Vol. 2.* (pp. 46-52): Hogrefe & Huber Publishers.

Perleth, C., Sierwald, W., & Heller, K.A. (1993). Selected results of the Munich Longitudinal Study of Giftedness: The multidimensional/typological giftedness model. *Roeper Review, 15,* 149-155.

Roe, A. (1952). *The making of a scientist.* New York: Dodd, Mead.

Schneider, W. (1993). Acquiring expertise: Determinants of exceptional performance. In K. A. Heller, F. J. Monks & A.H. Passow (Eds.), *International handbook of research and development of giftedness and talent* (pp. 311-324). Oxford: Pergamon Press.

Schneider, W. (1997). The impact of expertise on performance: Illustrations from developmental research on memory and sports. *High Ability Studies, 8,* 7-18.

Schneider, W., & Bjorklund, D.F. (1992). Expertise, aptitude, and strategic remembering. *Child Development, 63,* 461-473.

Schneider, W., & Korkel, J. (1989). The knowledge base and text recall: Evidence from a short-term longitudinal study. *Contemporary Educational Psychology, 14,* 382-393.

Schneider, W., Korkel, J., & Weinert, F.E. (1989). Domain-specific knowledge and memory performance: A comparison of high- and low-aptitude children. *Journal of Educational Psychology, 81*(3), 306-312.

Schofield, N.J., & Ashman, A.F. (1987). The cognitive processing of gifted, high average, and low average ability students. *British Journal of Educational Psychology, 57,* 9-20.

Schraw, G., Horn, C., Thorndike-Christ, T., & Bruning, R. (1995). Academic goal orientations and student classroom achievement. *Contemporary Educational Psychology, 20,* 359-368.

Scruggs, T.E., Mastropieri, M.A., Jorgensen, C., & Monson, J.A. (1986). Effective mnemonic strategies for gifted learners. *Journal for the Education of the Gifted, 9,* 105-121.

Shin, N., Jonassen, D.H., & McGee, S. (2003). Predictors of well-structured and ill-structured problem solving in an astronomy simulation. *Journal of Research in Science Teaching, 40,* 6-33.

Shore, B. M., Koller, M., & Dover, A. (1994). More from the water jars: A reanalysis of problem-solving performance among gifted and nongifted children. *Gifted Child Quarterly, 38*(4), 179-183.

Simonton, D.K. (2004). Creativity as a constrained stochastic process. In R.J. Sternberg, E.L. Grigorenko & J.L. Singer (Eds.), *Creativity: From potential to realization* (pp. 83-102). Washington: American Psychological Association.

Span, P., & Overtoom-Crosmit, R. (1986). Information processing by intellectually gifted pupils solving mathematical problems. *Educational Studies in Mathematics, 17,* 273-295.

Sriraman, B. (2003). Discovering mathematical generalizations via problem solving. *Beiträge zum Mathematikunterricht* (Dortmund, 2003). Proceedings of the 37th Annual Conference of the Gesellschaft für Didaktik der Mathematik (GDM), Dortmund, Germany.

Sternberg, R.J. (2001). Why schools should teach for wisdom: The balance theory of wisdom in educational settings. *Educational Psychologist, 36,* 227-245.

Sternberg, R.J., & Hovarth, J. (1995). A prototype view of expert teaching. *Educational Researcher, 24,* 9-17.

Swanson, H.L. (1989). The effects of central processing strategies on learning disabled, mildly retarded, average and gifted children's elaborative encoding abilities. *Journal of Experimental Child Psychology, 47*, 270-397.

Swanson, H.L. (1990). Influence of metacognitive knowledge and aptitude on problem solving. *Journal of Educational Psychology, 82*, 306-314.

Swanson, H.L. (1992). The relationship between metacognition and problem solving in gifted children. *Roeper Review, 15*, 43-48.

Swanson, H.L., O'Connor, J.E., & Carter, K.R. (1991). Problem-solving subgroups as a measure of intellectual giftedness. *British Journal of Educational Psychology, 61,* 55-72.

Winner, E. (2003). Creativity and Talent. In M.H. Bornstein, L. Davidson, C.L. Keyes, & K.A. Moore (Eds.), *Well-being: Positive development across the life course* (pp. 371-380). Mahwah, NJ: Erlbaum.

Zimmerman, B. J. (2000). Attaining self-regulation: A social cognitive perspective. In M. Boekaerts, P. R., Pintrich, & M. Zeidner (Eds.) *Handbook of self-regulation* (pp. 13-39). Academic Press, San Diego, CA.

In: Meta-Cognition: A Recent Review of Research...   ISBN: 978-1-60456-011-4
Editors: M.F. Shaughnessy et al. pp. 127-139   © 2008 Nova Science Publishers, Inc.

Chapter 7

MARGINALIA AS A METACOGNITIVE STRATEGY

Scott L. Hunsaker
Utah State University, USA

ABSTRACT

Marginalia, the practice of writing annotations in the margin of a text being read, is a long-standing practice that has been shown through research to improve university students' comprehension and has the poitential, because it requires students to record their thinking, to provide strong metacognitive feedback to gifted students. In this chapter, a typology, named marginal thinking, is introduced that guides teachers in instructing students about marginalia—both to increase their annotation skills and to make them more aware and reflective of their thinking practices during reading.

In many schools students are learning to "leave tracks of their thinking" (Harvey & Goudvis, 2000, p. 19) with the cognitive strategies taught through explicit reading comprehension instruction. In other words, students are encouraged to make a written record of their thinking while reading for later use in individual and small group discussions with the instructor. While such strategies are intended to help students "make meaning as they go" (p. 19), much of the instruction focuses on rebuilding meaning by "providing an opportunity ... to clarify confusions and misconceptions" (p. 20). Certainly it is important to provide struggling readers with strategies that will assist them in unlocking the meanings of what they read, however, the focus of this chapter is how leaving "tracks of their thinking" can be a valuable experience for advanced readers that will help them fathom the deeper meanings of text.

Creating a written record about one's thinking during reading can take different forms. Many readers keep notes in a separate journal. Some write notes directly in the margins of the book being read. These marginal notations are known as *marginalia*, the focus of this chapter.

HISTORICAL PERSPECTIVE

Writing marginalia is not necessarily an honored practice. For example, in her extensive treatise on marginalia, Jackson (2001) at first refers to the "reader-annotated book" (p. 1) as "a scruffy thing" (p. 1). She points out that people have mixed feelings about marginalia, "such as shame and disapproval" (p. 4). Libraries around the world post signs in their study areas, such as the one at Trinity University at Cambridge that read "Marking of Books is FORBIDDEN" (p. 10).

Yet, the practice of marginal note-taking is centuries old, going "back far beyond the birth of print" (Jackson, 2001, p. 5), perhaps even two thousand years. Indeed, the practice may be as old as the practice of writing itself. Jackson identifies several famous note-makers, including Erasmus, Alexander Pope, Thomas Hardy, Samuel Taylor Coleridge, William Ewart, Gladstone, and, in more modern times, Marilyn Monroe and Nelson Mandela. Medieval readers were apparently quite persistent annotators, using the "margins of manuscripts to discuss, critique, and learn from the annotations left behind by earlier readers" (Wolfe, 2002, p. 297). Though "monastic librarians placed 'anathemas' … and other drastic injunctions in books to dissuade potential abusers" (Garrett, 2002, p. 292).

In America's history, one of the greatest letter writers, John Adams, was also one of the most prolific annotators. McCullough (2001) notes:

> Unlike Jefferson, who seldom ever marked a book, and then only faintly in pencil, Adams, pen in hand, loved to add his comments in the margins. It was part of the joy of reading for him, to have something to say himself, to talk back to, agree or take issue with, Rousseau, Condorcet, Turgot, Mary Wollstonecraft, Adam Smith, or Joseph Priestly. … At times his marginal observations nearly equaled what was printed on the page. … In all, in … one book, Adam's marginal notes and comments ran to some 12,000 words. (p. 619)

RESEARCH PERSPECTIVE

To take advantage of the purported power of annotations to help students delve more deeply into text, many textbooks now contain marginal notations that range from simple contextual definitions of important terms, to summaries of major points, to enriching sidebars. Theses glosses, as they are called, are intended to improve comprehension of the text or to make suggestions for further study based on potential student interests. As an example, in composition textbooks, the practice of glossing is used to demonstrate how students might read an essay or letter or some other written communication with a critical eye. Glosses point out specific rhetorical devices in the reading or critical thinking practices that could be employed by the reader (Wolfe, 2002). The danger, however, is that students may not focus on the reading processes as a guide of how to think, but on their content as a clue of what to think. In her research with 122 students enrolled in a lower level composition course at a university, Wolfe indeed found this to be true. While students with annotated texts performed better on recall tasks than students with underlining only or with completely unaltered text, students with annotated text were also more strongly influenced by the general tone of an annotation, taking negative attitudes toward passages accompanied by negative annotations and positive attitudes toward passages accompanied by positive annotations. Further, students with annotated texts showed no greater propensity to annotate texts on their own than students with unannotated texts.

Another issue with author-annotated texts is that of cognitive load. When textbook writers provide gloss, it is possible that the information presented is redundant for the already-informed learner or that the information "exceeds the cognitive capacity of the learner" (Wallen, Plass, & Brünken, 2005, p. 61), thus, in either case, creating extraneous material that interferes with learning. In their research with 109 college students, Wallen, Plass, and Brücken found that this was indeed the case.

This begs the question of whether or not student-generated annotations are useful in helping students understand text at surface or deeper levels. There is apparently something powerful, let alone convenient, about the act of writing notes in the margins that makes it a preferred annotation strategy to others that might be used. In a study of three annotation practices, Tucker and Jones (1993), found that recording notes in the margins of a hard copy of a document was preferred to typing annotations with a word processor or to making voice recordings of comments. It may be that, nearly 15 years later, technology has improved so that word processing or voice recording may now be less cumbersome, but the research has not been replicated, and it still leaves the question of whether students actually benefit from making their own annotations.

In a study with 46 college freshmen studying the same novel, Hynd, Simpson, and Chase (1990) found that students writing marginal notes in the novel, versus those who wrote in reading response journals, performed better on recall task and, after receiving instruction on writing inferential marginal notes, on constructed response items. However, journal writers performed better on essay questions. Interestingly, all readers reported that they found the reading task to be relatively unchallenging, indicating that the relationship between the cognitive demands of the text itself, in addition to the note-taking strategy employed, may have suppressed the results of this study.

Moreland, Dansereau, and Chmielewski (1997) examined the use of a variety of annotation strategies that had been found in previous research studies to be useful for improving student comprehension. The strategies were basically of four types:

1. The use of underlining and circling, for identification, separation, and grouping of ideas to be further examined, connected, and questioned;
2. The development of connections within the information to identify relationships not previously specified by the experimenters (e.g., themes, similarity/dissimilarity, and causes);
3. The creation of elaborations; and
4. The generation of questions about information not fully understood. (p. 522).

They found, in their study with 73 undergraduate students, that question-asking and connection annotations were related to higher recall scores, while the use of elaborations was definitely unrelated to recall. The authors admitted that no direct instruction was given on what kinds of elaborations could be written, and this could have affected outcomes. Further, it may be that elaborations are not helpful for recall but may be associated with more complex intellectual tasks. The researchers also found that while readers of differing comprehension abilities do not differ in the number or type of annotations they make, learners with high comprehension ability seem to benefit more from the practice as it assists them with establishing an "integrated structure for information" (pp. 531-532).

In a qualitative study, Porter-O'Donnell (2004) instructed ninth graders in how to make different types of marginal notations, including summaries, predictions, opinions, connections, questions, critiques of author's craft, reflections, reactions, and patterns. Interviews with her students revealed the following benefits of annotating: (1) teaching reading as a process, (2) changing comprehension, (3) slowing down reading, (4) promoting more active reading, and (5) improving writing. These benefits were recognized by students even though many of them initially complained about having to do the annotations.

In sum, the most consistent finding in the research seems to be that the reader-generated marginal notes can be useful in improving recall of information read, especially for college-level students. Because of the unique abilities of advanced readers in elementary and secondary schools, in which their cognitive functioning may be more like that of college students than of their age-mates, is it possible that the similar benefits might be had for them? Further, might there be goals beyond simple recall that would be appropriate for advanced readers and that could be assisted by instruction in marginal annotations? The current corpus of research seems hopeful in this regard, but, in general the question has been ignored. It would seem, as a first step, that a system of marginal note-taking that would assist primary and secondary students in keeping a record of their thinking would be useful. The remainder of this chapter describes one such system.

THE "MARGINAL THINKING" TYPOLOGY

The typology proposed here draws primarily from the author's own experience as a voracious reader, but also draws on the work of Basile (1978), Nist and Hogrebe (1985), and Santa, Havens, and Maycumber (1996). The typology (see Figure 1) includes five general categories of marginal notes. There is a hierarchy of sorts from Type 1 through Type 5, beginning with basic notation types and moving to the more complex. Each of the five categories is divided into two subcategories, making a total of ten types of marginalia. The subcategories include a mnemonic word that begins with the letter blend *bl*. The mnemonic cues can assist the student in remembering the different types of marginalia that can be made, without having to keep a paper copy of the typology nearby. In addition to the explanation provided here, the entire typology is summarized with examples in the accompanying figure. Each type of notation is explained in the following material.

Type 1. Interrogative Notations

The first, and most basic type of marginal note is the interrogative notation also known as **questioning**. With this type of notation, the reader asks questions of the author. The reader can ask questions about general *comprehension* or for more specific *clarification*. The *comprehension* question is known as the <u>blank,</u> inferring that the reader has drawn a blank from what was just read. The *clarification* question is called a <u>blink,</u> representing the blink of the eye that occurs as part of a double-take and inferring the need for the reader to investigate further what he/she has just understood from the reading.

Typology of Marginalia					
Type #	Category	Label	Subcategory	Mnemo-nic	Example
1	Interrogative	Question-ning	Comprehen-sion	Blank	Huh?
			Clarification	Blink	Is the author saying that teachers are among the worst in supporting the profession?
2	Summative	High-lighting	Exclamation	Blurt	Right!
			Explanation	Blurb	Main Point: Excellence is not always rewarded in the system.
3	Evaluative	Criti-qu-ing	Strengths	Blessing	The author's writing style makes it easy for me to find the main point of every paragraph. Its always in the first sentence.
			Weaknesses	Blasting	This author uses so many words that I don't know, I'll never understand this material.
4	Applicative	Connec-ting	Emotional	Blubbering	What I'm reading here about professionalism makes me angry that I didn't see more of this type of behavior in my teachers.
			Experiential	Blabbering	Once in second grade, I experienced humiliation from the teacher. She literally labeled me a nincompoop.
5	Argumentative	Arguing	Affirming	Blender	This is supported by Bloom's notion that the curriculum is what is taught when the teacher closes her classroom door.
			Negating	Blunder	The author has been inconsistent here. See page 12 where he discusses child-centeredness.

Figure 1. Marginal Thinking Typology.

Type 1. Interrogative Notations

The first, and most basic type of marginal note is the interrogative notation also known as **questioning**. With this type of notation, the reader asks questions of the author. The reader can ask questions about general *comprehension* or for more specific *clarification*. The *comprehension* question is known as the <u>blank,</u> inferring that the reader has drawn a blank from what was just read. The *clarification* question is called a <u>blink</u>, representing the blink of the eye that occurs as part of a double-take and inferring the need for the reader to investigate further what he/she has just understood from the reading.

Type 2. Summative Notations

The second type of marginal note is the summative notation also known as **highlighting**. Here the reader focuses on important ideas in the text, either through *exclamation* or *explanation*. The *exclamation*, or <u>blurt</u>, is usually a brief positive or negative reaction to ideas the reader him/herself finds important. The *explanation*, or <u>blurb</u>, is a restatement, outline, or graphic representation of the main points the author is making.

Type 3. Evaluative Notations

The Type 3 marginal note is the evaluative notation, also known as **critiquing**. In critiquing, the reader points out the *strengths* and *weaknesses* of the author's presentation of material. A comment on *strengths*, also called a <u>blessing</u>, provides comments on the manner in which the author's writing style aids the reader in understanding and engaging with the text. A comment on *weaknesses*, also called a <u>blasting</u>, provides comments on the manner in which the writing style hinders the reader in understanding and engaging with the text. In both subcategories, comments on the editing of the text would also be appropriate.

Type 4. Applicative Notations

The fourth type of marginal note is the applicative notation, also know as **connecting**. This type of note permits the reader to express his/her *emotional* or *experiential* connections with the text. The *emotional* note is mnemonically referred to, with a bit of tongue-in-cheek attitude, as <u>blubbering</u>. Here the reader indicates the positive or negative feeling encountered during the textual reading. The *experiential* note, also with the tongue-in-cheek attitude, is referred to as <u>blabbering</u>. Here the reader recounts a personal experience related to the content of the reading, though it is not necessary for the note to be overly lengthy, as blabbering might imply.

Type 5. Argumentative Notations

The final, and most complex, type of marginal note is the argumentative notation, or **arguing**. With this type of note the reader undertakes a substantive conversation with the author, either *affirming* or *negating* the author's arguments. The *affirming* note is an opportunity for the reader to provide additional thinking that supports the author's thesis. This is mnemonically referred to as the <u>blender</u> because the reader is blending his/her arguments with those of the author. The *negating* note is an opportunity for the reader to provide thinking opposed to the author's thesis. This is mnemonically referred to as the <u>blunder</u> because the reader is attempting to point out the blunders the author has made in his/her thinking. At his/her best, the excellent critical thinker would include both blenders and blunders in the marginalia for any particular text.

INTRODUCING MARGINAL THINKING TO STUDENTS

The first stage in presenting the marginal thinking typology to students is to be very familiar with the typology and its uses as a teacher. This means taking the time to personally practice using the typology in one's own reading. As marginal thinking is recorded, the reader should become explicitly aware of the specific passage causing a response. This is illustrated in Figure 2, which provides a record of the stimulus passage and the marginal notation for the text *Why Education Is Useless* by Daniel Cottam (2003). The sample figure includes the labels and mnemonics because these are the terms for the annotations that will most often be used with children. Older or more capable students can be taught the vocabulary of the categories and subcategories.

Once the teacher becomes comfortable with using marginal thinking, she or he is ready to instruct students in the process. It is usually best to teach the annotations from simplest to most complex. Thus, the blank, blink, and blurt can be taught right away, followed by the blurt. As students become skilled at these, then the blurb can be added. Students usually easily add in the blubbering and blabbering, with blessings, blastings, blenders, and blunders being included in instruction last.

Because it is usually frowned upon actually to write in the books, teachers may want to prepare photocopies of materials to be used for training. If this is not possible, sticky notes or highlighter tape can be use. The size of the sticky notes should take into account the fine motor skills of the children who will be using them to write their marginal thinking—the younger the child, the larger the sticky note (Porter-O'Donnell, 2004). When students become facile with the system, it may be appropriate to have them write their marginal thinking in a dialectical journal, but this should not be done until students are very clear about identifying the stimulus passage in addition to writing the marginal thinking annotation.

Introducing the typology in small groups is preferred to whole class instruction when the introduction in done through *interrupted reading*. In interrupted reading, the teacher introduces a type of marginal thinking. As the teacher reads aloud to the group, students are invited to interrupt the teaching with a hand raise and vocal signal. The student then identifies what the stimulus passage was and articulates his or her response. The teacher records the response on a sticky note and places it on the text next to the stimulus passage. Consider this script of a session with third graders who read above grade level as an example. The text being read is from the book *Why Are All Families Different? Questions Children Ask about Families* (Melvin, 1997).

Marginal Thinking Examples			
Label	Mnemonic	Stimulus Passage	Sample Marginal Notation
Questions	Blank	"Education is useless because it leads to doubt" (p. 10).	Are doubt and skepticism the same thing?
	Blink	"Education is useless because it isolates us from the rest of humanity" (p. 3).	So the "gifted education is elitist" argument applies to all education!?
Highlights	Blurt	"Education is useless because it swells our heads" (p. 5).	Okay, I admit it!
	Blurb	"Education is useless because it dulls our personalities" (p. 6).	Cultural transmission v. cultural transformation. Transmission does seem to dominate currently.
Critiques	Blessing	"Education is useless because it makes us optimists. ... Education is useless because it makes us pessimists" (p. 9).	Clearly by making both these arguments, Cottam is presenting the case of others. Though he, like I, clearly loves a paradox.
	Blasting	"... beauty ..." (p. 95)	Amazing that in a chapter on beauty this is only the second time some form of the word has been used (not counting the reference to *A Beautiful Mind*). This is an interesting essay on outsider art, but the connection to beauty has not been made.
Connections	Blubbering	Response to the poem "Insomnia" by Elizabeth Bishop (p. 68)	I know about going sleepless over unrequited love.
	Blabbering	"Education is useless because it weakens our bodies" (p. 5).	It is a sedentary profession, but my education also has given me access to resources that have made me aware of how to be healthier in body and has led to action, finally, to do something about it.
Arguments	Blender	"...'the genetic fallacy' ... indicting ideas by relating them to the accident of origins (p. 29).	More on "genetic fallacy." This error was committed by the Apostle Nathaneal when he said, "Can any good thing come out of Nazareth?" prior to his calling (John 1:46).
	Blunder	Response to the whole of Chapter 1.	It's not that education makes us better people, but that it makes it *possible* for us to be better. Education does not take away our agency but enhances it, giving us a greater *range* of choices and more *important* choices—choices with greater consequences to self and others. Thus it makes sense that greater evil has come from those with more education—the possibility to do greater good comes with the possibility to do greater evil. This is necessary to keep agency in balance. Example: Greater "schooling" in nuclear physics gives me the possibility of making a bomb or of curing cancer. The choice is still mine. Education doesn't make me more or less good or evil, it makes me more free.

Figure 2. Marginal Thinking Examples.

Teacher [reading from the text]: "It's usually the people in our family who take care of us and teach us about the world as we grow up. Our parents, brothers, sisters, and other relatives love us and watch over us. They …"

Student [raising hand]: Beep!
Teacher: Yes, Amanda.
Student: I have a blink!
Teacher: All right. What part are you reacting to?
Student: Where it said, "Our parents, brother" and everybody "love us."
Teacher: Okay, and what do you have to say about that?
Student: Is the author saying *all* families love each other?
Teacher [writing exactly what student said]: Thank you, Amanda. Okay, now where were
    we? Oh, yes. "They do their best to help us grow up happy."

The following script shows how interrupted reading may sound once students have been taught critiquing. This example is from the same group of third graders using the same text.

Teacher [reading from text]: "When grown-ups tell you to go and play, they still love
    you, they just need some quiet time to themselves. They may want to rest or
    concentrate on their work for a little while."
Student [raising hand with big smile on her face]: Beep! I have a blasting!
Teacher: All right, Ashland, tell me what you're responding to.
Student [now with a look of indignation]: The whole thing you just read. Why doesn't the
    writer see the kid's point-of-view?
Teacher [writing what student said on sticky note]: Thank you, Ashland.
Student: You're welcome!

As a follow-up to small group work or as another method of introduction, a whole class can also work on marginal thinking together. This method is especially good to use with photocopied versions of the material, but could easily be adapted for use with sticky notes. In this method, each student has her or his own copy of the text (and a pad of sticky notes, if those are being used). As the teacher reads aloud, the students are invited to raise their hands to indicate when they have a reaction. When called upon by the teacher, the student then indicates the stimulus passage, what kind of marginal thinking she or he is doing, and what the annotation is. The teacher and all the students then mark the stimulus passage (with underlining or highlighting) and record their own paraphrase of what the responding student said. This provides all students with practice in writing appropriate annotations.

As students become familiar and facile with the marginal thinking system, it becomes relatively easy to vary marginal thinking assignments and challenges based on the texts being studied. For example, for a difficult science text, the teacher might indicate, "Students, please notice the bolded heading in this science chapter. See, in this chapter there are six different sections. For marginal thinking on this chapter today, I'd like you to stop at the end of each bolded section and write a blurb of the main ideas the section contained." Or, for reading a particular powerful passage of literature, "Students, as you are reading these assigned pages for tomorrow, I want you to concentrate on the emotions you experience. Make sure to use your marginal thinking skill of blurting. Put in a blurt note every time you can tell your emotions are changing."

MARGINAL THINKING AS AN INSTRUCTIONAL STRATEGY

The marginalia described above provide a systematic way for a student to respond to text at various stages of the reading process. Prior to reading, the student can review the typology as a cue to attend to his or her thinking during the reading and to make note of that thinking. During the reading the student, of course, writes the actual marginalia. Following the reading, the student can conduct a metacognitive audit for the following purposes; (1) to determine the frequency of marginalia use, (2) to establish the categories of marginalia used, (3) to summarize generally or specifically what was learned from the reading, (4) to set goals to increase or decrease the frequency of use to optimal levels so the learning is enhanced, and (5) to challenge him/herself to use higher levels of marginalia so that understanding is deepened.

A primary purpose of marginal thinking is to enhance the breadth and depth of discussion about text. This can be done with small instructional groups or as a whole class. Generally, the use of small instructional groups is preferred because it gives greater opportunity to more students to participate in the discussion. Groups can be formed based on the difficulty of the text being read (assuming that texts have been matched to readers based on reading level). In this type of discussion, students read and respond to the text before coming to group. When students are gathered into group, the teacher asks the students to indicate, page by page, when they have written a note. The student then reads the stimulus passage and his or her annotation. Other students who have written responses to the same passage are invited to share their responses. The teacher then asks questions to explore further the points, issues, or emotions raised by the students' responses, always looking for opportunities to challenge the students with alternative perspectives or deeper thinking. This same process is followed as the group moves through each page of the assigned reading.

A teacher might also group students according to the passages students have responded to or the types of notes being written. For instance, consider a fourth grade class that has been assigned to read *Ida B ...and Her Plans to Maximize Fun, Avoid Disaster, and (Possibly) Save the World* by Katherine Hannigan (2004). Several students in the class wrote blanks such as "What does *utmost* mean?" or "What's *forbearance*?" and other notes related to issues of the vocabulary in the text. These students could readily be grouped to assist one another in understanding the vocabulary. With this group the teacher could also focus instruction on how to use context clues to ascertain the meanings of words.

Another group of children responded to these passages:

> Well, that stopped me in my tracks. Because what Daddy said might have seemed all right to him, but it was sitting about two miles beyond wrong with me. I wasn't going to be able to put away another tiny teaspoon till I set things straight. (p. 3)
>
> Now, a school of goldfish could go swimming in the pool of drool that dog makes while he's sleeping. (p. 4)

The students' marginal thinking annotations included blanks such as "Now, what?" and blurts such as "She talks funny!" to the first passage. Responses to the second passage included blurts—especially "Oo, Gross"—and one extended blabbering from a girl whose family owns a St. Bernard with similar drooling issues. A teacher could combine these students in a group to become experts on other examples of hyperbole in the text and how this literary device is used to establish Ida B's character.

A third group of children responded to passages with more thematic elements such as "And staring right into his eyeballs I told him, 'There is never enough time for fun.'" (p. 3) and this more extended passage:

> When I got up in the morning, I'd have to wash my face and hands. And before I could eat my supper or go to the store or go visiting, I'd have to wash them again. It seemed like just about every time I'd get excited and want to get on with life I'd have to stop and wash up. And by the time I was done with it, who knows what opportunities had passed me by. (p. 21)

Some students responded to this with blurts such as "Right on" or "Me, too." Others, however, responded more thoughtfully with blenders defending the importance of fun or blabberings detailing their own conflicts with the adults in their lives about what is important and what is not, including one delightful annotation about a boy's mother who is always interrupting his activities with reminders to use the bathroom. These students clearly are thinking more deeply about the text and should be given the opportunity to meet together to explore the themes of the book and to challenge one another's thinking. In fact, it should be noted that the groupings just suggested, while not strictly organized around students' tested reading levels, sorted themselves out in much the same way, with more struggling readers needing help with a basic skill such as using context clues to unlock meaning and more gifted readers needing challenge in delving deeply into thematic elements.

It is important to develop students' cognitive abilities in relations to reading, and marginal thinking is clearly a strategy that can facilitate that. It is also important, however, to attend to the affective responses students have to their reading, and marginal thinking can be useful for this purpose as well. Consider these marginal notations from a group of third and fourth graders reading well above grade level: "I agree!!!" "I disagree!!!" "What the heck does that mean?" "What does racism mean?" "Why don't young children know about races?" "Why is *negro* thought of as a bad word?" "I hate that rule!" "WHY?" "WOW!" "I could punch white people." The text being read was *Through My Eyes* by Ruby Bridges (1999). Interestingly the readers were all White. Obviously these students have had an emotional reaction to the text, as shown through the use of multiple exclamation points, all capitals, and strong words like *heck*, *hate*, and *punch*. The teacher's role in such situations goes beyond defining *racism* or *integration* or building background knowledge about the civil rights movement. Students must be given opportunities to explore their emotions—why they've reacted this way, whether it's helpful or not, and how to manage the emotions or use them as an impetus for action.

CONCLUSION

In this chapter, the practice of teaching students to "leave tracks of their thinking" (Harvey & Goudvis, 2000, p. 19), in their reading material has been explored. However, the goal for this practice of filling in gaps of understanding has been questioned, because advanced readers often do not need the gaps filled in. Rather, they need opportunities to read and understand more deeply. Following from research that demonstrates the positive effects of annotation on higher education students, a systematic taxonomy of marginal notations, called marginal thinking, was introduced as one strategy for assisting elementary and secondary students to approach text in different ways. The system gives students opportunities to interact with text through questioning, highlighting, critiquing, connecting, and arguing. Approaches for presenting and implementing the system were discussed, with an emphasis on deepening the discussions students can have about text.

This systematic approach can be particularly useful in addressing the needs of gifted level readers. It addresses several of their characteristics, including possession of a large vocabulary, ability to conceptualize, development of metacognitive awareness, and hypersensitivity to global issues. Teachers who employ the marginal thinking system are likely to find their students will perceive greater challenge in the reading task and will appreciate the opportunity to grow.

REFERENCES

Basile, D. D. (1978). Helping college students understand their textbooks. *Reading World, 17,* 289-294. (Abstract retrieved September 6, 2001 from PsychInfo database).

Bridges, R. (1999). *Through my eyes.* New York: Scholastic.

Cottam, D. (2003). *Why education is useless.* Philadelphia: University of Pennsylvania Press.

Garrett, J. (2002, May). [Review of the book *Marginalia: Readers writing in books*]. *College & Research Libraries,* 63(3) pp. 292-294.

Hannigan, K. (2004). *Ida B: ...And her plans to maximize fun, avoid disaster, and (possibly) save the world.* New York: Greenwillow.

Harvey, S., & Goudvis, G. (2000). *Strategies that work: Teaching comprehension to enhance understanding.* Portland, ME: Stenhouse.

Hynd, C. R., Simpson, M. L., & Chase, N. D. (1990). Studying narrative text: The effects of annotating vs. journal writing on test performance. *Reading Research and Instruction, 29*(2), 44-54.

Jackson, H. J. (2001). *Marginalia: Readers writing in books.* New Haven, CT: Yale University Press.

McCullough, D. (2001). *John Adams.* New York: Simon & Schuster.

Melvin, D. [Consultant]. (1997). *Why are all families different? Questions children ask about families.* New York: DK Publishing.

Moreland, J. L., Dansereau, D. F., & Chmielewski, T. L. (1997). Recall of descriptive information: The roles of presentation format, annotation strategy, and individual differences. *Contemporary Educational Psychology, 22,* 521-533.

Nist, S. L., & Hogrebe, M. C. (1985, December). *The effects of high and low relevant text underlining on test performance*. Paper presented at the 35th Annual National Reading Conference, San Diego, CA. (ERIC Document Reproduction Services No. ED265520).

Porter-O'Donnell, C. (2004). Beyond the yellow highlighter: Teaching annotation skills to improve reading comprehension. *English Journal, 93*(5), 82-89.

Santa, C. M., Havens, L. T., Maycumber, E. M. (1996). *Project CRISS: Creating independence through student-owned strategies* (2nd ed.). Dubuque, IA: Kendall/Hunt.

Tucker, P. & Jones, D. M. (1993). Document annotation: To write, type, or speak? *International Journal of Man-Machine Studies, 39*, 885-900.

Wallen, E., Plass, J. L., & Brünken, R. (2005). The function of annotations in the comprehension of scientific text: Cognitive load effects and the impact of verbal ability. *Educational Technology Research and Development, 53*, 59-72. (WN 0500303447006; Downloaded from Wilson Web, January 9, 2007).

Wolfe, J. (2002). Marginal pedagogy: How annotated texts affect a writing-from-source task. *Written Communication, 19*, 297-333.

In: Meta-Cognition: A Recent Review of Research...   ISBN: 978-1-60456-011-4
Editors: M.F. Shaughnessy et al. pp. 141-159   © 2008 Nova Science Publishers, Inc.

Chapter 8

SELF-AWARENESS AND SELF-MAPPING OF COGNITIVE PROCESSES FROM EARLY CHILDHOOD TO ADOLESCENCE

Smaragda Kazi[1]*, Nikolaos Makris[2], and Andreas Demetriou[3]
[1]Panteion University of Social Sciences, Greece
[2]University of Thrace, Greece,
[3]University of Cyprus, Cyprus

ABSTRACT

This chapter focuses on self-awareness and self-representation of cognitive processes. Specifically, we will present a series of studies that examined if persons from early childhood to late adolescence were aware of the similarities and differences between cognitive processes used to solve different types of problems, such as problems requiring spatial, mathematical, and causal reasoning. Obviously, answering this question is important both for the general theory of intelligence and mind, but also for practical reasons. In the general theory of mind, self-awareness and awareness about other persons' minds is an important quality of the mind itself. That is, to be mindful implies, by definition, to be aware of one's own mind's functioning and its products. In fact, modern cognitive science takes consciousness and ensuing self-awareness for granted and attempts to specify how it emerges, how it works, and how it affects processing of real world problems. The general theory of intelligence, strangely, has remained rather impervious to these modern trends. That is, modern theories of intelligence (Carroll, 1993; Jensen, 1998; Gustafson & Undeheim, 1996) still continue, like the good old days when the study of intelligence was culminating (Guilford, 1967; Thurstone, 1938), to conceive of the human intellect as devoid of awareness and consciousness. As a result,

* Correspondence: Andreas Demetriou, Department of Psychology, University of Cyprus, P. O. Box 537, 1678 Nicosia, Cyprus. Phone: +35722892080; Fax: +35722892071; Email: ademetriou@ucy.ac.cy

the IQ measurement enterprise has not yet shown any interest in integrating measures of these processes into tests of intelligence.

Obviously, further progress in our understanding of the human mind requires, first, to map the state and development of awareness about cognitive functions along with growth. Second, it also requires us to examine the relations between awareness and intellectual abilities in order to specify how, if at all, individual differences in intellectual competence are related to individual differences in awareness. Progress in these directions will have beneficial practical implications because it may expand our means for enhancing self-regulation of learning, thereby improving clinical or educational practice.

The studies to be presented here were designed in the context of our model of the architecture of the human mind. Thus, in the pages below we will first summarize this model and then describe our empirical studies. In the concluding section of the chapter, we will elaborate on the implications of these findings.

THE ARCHITECTURE OF THE HUMAN MIND

According to our model, the mind involves three general levels of functioning. The most basic of these levels involves general processes and functions, such as processing efficiency and representational capacity, which define the processing potentials available at a given time. Thus, the condition of the processes comprising this level constrains the condition and functioning of the systems included in the other two levels to be discussed below (see Demetriou, Christou, Spanoudis, & Platsidou, 2002; Demetriou, Mouyi, & Spanoudis, in press). This level will not be discussed any further in this chapter because the studies to be presented here are not related to it. The other two levels involve systems and functions underlying understanding and problem solving. One of these levels is oriented to the environment, and the other is oriented to the self.

The Environment-oriented Level of the Mind

This level comprises representational and understanding processes and functions that specialize in the representation and processing of information coming from the environment. Empirical research has identified and delineated the following seven environment-oriented systems: (1) The *categorical system* deals with similarity-difference relations. Forming concepts about class relationships is an example of the domain of this system. (2) The *quantitative system* deals with quantitative variations and relations in the environment. Mathematical concepts and operations are examples of the domain of this system. (3) The *causal system* deals with cause-effect relations. Operations such as trial-and-error or isolation of variables and strategies that enable a person to decipher the causal relations between things or persons and ensuing causal concepts and attributions belong to this system. (4) The *spatial system* deals with orientation in space and the imaginal representation of the environment. Mental images and operations on these images belong to this system. (5) The *propositional system* deals with the truth/falsity and the validity/invalidity of the flow of information in the environment and in systems of representation about the environment. Different types of logical relationships such as implication and conjunction belong to this system. (6) The *social system* deals with the understanding of social relationships and interactions. Mechanisms for monitoring non-verbal communication or skills for manipulating social interactions belong to this system. (7) The *pictographic system* underlies the representation of the environment or of thoughts themselves by means of drawings or other kinds of signs. Manual skills or skills enabling the translation of a mental image into a picture on paper belong to this system (Case, Demetriou, Platsidou, & Kazi, 2001; Demetriou & Efklides, 1985, 1989; Demetriou & Kazi, 2000; Demetriou, Efklides, & Platsidou, 1993; Kargopoulos & Demetriou, 1998; Shayer, Demetriou, & Pervez, 1988).

Each of these systems is domain-specific in that it includes a characteristic set of operations and processes which are appropriate for thinking and problem solving within its own domain of application (Kargopoulos & Demetriou, 1998). Hence, their name: Specialized Capacity Systems (SCS). Moreover, each SCS is biased to a different symbol system, which is more appropriate than others to represent the type of relations and information that is characteristic of the domain concerned. For instance, language is more appropriate for verbal propositional reasoning, mental images for spatial reasoning, and mathematical symbolisms for quantitative reasoning (Demetriou & Efklides, 1988). Finally, because of these differences, the development of each system may be relatively autonomous from the development of the other systems.

The Self-oriented Level of the Mind

Possession of problem-solving abilities affiliated with the domains above is not sufficient to credit a thinking creature, be it living or artificial, with mind. For this to be possible, a cognitive system must be capable of *self-monitoring, self-mapping,* and *self-representation.* That is, it must be able to observe and record its own cognitive functioning and experiences and keep maps of them that can be used in the future, if the need arises (Demetriou, 2000; Demetriou & Efklides, 1989; Demetriou et al., 1993; Demetriou & Kazi, 2000; Demetriou, Kyriakides, & Avraamidou, 2003).

Positing this principle implies that creatures capable of self-monitoring and self-mapping possess a second-order level of knowing. In our terms, this is the *hypercognitive system* (the adverb "hyper" in Greek means "higher than" or "on top of" or "going beyond", and when added to the word cognitive, it indicates the supervising and coordinating functions of the hypercognitive system). The input to this system is information coming from the other levels of the mind (sensations, feelings, and conceptions caused by mental activity). This information is organized into the maps or models of mental functions to be described below. These are used to guide the control of the functioning of the domain-specific systems and the processing potentials available. Thus, the hypercognitive system involves self-awareness and self-regulation knowledge and strategies and is conceived as the interface between (a) mind and reality, and (b) any of the various systems and processes of the mind. The hypercognitive system involves *working hypercognition* and *long-term hypercognition.*

Working hypercognition revolves around a strong directive-executive function that is responsible for setting and pursuing mental and behavioral goals until they are attained. Thus, working hypercognition includes the following functions: (i) a goal setting function; (ii) a planning function setting the steps to be made for the sake of the goal; (iii) a monitoring function examining goal attainment; (iv) a control function registering discrepancies between the present state and the goal; (v) an evaluation function enabling the system to evaluate each step's processing demands vis-à-vis the available structural possibilities and necessary skills and strategies of the system so as to make decisions about the value of continuing or terminating the endeavor and evaluate the final outcome achieved. These processes operate recursively, so that goals and subgoals may be renewed according to every moment's evaluation of the system's distance from its ultimate objective (Demetriou, 2000; Demetriou & Efklides, 1989; Demetriou & Kazi, 2000).

Long-term Hypercognition

Consciousness is an integral part of the hypercognitive system. That is, the very process of setting mental goals, planning their attainment, monitoring action vis-à-vis both the goals and the plans, and regulating real or mental action requires a system that can remember and review and therefore know itself. Therefore, conscious awareness and all ensuing functions, such as a cognitive self-theory (that is, a representation of similarities and differences between mental processes and functions), a cognitive self-concept (that is, awareness of one's own strengths and weaknesses in concern to the various mental processes and functions), and a theory of mind (that is, awareness of other persons' mental functions and states) are part of the very construction of the system. In fact, long-term hypercognition comprises the models and representations concerning past cognitive experiences that result from the functioning of working hypercognition. These models involve descriptions about the general structural and dynamic characteristics of the mind—for example, that there are different cognitive functions, such as perception, attention, and memory, and different cognitive structures, such as the domain-specific systems described above. Moreover, these models involve prescriptions and rules about the efficient use of the functions. For instance, that excessive information requires organization if it is to be retained in memory or that rehearsal is needed if one is to learn quickly and permanently.

Optimum performance at any time depends on the interaction between the two knowing levels of the mind, because efficient problem-solving or decision-making requires the application of environment-oriented functions and processes under the guidance of representations held about them at the level of self-oriented processes. This interaction between the two levels of mind ensures flexibility of behavior, because the self-oriented level provides the possibility for accessing alternative environment-oriented representations and actions and thus it provides the possibility for planning.

STUDY ONE: AWARENESS OF COGNITIVE PROCESSES IN EARLY CHILDHOOD

According to Flavell, Green, and Flavell, (1995) preschoolers seem to "have at least a minimal grasp of the bare-bones essentials of thinking: namely that it is some sort of internal, mental activity that people engage in that refers to real or imaginary objects or events " (1995, p. 75). Moreover, they also realize that thinking is different not only from perceiving but also from other cognitive processes, such as knowing. However, there are important aspects of thinking that preschoolers do not understand; specifically, preschoolers do not understand what William James called the "stream of consciousness". That is, they do not realize that thinking is a process which goes on continuously, even during physically inactive periods such as waiting in a doctors office. Preschoolers also seem unable to realize that cognitive activities such as looking, listening, reading, and talking necessarily entail thinking and the experience of thought. Although they can at times recognize that mental activity is going on in a person's mind, they are unable to specify the content of the thinking in spite of very clear signs. Finally, according to these studies, preschoolers do not conceive of intellectual ability as an internal quality of the mind; rather they seem to associate it with various external characteristics, such as work habits and conduct, and therefore believe that it may be increased by practice and hard work (Flavell, Green, & Flavell, 1995; see also Demetriou, 2000).

Our model summarized above, is not fully consistent with the evidence summarized above. That is, we would predict that some awareness of cognitive processes must be present from the early preschool years, due to the very nature of the human mind. That is, the two-level nature of the mind suggests that some kind of awareness of cognitive processes must go hand in hand with cognitive activity itself. Obviously, development of experience and ability should lead to development and refinement of hypercognitive skills and knowledge, but they must be somehow present from the beginning. Therefore, this study was designed to probe early awareness about cognitive processes further. Specifically, this study aimed to answer the following questions: When does awareness of the cognitive processes begin in early childhood? Are young children able to notice the similarities and differences between the processes activated to solve tasks addressed by the various SCSs mentioned above? Does this awareness develop during early childhood? How does cognitive processing affect hypercognitive awareness and vice-versa?

The Study

To answer these questions, a total of 100 children were examined. These children were equally drawn from five age groups, that is, from each of the age years 3 through 7. Boys and girls were equally represented in each age group.

Children were tested in three of the SCSs mentioned above, that is, the quantitative, the categorical, and the spatial SCS. Each domain was examined by two tasks, representing different component skills of the domain.

The quantitative tasks addressed counting and arithmetic operations. For counting, children were asked to count up to 12 objects arranged either in a line or randomly. Children were asked to count two different objects: cubes and pencils. Counting started from 2 objects and it stopped after two failures in succession. One point was given for each successful trial. The arithmetic operations tasks involved 12 items organized in four levels of difficulty, specified in reference to the size of the result of numerical operation to be performed (i.e., 3, 5, 7, and 11). Two items in each level required addition and one required subtraction. Each item was actualized by the experimenter by putting in or taking out from a box as many cubes as required. The child's task was to specify the result of each of these actions. One point was given for each item answered successfully.

The categorical tasks addressed classification. One of the tasks involved different types of vehicles and the other involved geometrical objects. Specifically, in the vehicles task, children were asked to classify various types of toy vehicles in groups. In the geometrical figures task, children were asked to classify different geometrical shapes. There were three levels of difficulty depending upon the type (flying vehicles, such as airplane and helicopter, sea vehicles, such as ship and boat, and wheel moving vehicles, such as cars, bus, and lorry) and the number of items involved. One point was given for each task answered successfully.

The spatial tasks addressed the ability to compose an object by properly arranging its component parts. The first task involved nine items requiring the reproduction of geometrical figures. Children were asked to reproduce a model figure on a blank card by properly arranging its component parts, which were randomly arranged on the side of the model figure. Difficulty was manipulated in reference to the number and shape of the components involved. For example, the easiest was a circle made of two semicircles whereas the most difficult was a complex figure made of a diamond and four triangles, each attached to one of the diamond sides. The second task was a wooden puzzle involving six pieces organized in tiers. One, two, and three pieces fit into the three tiers, respectively. Children were given one point for each piece that was placed at the right place.

Children were led to compare pairs of tasks addressing either the same or different SCSs in order to examine if they were aware of the processes activated by them. Specifically, children were presented with pairs of cards, each of which showed a child trying to solve a cognitive task. The cognitive tasks presented in each card were exact depictions of the cognitive tasks described above and the children were asked to evaluate if the tasks of the two children in each pair were similar to each other and explain their answers. There were nine pairs of cards. In sets of two, there were pairs where the two children were required to use the same processes, applied either on the same, or on different objects. Specifically, two of the pairs addressed classification (in the first pair, both children were described as trying to classify geometrical objects, but the one child was classifying 4 geometrical objects; whereas the second child was classifying 6 geometrical objects; in the second pair both children were again trying to classify, but the one child was classifying vehicles whereas the second child was classifying geometrical objects); two pairs addressed counting (counting same objects of different number in the first pair and counting different objects in the second); and two addressed spatial reasoning (reproduction of model figures comprising of different number of parts in the first pair, and puzzle construction and reproduction of model figure in the second pair). Finally, there were three pairs where the two children depicted were required to use different mental processes. That is, in one pair, one of the children was supposed to classify and the other to count. In another pair, one of the children was supposed to classify and the other to reproduce a model figure. Finally, in the last pair, one of the children was supposed to count and the other to reproduce a figure. The nine pairs of cards were presented in random order to children.

Responses on each of these nine tasks was scored on a four-point scale as follows: 0 for wrong or irrelevant responses; 1 for answers indicating focusing on the perceptual similarity of the objects involved; 2 for answers indicating focusing on the symbolic/generic characteristics of the tasks (e.g., here he has cubes and here he has a figure to work on); 3 for answers explicitly referring to the mental operation or processes involved (e.g., they are both counting; one is counting, the other is classifying, etc.).

The Organization of Cognitive and Hypercognitive Processes

To examine if the experience of solving the tasks influences awareness of the processes involved, half of the children in each age group were presented with the cognitive tasks first, and the hypercognitive tasks second, whereas, the other half of the children were presented with the hypercognitive tasks first and the cognitive tasks second.

A basic prediction suggested by our claim that the hypercognitive system accurately registers similarities and differences between cognitive processes, is that the domains of thought described above must be discernible on both the level of performance and the level of hypercognitive evaluations. In the present study, the three domains must stand up as distinct entities on both levels. To test this prediction, a series of structural equation models were fitted to the performance attained on the various cognitive tasks and the hypercognitive evaluations. One of these models is shown in Figure 1. It can be seen that performance on each pair of tasks addressed to an SCS was associated to a different factor and that evaluations on each pair of tasks concerning the same SCS were associated with another factor. The three performance factors were associated with a second-order factor. This factor stands for general inferential ability underlying the environment-oriented level of the mind. The three hypercognitive-evaluation factors were associated with another second-order factor. This factor stands for general self-monitoring, self-recording, and self-representation skills and processes underlying the hypercognitive level of the mind. Finally, these two second-order factors were regressed on a common third-order factor which may be taken to represent the integrative inferential and reflective processes underlying the interactions between the two main knowing levels of the mind. It can be seen in Figure 1 that the fit of this model was excellent. All domains are present and very powerful on both levels of the mind. Moreover, they are closely related despite their functional autonomy. It must be emphasized that this finding is all the more interesting due to the very young age of our participants. This suggests that the architecture of mind, as depicted by our model, is in place from early childhood.

Development of Self-awareness

Several multivariate analyses of variance were employed to specify the changes in the various processes examined and their interactions during development. The main trends uncovered by these analyses are illustrated in Figures 2 and 3.

Specifically, it can be seen in these figures that both cognitive performance (Figure 2) and hypercognitive evaluations (Figure 3) improved systematically across all three SCSs throughout the age phase examined. In concern to hypercognitive evaluations, it can also be seen that there was an interaction between age and order of presentation. This interaction reflected the fact that the experience of solving the tasks before taking the hypercognitive tasks did positively affect hypercognitive performance among younger children (3 ½ to 6 ½ years old), but not the latter because they already reached their ceiling.

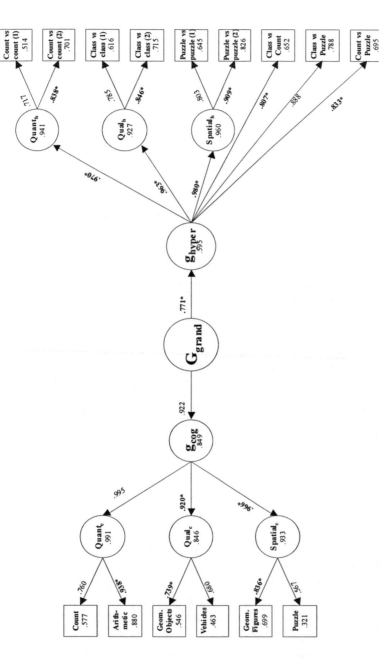

Note 1: Free parameters are denoted by bold characters. Significant coefficients are denoted by asterisk. Numbers in squares and circles indicate variance accounted for.

Note 2: The error terms of the following variables were allowed to correlate: (1) the wooden puzzle task with the evaluation of similarity between the counting and the wooden puzzle task, (2) the counting task with the evaluation of similarity between the classification and the wooden puzzle task, and (3) the evaluation of similarity between the classification task and the evaluation of similarity between the two counting tasks.

Figure 1. The confirmatory faxtor analysis model for cognitive performance and self-awareness of cognitive processes examined in Study 1. Model's fit indices were: x^2 (79)=105.004, p=0.03, CFI=.976, RMSEA=.058, (10% confidence interval=.021-.085)

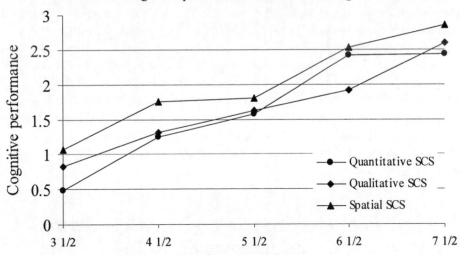

Panel A: Cognitive performance as a function of age and SCS

Note 1: Scores on cognitive tasks were standardized and transformed to a 0 to 3 scale, so that cognitive and hypercognitive performance is comparable.

Figure 2. Mean performance on the cognitive tasks as a function of age.

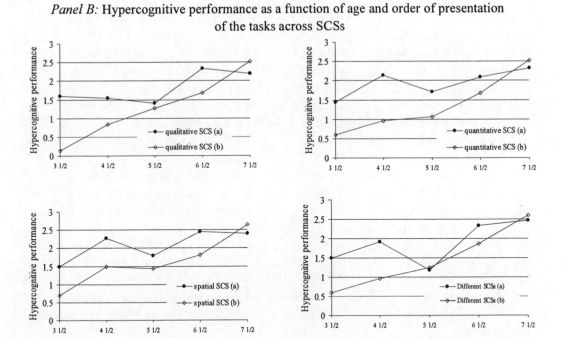

Panel B: Hypercognitive performance as a function of age and order of presentation of the tasks across SCSs

Figure 3. Mean hypercognitive performance on the three SCSs and the cross-SCS comparison task as a function of age and order of presentation of the hypercognitive tasks (i.e., (a) before and (b) after solving the cognitive tasks).

This pattern of relations between age and hypercognitive evaluations is highly interesting in its implications for the development of awareness about cognitive processes. Specifically, it suggests that early in childhood this kind of awareness is very weak. Thus, it does not show up when required independently of any relevant cognitive experiences. However, when these experiences are available and recent, evaluations do reflect the peculiarities and demands of cognitive processes activated by the tasks at hand. In other words, from this early age, the hypercognitive level of the mind does register the functioning of its cognitive level and it organizes its cognitive experiences into maps reflecting similarities and differences between tasks and domains. By early childhood, these maps are already available in long-term hypercognition and can be called upon, independently of the availability of cognitive experiences.

STUDY TWO: AWARENESS OF COGNITIVE PROCESSES IN ADOLESCENCE

The second study to be summarized here focused on the development of awareness about cognitive processes in adolescence. This study aimed to examine if adolescents are able to associate different component processes with the SCS they are assumed to be associated with, rather than with a different SCS. In order to explore this idea, our participants were asked do work on cognitive tasks and also explicitly associate different cognitive processes, supposedly activated by these cognitive tasks with each of them. If our assumptions about the functioning of hypercognition are accurate, we should observe that estimations of process use would be structured in the same SCS-specific factors as performance itself. This would indicate that the hypercognitive maps of cognitive processes include the same constructs as the maps reflecting the organization of performance emanating from these processes. It is also expected that each component process would have to be associated more closely with its own SCS rather than with a different SCS.

To test these assumptions, a total of 261 participants, about equally drawn among 12- through 16-year-old adolescents, were examined. These participants were asked to do the following: First, they were asked only to read six tasks addressed, in pairs, to three different SCSs, that is, the spatial, the quantitative, and the causal SCS. Second, they were given descriptions of three different component processes for each SCS and they were asked to specify how much each of these component processes will be used when working on each of the tasks. Finally, after actually solving the tasks, they were asked again to specify how much each of these component processes were used when working on the tasks. In order to examine the influence of task difficulty and content on hypercognitive estimations, a rather complex experimental design was employed where these factors were systematically manipulated.

Specifically, for each SCS, we created a pool of four tasks. In pairs, these tasks addressed two component processes within each SCS and two levels of difficulty. The quantitative SCS was addressed by numerical estimations and proportional reasoning tasks. The spatial SCS was addressed by mental rotation and picture integration tasks. The causal SCS was addressed by isolation of variables and hypothesis formation tasks. Of the two tasks addressing the same component process within each SCS, one was easy (i.e., it could be solved by 12-yr-old persons) and the other was difficult (i.e., it could be solved by 14-yr-old persons), according to earlier research (Demetriou & Efklides, 1985; Demetriou, Efklides, Papadaki, Papantoniou, & Economou, 1993).

Participants in each age group were randomly allocated to one of five groups that were specified according to combinations of task difficulty and task content. Specifically, for each group, two cognitive tasks per SCS (a total of six tasks) were selected from the pool, according to the following rationale: The first group received, for each SCS, the two tasks addressing the same component process at the two levels of difficulty (same component-different levels). The second group received the easy tasks addressing the two component processes within each SCS (different components-easy level). The third group differed from the first in that it addressed the second component process for each SCS at the two difficulty levels (same component-different levels). The fourth group received the difficult tasks addressing the two component processes within each SCS (different components-difficult level). Finally, the tasks given to the fifth group differed in both their difficulty level and component processes (different components-different levels). It is clear that we attempted to systematically manipulate the complexity as well as the content of the tasks across the five groups. This manipulation was considered able to reveal the effect of complexity of cognitive processes on self awareness.

The hypercognitive estimation battery included nine statements describing three component processes or skills for each SCS. Each of these statements was presented together with an example instantiating how this function or skill may be used when solving common, everyday problems.

The three statements representing the causal SCS referred to combinatorial, isolation-of-variables, and hypothesis-formation processes. The statement addressing isolation of variables was as follows: "To solve this problem, you have to proceed to test each of its elements while making sure that all the others remain the same (e.g., if you suspect that either the juice, the honey, or the milk was responsible for a certain recipe not succeeding, you have to make a number of tests changing only one of these constituents each time in order to find out what was really to blame)".

Those representing the quantitative-relational SCS, referred to the processes enabling one to apply the basic arithmetic operations, order things along a quantitative dimension, and estimate proportional relations. The statement referring to proportional relations was as follows: "To solve this problem, you must first understand that two different measurements can change in the same way (e.g., when the one increases, the other increases also) or that they can change in different ways (e.g., when one increases, the other decreases) (in general, e.g., when you know the relation between width and height, you can find the measurement for one if you know the measurement for the other)".

Finally, the statements addressing the spatial SCS referred to the processes enabling one to apply mental rotation, integrate the different perspectives from which one can see an object, and integrate the different pieces of an image into the integrated image. The statement referring to mental rotation was as follows: "To solve this problem, you have to imagine that a certain shape turns in space either as a whole or only in part and to know the form that it will have when it stops rotating (e.g., you are shown the position of the hands of a clock when the time is 3 o'clock and then asked to describe their position when the time is 12 o'clock)".

Participants were first presented with the cognitive tasks, and they were instructed as follows: "Do not try to solve them, just read them carefully". Each cognitive task was given a label, which appeared on the top of the task. Immediately after reading the tasks, the hypercognitive battery was presented. The labels of the cognitive tasks were listed in a column to the right of each of the statement-example blocks and for each cognitive task participants were asked to indicate "how much they will use" the skill described in the left-hand column when solving it. Estimations were given on a five-point scale (from not at all to very much). After solving the cognitive tasks, participants were again instructed to answer the hypercognitive statements (this time: "how much they used" the skill described in the left-hand column when solving each task).

Cognitive and Hypercognitive Maps

The model shown in Figure 4 presents the structural organization of cognitive performance and hypercognitive estimations for one of the five participant groups. It needs to be noted that the models for the other four groups were very similar to this one in both the relations between measurement and constructs and fit indices. It can be seen in Figure 4 that each pair of cognitive tasks was associated with a different factor that stands for ability on the SCS concerned. Estimations given to the three statements representing component processes associated with the same SCSs before solving the tasks were associated with one factor, and estimations given to the same statements after solving the tasks were associated with another factor. Thus, for each SCS, there were two hypercognitive estimation factors: one representing estimations before, and one representing estimations after, working on the tasks. Each set of factors (i.e., SCS-specific estimation factors before solving the tasks, cognitive performance factors, and SCS-specific estimation factors after solving the tasks) was regressed on a separate second-order factor. To specify the relations between the three types of factors that stand for measurements taken in succession, the cognitive performance second-order factor was regressed on the "before" second-order hypercognitive estimation factor and the "after" hypercognitive estimation factor was regressed on the cognitive performance factor. The fit of this model was excellent (see fit indices in Figure 4). It is suggested, therefore, that hypercognitive maps do mirror accurately the organization of cognitive processes. Moreover, it is also suggested that their condition does affect the quality of performance at a given time and that, in turn, actual performance itself does affect the hypercognitive estimations to be given at a point in time. In other words, the two knowing levels of the mind seem to interact dynamically in adolescence.

Perceived Relations between SCS and Specific Components Skills

To uncover the perceived relations between SCSs and specific component skills five MANOVAs were conducted, one for each experimental group. These analyses involved age as between subjects factor and time (before vs. after), SCS (spatial vs. quantitative vs. causal), and component skills (three for each SCS) as within subject factors. Due to space limitations, presentation here will focus only on those results that highlight the relations between cognitive attainment and self-awareness. It is to be stressed that the effect of SCS was very strong in all analyses, indicating that thinkers differentiate the three SCSs in the processes that they evoke. Also, it is to be stressed that the interaction between component skills and

SCS was highly significant and strong in all five analyses, indicating that thinkers associated each SCSs with the component skills they are theoretically associated with more than with component skills associated with the other SCSs. An example of this strong trend is illustrated in Figure 5, both before and after solving the tasks, for the spatial SCS. It can be seen in this Figure that spatial component skills are rated higher in their use when working on the spatial tasks, than when working with quantitative or causal tasks. Likewise, quantitative component skills were associated more with quantitative tasks, and causal component skills were associated more with causal tasks, rather than with tasks representing the other SCSs.

Interestingly, the age effect was weak. However, there was an interaction between age, SCS, and component skills, suggesting that the trends described above concerning the association of component skills with the appropriate SCS, are non existent at the age of 13, it starts at 14, and tends to improve later, especially for the quantitative and the causal SCS. Thus, awareness of cognitive processes and their function in processing and problem solving develops throughout adolescence.

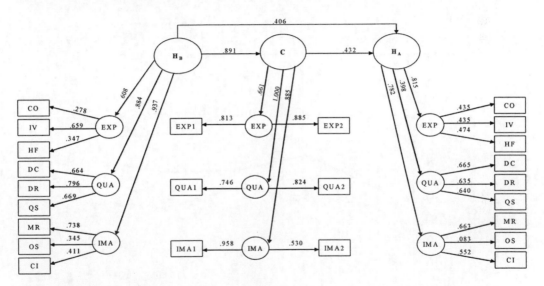

Figure 4. Indicative model of the structural relations between SCSs, specific components skills and actual performance. This model was fitted excellently to the data from each of the five groups. IV= isolation of variable, HF=hypothesis formation, CO= combinatorial abilities, DC= dimensional construction, DR= dimensional coordination, QS= quantitative specification, MR= mental rotation, OS= orientation in space IMA= integration of image, EXP= experimental SCS, QUA= quantitative SCS, SPA=spatial SCS, EXP1, EXP2 = first and second task addressed the experimental SCS, QUA1, QUA2 = first and second task addressed the quantitative experimental SCS, SPA1, SPA2 = first and second task addressed the spatial SCS, H$_B$= hypercognitive awareness before, H$_A$= hypercognitive awareness after, C= cognitive performance. Model's fit indices were: Group: 1 χ2 (224)=258.327, p=.06, CFI=.919, Group 2: χ2 (234)=259.487, p=.12, CFI=.926, Group 3: χ2 (213)=244.131, p=.07, CFI=.924, Group 4: χ2 (230)=257.484, p=.10, CFI=.881, Group 5: χ2(226)=261.020, p=.54, CFI=.879.

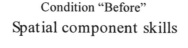

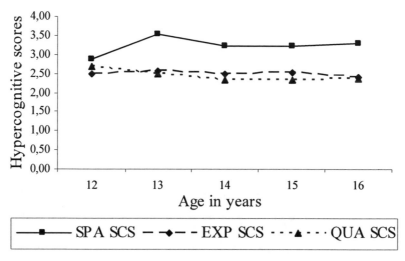

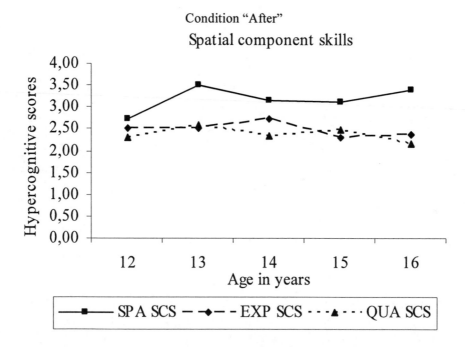

Figure 5. The effect of age on the subjective affiliation between SCS and specific component skills as it appeared in the conditions "before" and "after" the processing of the tasks. The pattern illustrated in the Figure represents the development of hypercognitive awareness regarding the Spatial SCS. SPA SCS= Spatial SCS, EXP SCS=Experimental SCS, QUA SCS= Quantitative SCS.

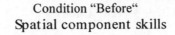

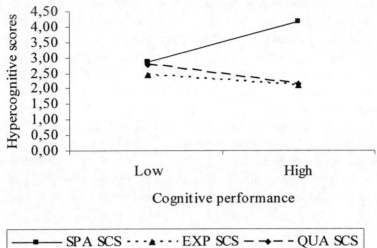

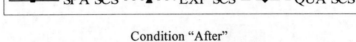

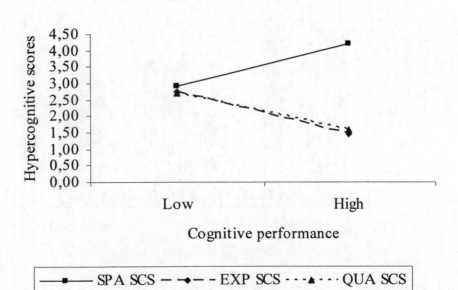

Figure 6. The effect of cognitive performance on the subjective affiliation between SCS and specific component skills. The pattern illustrated in the Figure represents the effect of cognitive performance on the hypercognitive awareness regarding the Spatial SCS. The symbol SPA, EXP, and QUA have the same meaning as in Figure 4.

Cognitive and Hypercognitive Performance

To determine how hypercognitive awareness was related to cognitive performance, a hypercognitive accuracy index was formulated. This index reflected the thinker's ability (a) to choose the most appropriate specific skill for the processing of a given task and (b) to reject the non appropriate ones. Participants whose hypercognitive accuracy index was one standard deviation (or more) above the mean score were considered as *high* in hypercognitive accuracy, while these whose index was one standard deviation (or more) below the mean score were considered as *low*. Participants with scores around the mean were excluded from the analyses presented below.

The level of hypercognitive accuracy was analyzed in its relations with cognitive performance as such. The relation between cognitive performance and hypercognitive accuracy in the spatial SCS is shown in Figure 6. It can be seen that high performers demonstrated a higher hypercognitive accuracy index. Likewise, it can be seen in Figure 7 that thinkers high in hypercognitive accuracy performed better in all three domains.

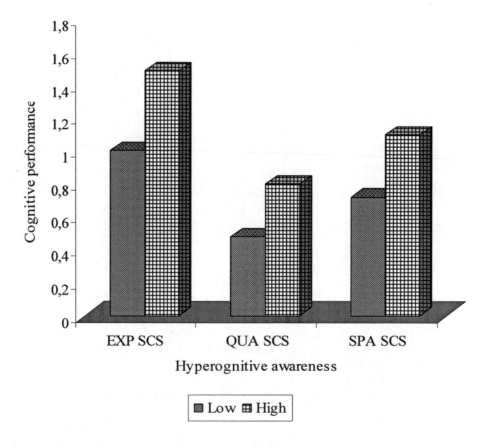

Figure 7. The effect of the level of hypercognitive awareness on cognitive performance. EXP= Causal-Experimental SCS, QUA= Quantitative SCS, SPA=Spatial SCS, Low= Low hypercognitive awareness score, High=High hypercognitive awareness score.

CONCLUSIONS

The two studies summarized here do support the architecture of mind depicted by our model. Specifically, these studies suggest the following conclusions.

First, domain-specific cognitive processes are organized in the same SCS-like structures in both actual performance on cognitive tasks and evaluations and estimations about this performance. This mirror-like organization of cognitive and hypercognitive processes conforms to the two-level architecture of knowing processes and suggests that there are common inferential and reflective processes interconnecting the two levels.

Second, this architecture is present since the early preschool years. Our first study is probably the only one in the literature to show that self-monitoring and self-representation of cognitive processes is in place from this early age.

Third, being in place does not imply a lack of development. On the contrary, the sensitivity of the hypercognitive system to the functioning of cognitive processes and the accuracy of hypercognitive maps does develop systematically and extensively with age. In infancy, toddlers need the experience of working on tasks to have reflections about cognitive processes. In middle childhood, reflections of this kind are already organized in mental maps that can be activated before actually working on cognitive tasks. Even so, however, children may differentiate between SCSs but are not able to differentiate between cognitive processes with SCSs until early adolescence. Moreover, there are changes throughout adolescence, leading to refinement of hypercognitive maps and to their emancipation from task contents and phenomenal appearances.

Overall, our studies suggest that reflective abstraction, in Piaget's terms, is always present and that its products form an integral part of the human mind from the very beginning. For developmental cognitive science, this implies that self-mapping, self-recording, and self-representation are products and causes of cognitive development. Thought generates hypercognitive processes and they themselves direct and shape thought. The development of reasoning as such, which grows from being content-dependent and concrete to content-free and formal is a product. We have argued elsewhere (Demetriou, Mouyi & Spanoudis, in press) that "metarepresentation is a hypercognitive process which looks for, codifies, and typifies similarities between mental experiences (past or present) to enhance understanding and problem-solving efficiency. So defined, metarepresentation is the constructive aspect of working hypercognition that integrates the contents of the episodic buffer, in Baddeley's (1990) terms, or the screen of conscience, in James's terms (1890), thereby generating new mental schemes and operations. In a sense, metarepresentation is inductive inference applied to mental experiences, representations, or operations, rather than to environmental stimuli and information as such. As a result, domain-specific inferential patterns are compacted into general reasoning patterns. In other words, we maintain that general reasoning patterns do not exist at the beginning. Instead, they are constructed by mapping domain-specific inference patterns onto each other. Therefore, a general language of thought is an emergent product of guided and reflected-upon domain-specific functioning. That is, this general language of thought is a construction that gradually expands and stabilizes through the interaction between domain-specific processing and executive, self-awareness, and self-regulation processes of the hypercognitive system.

These studies also have some strong implications for general psychometric theory of intelligence as well. Specifically, these studies suggest that self-awareness is part of general intelligence on a par with general processing efficiency (mainly associated with speed of processing, control of processing, and working memory, which were not discussed here) and general inferential processes traditionally associated with fluid intelligence. Therefore, tests of various components of self-awareness must be integrated into tests of general intelligence to increase their validity and predictive power (see Demetriou & Kazi, 2006). In fact, recent research suggests that experimental manipulation of these processes greatly enhances learning in demanding topics such as science (Kuhn & Pease, 2006) and mathematics (Panaoura, Demetriou, & Gagatsis, 2007).

ACKNOWLEDGEMENT

This chapter is based on work first presented in the doctoral dissertations of the first two authors, which were contacted under the supervision of the third author.

REFERENCES

Baddeley, A. D. (1990). *Human memory: Theory and practice*. Hillsdale, NJ: Erlbaum.

Carroll, J. B. (1993). *Human cognitive abilities: A survey of factor-analytic studies*. New York: Cambridge University Press.

Case, R., Demetriou, A., Platsidou, M., & Kazi, S. (2001). Integrating concepts and tests of intelligence from the differential and the developmental traditions. *Intelligence, 29*, 307-336.

Demetriou, A., (2000). Organization and development of self-understanding and self-regulation: Toward a general theory. In M. Boekaerts, P. R. Pintrich, & M. Zeidner (Eds.), *Handbook of self-regulation* (pp. 209-251). Academic Press.

Demetriou, A., Christou, C., Spanoudis, G., & Platsidou, M. (2002). The development of mental processing: Efficiency, working memory, and thinking. *Monographs of the Society of Research in Child Development, 67*(1, Serial No. 268).

Demetriou, A., & Efklides, A, (1985). Structure and sequence of formal and postformal thought: General patterns and individual differences. *Child Development, 56*, 1062-1091.

Demetriou, A., & Efklides, A, (1988). Experiential Structuralism and neo-piagetian theories: Toward and integrated model. In A. Demetriou (Ed.), *The neo-piagetian theories of cognitive development: Towards an integration* (pp. 173-222). Amsterdam: North-Holland.

Demetriou, A., & Efklides, A, (1989). The person's conception of the structures of developing intellect. *Genetic, Social, and General Psychology Monographs, 115*(3), 371-423.

Demetriou, A., Efklides, A., Papadaki, M., Papantoniou, A., & Economou, A (1993). The structure and development of causal–experimental thought. *Developmental Psychology, 29*, 480-497.

Demetriou, A., Efklides, A., & Platsidou, M. (1993). Experiential Structuralism: A frame for unifying cognitive developmental theories. *Monographs of the Society for Research in Child Development, 58*(1, Serial No. 234).

Demetriou, A., & Kazi, S. (2000). *Unity and modularity in the mind and the self: Studies on the organization and development of personality, mind, and the self from childhood to adolescence.* London: Routledge.

Demetriou, A., & Kazi, S. (2006). Self-awareness in g (with processing efficiency and reasoning). *Intelligence, 34,* 297-317.

Demetriou, A., Kyriakides, L., & Avraamidou, C. (2003). The missing link in the relations between intelligence and personality. *Journal of Research in Personality, 37,* 547-581.

Demetriou, A., Mouyi, A., & Spanoudis, G. (in press). Modeling the structure and development of g: Towards a neuro-cognitive model. *Intelligence.*

Flavell, J.H., Green, F.L., & Flavell, E.R. (1995).Young children's knowledge about thinking. *Monographs of the Society for Research in Child Development, 60*(1, Serial No. 243).

Gustafson, J. E., & Undeheim, J. O. (1996). Individual differences in cognitive functions. In D. C. Berliner, & C. Calfee (Eds.), *Handbook of educational psychology* (pp.186-242). New York: Macmillan.

Guilford, J. P. (1967). *The nature of human intelligence.* New York: McGraw-Hill.

James, W. (1890). *Principles of psychology.* Chicago: Encyclopedia Britannica.

Jensen, A. R. (1998). *The g factor. The science of mental ability.* New York: Praeger.

Kargopoulos, P., & Demetriou, A. (1998). Logical and psychological partitioning of mind. Depicting the same map? *New Ideas in Psychology, 16,* 61-87.

Kuhn, D., & Pease, M. (2006). Do children and adults learn differently? *Journal of Cognition and Development, 7,* 279-293.

Shayer, M., Demetriou, A., & Pervez, M. (1988). The structure and scaling of concrete operational thought: Three studies in four countries. *Genetic, Social, and General Psychology Monographs, 114*(3), 307-376.

Thurstone, L. L. (1938). Primary mental abilities. *Psychometric Monographs,* (Whole No.).

In: Meta-Cognition: A Recent Review of Research...
Editors: M.F. Shaughnessy et al. pp. 161-174

ISBN: 978-1-60456-011-4
© 2008 Nova Science Publishers, Inc.

Chapter 9

EPISTEMIC DEVELOPMENT AND THE PERILS OF PLUTO

David Moshman[*]

Department of Educational Psychology, University of Nebraska–Lincoln, Lincoln, NE 68588-0345, USA

ABSTRACT

Epistemic cognition is knowledge about knowledge. Epistemic development is progress in epistemic cognition—that is, progress in knowledge about knowledge. Children have epistemic cognition from the time they understand that beliefs may be false, about age four. Over the elementary school years, they increasingly distinguish (1) an objective domain of truth, (2) a subjective domain of taste, and (3) a rational domain of reasonable interpretation. Questions about the truth, falsity, or justification of particular beliefs and inferences arise and are addressed within these epistemic domains. Adolescents and adults, unlike children, theorize about the general nature and justification of knowledge. Advanced epistemic development proceeds from (1) objectivist epistemologies , which take verifiable facts and logical proofs as paradigm cases of knowledge ; to (2) subjectivist epistemologies, which view knowledge as opinion and thus a matter of taste ; to (3) rationalist epistemologies , which construe knowledge, in a world of interpretation and inference, as justified beliefs.

At the start of the year 2006, the Earth was the third from the sun among the nine planets in its solar system. By the end of that year, Earth was the third of eight planets on a list that now ended with Neptune. How did that come about? What happened to Pluto?

One possibility is that Pluto was destroyed by a starship from another part of the galaxy, or perhaps from the future. Perhaps the intent was to destroy the Earth but the ship mistakenly targeted Pluto instead. Or maybe it was an accident. Perhaps Pluto was destroyed by a

---

[*] Email: dmoshman1@unl.edu

collision with some other object way out there. It's a dangerous universe. Or perhaps it had some sort of internal, geological catastrophe. There are many potential scenarios in which Pluto is destroyed, leaving just eight planets.

But none of this happened in 2006. Pluto was not blasted out of space. It was redefined. More precisely, the definition of planet was changed, after years of contentious debate among astronomers and others, so as not to include Pluto. The object of this astrolexical brouhaha meanwhile continues on its vast course around the sun, sublimely oblivious to all the turmoil surrounding its conceptualization by a primate species on the third planet. Nothing happened to Pluto out there beyond Neptune but plenty happened to it here on Earth. To understand why there are no longer nine planets we need to look into our own minds.

But how can that be? Is the world a function of our minds? As it turns out, moreover, it's not just Pluto that perplexes us, and not just the number of planets—and not just astronomy. Things we thought we knew often turn out to be false. Sometimes we examine how we know that something is true. Sometimes we realize we don't know what's true. Sometimes we don't know how to tell what's true. Sometimes we think about what it means for something to be true. Sometimes we consider how we can tell whether anything is true. Sometimes we wonder whether we can ever really know anything at all. Sometimes we worry about how we can live our lives in the light of that. Sometimes we find our way through such epistemic doubts. Sometimes we don't.

But is there any pattern to all this? Do we simply mull over such questions or do we make progress in our understanding of knowledge? Do we simply come up with a variety of beliefs about knowledge or does our knowledge about knowledge develop? Research indicates that children know something about knowledge as early as age 4 and make remarkable progress for many years thereafter. To the extent that they have knowledge about knowledge, they may be said to have epistemic cognition. To the extent that they make progress in such knowledge, their progress is epistemic development. That is:

1. Epistemic cognition is knowledge about knowledge.
2. Epistemic development is progress in epistemic cognition.

Epistemic development, then, is progress in knowledge about knowledge. In this chapter, I propose a theoretical account of epistemic development that draws on several discrete literatures: (a) a literature on epistemic cognition in adolescents and adults in the tradition of William Perry (1970; Chandler, 1987; Chandler, Boyes, & Ball, 1990; Chandler, Hallett, & Sokol, 2002; King & Kitchener, 1994, 2002; Kuhn, 2005; Kuhn, Cheney, & Weinstock, 2000; Kuhn & Franklin, 2006; Kuhn & Weinstock, 2002; Mansfield & Clinchy, 2002; Moshman, 2005); (b) a literature on young children's theories of mind, including their understanding of the possibility of false belief (Wellman, Cross, & Watson, 2001); (c) a literature on the development of interpretive and constructivist theories of mind in the elementary school years (Carpendale & Chandler, 1996; Fabricius & Schwanenflugel, 1994; Lalonde & Chandler, 2002; Pillow & Henrichon, 1996; Rowley & Robinson, in press; Schwanenflugel, Fabricius, & Noyes, 1996); (d) a literature on the development of metalogical understanding (Miller, Custer, & Nassau, 2000; Moshman, 1990, 2004, forthcoming; Pillow, 2002); and (e) a literature on domain specificity in cognition (Komatsu & Galotti, 1986; Nicholls & Thorkildsen, 1988; Wainryb, Shaw, Langley, Cottam, & Lewis, 2004). With regard to previous theoretical approaches, the present account draws on (a)

Wainryb et al.'s (2004) conception of distinct epistemological domains differentiated even by young children; (b) Chandler's (1987; Chandler et al., 2002) distinction between "retail" and "wholesale" levels of epistemic cognition; and (c) the standard three-stage conception of advanced epistemic development as the reflective coordination of objectivity and subjectivity (Kuhn & Franklin, 2006, Mansfield & Clinchy, 2002; Moshman, 2005).

The theory, in two paragraphs, is as follows: Children may be said to have epistemic cognition from the time they understand that beliefs may be false, about age 4. Over the course of the elementary school years, children increasingly distinguish at least three epistemic domains: (1) an objective domain of truth, (2) a subjective domain of taste, and (3) a rational domain of reasonable interpretation. Questions about the truth, falsity, or justification of particular beliefs and inferences arise and are addressed within these domains.

Adolescents and adults, unlike children, often theorize more abstractly about the nature and justification of knowledge in general. Development beyond age 11 or 12 is much less universal and predictable than earlier development. To the extent that adolescents and adults construct advanced forms of epistemic cognition, however, they progress in a universal sequence from (1) objectivist epistemologies, which take verifiable facts and logical proofs as paradigm cases of knowledge; to (2) subjectivist epistemologies, which view knowledge (if we even call it that) as opinion, and opinion as a matter of taste; to (3) rationalist epistemologies, which construe knowledge, in a world of interpretation and inference, as justified belief.

THE PERILS OF PLUTO

Consider the following questions:

1. Is Pluto a planet?
2. How many planets are there in our solar system?
3. Which planet is best?
4. Which planet(s) can support life?

For most of the 20th century, the first two questions seemed simple. Pluto, which was discovered in 1930, was a planet. There were nine planets. These were matters of fact. You could learn things like this from teachers, parents, and experts. You could look them up in books. In principle, with sufficient expertise and technology, you could observe for yourself that Pluto is a planet and could count the number of planets. On matters of fact, you can perceive the truth. (Or so it would seem.)

Which planet is best? This seems a different kind of question. No planet is "better" than another, at least not in any general sense. We might instead ask, "Which is your favorite planet?" That formulation acknowledges that choosing a planet as best, in some general and undefined sense, is a matter of personal preference about which people legitimately differ. Even with full access to information, careful reflection, and extended discussion, we cannot count on consensus.

Which planets can support life? We know the Earth can, because it does. Can Mars? Venus? Jupiter, or maybe it's volcanic moon Io? If we go beyond planets, how about one of the larger asteroids? Come to think of it, how about Pluto, whatever it is? These questions seem different from questions about which planet is best, but also different from questions about the number of planets. We can get evidence relevant to whether various planets (or other heavenly bodies) could support various kinds of life, but such evidence is open to multiple interpretations. There can also be different conceptions of what counts as "life" and what it means to "support" it. The question of whether a planet can support life is more factual than the question of how "good" it is, but less a matter of simple truth than the question of whether it is a planet. The question of potential support for life, and other questions of this sort, are neither matters of truth nor matters of taste. Instead, they are matters of interpretation.

It thus appears that we can distinguish three categories: (1) matters of truth, (2) matters of taste, and (3) matters of interpretation. Matters of truth fall within an objective domain in which truth and falsity can be clearly and sharply distinguished. In this domain we expect agreement unless someone is making a mistake. Matters of taste fall within a subjective domain in which truth and falsity are irrelevant. In this domain we neither expect agreement nor try to achieve it. Finally, matters of interpretation fall within a domain of reasonable judgment in which some ideas are better justified than others but truth cannot be proven. In this domain, we acknowledge that different minds may reach legitimately different conclusions but we believe evidence and argument may generate progress in understanding.

And now, in the present, let us reconsider the first two questions. Is Pluto a planet? No. How many planets are there? Eight. But what are we to make of the changes in our answers? Did Pluto used to be a planet, but now it isn't? Did there used to be nine planets, but now there are eight? But how could that happen, given that Pluto is still there and nothing about it has changed? Maybe Pluto was never a planet. Did we used to think Pluto was a planet, but new evidence showed it is not? But Pluto's deplanetization was not the result of new evidence about it. So why is it not a planet, and how sure are we that this time we have finally got it right? All we really know for sure, it appears, is that we used to consider Pluto a planet and now we don't. Are all facts subject to such radical change? Can any truth turn out to be false? If so, do we really know anything at all?

The purpose of the present chapter, of course, is not to set things straight about Pluto, but rather to consider what people know about knowledge and how knowledge about knowledge develops. With that in mind, we can make an initial distinction between two aspects of epistemic cognition, both illustrated by the above questions. Epistemic cognition includes both (a) knowledge about the epistemic status and properties of specific beliefs and inferences and (b) knowledge about the general nature and justification of knowledge. Research on epistemic development shows that epistemic cognition regarding specific beliefs and mental processes shows substantial development over the course of childhood, whereas epistemological theories of a more general, abstract, and explicit sort are not seen in childhood but often develop over the course of adolescence and early adulthood. It thus appears useful to distinguish two levels of epistemic development, one associated with childhood and the other with adolescence and adulthood (Chandler, 1987; Chandler et al., 2002).

EPISTEMIC DEVELOPMENT IN CHILDHOOD

The origin of epistemic cognition lies in the recognition that beliefs can be false. This creates a distinction between truth and falsity and raises questions about the justification of beliefs. Developmental research indicates that comprehension of the possibility of false belief develops dramatically between ages 3 and 5 (Wellman et al., 2001). By age 4 or 5, but rarely much before that, children clearly understand that lack of information can result in false beliefs, in themselves and others, and that they and others act on the basis of their beliefs even when those beliefs are false. Thus epistemic cognition begins in the preschool years (Kuhn, 2005; Kuhn & Weinstock, 2002; Moshman, forthcoming). Evidence from several distinct literatures indicates that over the course of middle childhood (roughly ages 6-10) children increasingly distinguish the three epistemologically relevant domains noted earlier: (1) a domain of truth, (2) a domain of taste, and (3) a domain of interpretation.

The domain of truth is where objectivity prevails. Assertions are true or false. If I say there are nine planets, and you say there are eight, and if we're still in the 20th century, we can look in a book and determine that my assertion is true and yours is false, which settles the matter. If I say there are at least as many planets in our galaxy as there are in our solar system, it can be proved logically that this must be true. If I say harming innocent people for no good reason is wrong, we can agree on the correctness of my claim. The domain of truth, then, includes factual, logical, and moral truths.

With regard to matters of fact, children understand by the age of about 4, as we have seen, that they and others can hold demonstrably false beliefs (Wellman et al., 2001). They understand that a belief can be true or false, and that its truth or falsity can be determined by examining the relation of the belief to reality. Beliefs that correspond to reality are true and those that do not are false.

With regard to logic, preschool children also make inferences, including deductive inferences, but they are largely unaware of, and thus unable to evaluate, their inferences. By age 6, however, children recognize inference as a source of knowledge (Rai & Mitchell, 2006; Sodian & Wimmer, 1987). Over the next few years they increasingly recognize the logical necessities inherent in class hierarchies (for example, that there must be at least as many flowers as daisies), mathematical truths (3 is always and everywhere bigger than 2), and deductive inferences (as distinct from inductive inferences and partially informed guesses) (Miller et al., 2000; Moshman, 1990, 2004, forthcoming; Piaget, 1987, 2001, 2006; Piéraut-Le Bonniec, 1980; Pillow, 2002; Pillow & Anderson, 2006; Smith, 1993).

Finally, with regard to morality, there is extensive evidence from social cognitive domain theorists that by age 5, if not before, children distinguish moral from other values on the basis of objective and universal standards of right and wrong. Failing to sit in your assigned seat, for example, is wrong if there is a rule that children must sit in assigned seats, but would be acceptable in another school without such a rule. Hitting another child, however, is wrong regardless of whether there is a rule against this because it hurts the other child. More generally, even children as young as 5 years see issues of rights, justice, harm, and welfare—as distinct from issues of authority, convention, and personal choice—as constituting a moral domain in which objective standards prevail (Wainryb et al., 2004).

In the domain of taste, in contrast, subjectivity prevails. Idiosyncratic preferences are neither true nor false, and efforts to argue for them are pointless. These may be personal preferences for particular flavors of food—taste in the most literal sense—or cultural preferences for particular social conventions, but we do not expect to convince others that chocolate really tastes better than vanilla, or vice versa, or that a particular manner of assigning seats is the one true way. We can say that a food tastes good to a particular person or that a social convention feels right to those brought up with it, but there is no rational basis for claiming that all people ought to enjoy the taste of that food or ought to practice that social convention.

Research shows that at least some children recognize the subjectivity of taste as early as age 5 and that matters of taste are increasingly distinguished from matters of truth over the elementary school years (Carpendale & Chandler, 1996; Kuhn et al., 2000; Rowley & Robinson, in press; Wainryb et al., 2004). Wainryb et al. (2004), for example, presented children ranging in age from 4 to 9 years with disagreements reflecting matters of taste (e.g., whether chocolate ice cream is "yummy" or "yucky"), fact (e.g., whether pencils "go up" or "fall down" when released), and morality (e.g., whether it is "okay" or "wrong" to hit and kick other children). Regardless of age, children were virtually unanimous in maintaining that there was one right answer with regard to matters of fact and morality. With regard to matters of taste, in contrast, even some of the younger children saw both opinions as legitimate and justified their responses on the basis of the subjectivity of taste. Acceptance of diversity and acknowledgment of subjectivity with regard to taste increased substantially with age. The domains of taste and truth may be at least partially distinct as early as age 5, it appears, and become increasingly differentiated over the course of middle childhood (see also Komatsu & Galotti, 1986; Nicholls & Thorkildsen, 1988).

The domain of interpretation is the domain where reasons may be less than definitive without being entirely personal, cultural, or arbitrary. Given the constructive nature of the mind, diversity of interpretation is to be expected. Within the domain of interpretation, however, such diversity is not associated with an ultimate and nonnegotiable subjectivity. On the contrary, interpretation of an object must in some way be true to that object in order to qualify as an interpretation rather than a pure act of imagination. Thus interpretation has an objective aspect of accommodation to reality in addition to its subjective aspect of assimilation by an active mind.

Carpendale and Chandler (1996) presented children of ages 5 through 8 with tasks in which two puppets disagreed with each other about the interpretation of (a) ambiguous figures (such as the classic "duck-rabbit"), (b) lexical ambiguity (e.g., "wait for a ring"), or (c) ambiguous referential communication (eliminating one possibility but leaving two others). They also provided control tasks in which (a) an additional puppet provided a deviant interpretation (e.g., interpreting the duck-rabbit as an elephant) or (b) the puppets disagreed about matters of taste (e.g., whether a particular soup tastes "good" or "bad"). In addition, every child received, and passed, a standard false belief task. The 5- and 6-year-olds seemed mostly unable to comprehend the legitimacy of different interpretations in these tasks, though they were somewhat more able to recognize and explain differences in taste. The 7- and 8-year-olds, in contrast, often recognized and explained that the two interpretations were both reasonable given the ambiguous nature of the stimulus and that the response of a new child could not be predicted. They usually recognized, moreover, that the deviant interpretations were not reasonable. Further, children's explanations showed an emerging distinction between the domains of interpretation and taste. At least some of them recognized that in the domain of interpretation, in contrast to that of taste, responses must be grounded in evidence and reasons concerning the object to be interpreted. Thus they distinguished the domain of interpretation not only from the objective domain of truth, in which everything is true or false, but also from the subjective domain of taste, in which nothing is true or false, or even better or worse. It appears that by age 7 or 8, many children are beginning to see interpretation as distinct from both matters of truth and matters of taste (see also Lalonde & Chandler, 2002; Pillow & Henrichon, 1996).

By age 7 or 8, then, children are beginning to distinguish (a) an objective domain of truth, (b) a subjective domain of taste, and (c) a domain of reasonable interpretation that is distinct from both. These distinctions become increasingly clear over the next few years (Rowley & Robinson, in press; Wainryb et al., 2004). Children's epistemic cognition, however, remains focused on particular beliefs, inferences, interpretations, and judgments. Children do not think about knowledge in the abstract or in general (Chandler et al., 2002). Children intuitively distinguish at least three epistemic domains in thinking about questions and issues of knowledge, but they do not think about the domains themselves, they do not reflect on the interrelations and coordinations of subjectivity and objectivity, and they do not think about the general nature of knowledge and justification. Many adolescents and adults, however, do indeed think about such matters.

EPISTEMIC DEVELOPMENT IN ADOLESCENCE AND BEYOND

Suppose you are a child of 9 or 10 in 2006. How might you react to the news that Pluto is no longer a planet and that there are now eight planets? If you hear it first from a friend, you might assume you are being tricked. Assuming you also hear this from teachers, parents, television, and other sources, however, you would soon accept the change. You already knew that people can turn out to be wrong. Now you know, if you didn't already, that even scientists can turn out to be wrong. But you are unlikely to perceive a problem with the distinction between truth and falsity or with the status of the domain of truth as a distinct domain. If you are sufficiently interested in astronomy you may learn, perhaps with surprise, that nothing whatsoever happened to Pluto, and that scientists have not learned anything new about it that changed their minds regarding its planetary status. In response to your questions, you may learn that scientists decided Pluto is no longer a planet because they have a new definition of planet. Even if you find this perplexing, however, you almost surely see it as a problem of astronomy, not epistemology.

Suppose now you are in your early teens, or beyond, and very interested in astronomy. You like it, perhaps, because it is so scientific. You like it better than, say, art or literature, where everyone just spouts their opinions. Scientists work with facts. Even their theories are based on facts and tested against facts, so we can tell what's true and what's false. This is real knowledge. Of course you can have knowledge about a novel, such as the names of the characters and what they did, or about a work of art, such as the colors and the name of the artist, but once you get into the realm of opinion, it's all a question of taste, not knowledge. This objectivist epistemology takes the objective domain of truth as paradigmatic of knowledge. Matters of taste are not matters of knowledge. As for interpretation, to the extent that it involves logical inference and affords the potential for consensus, it qualifies as knowledge. All the rest is mere opinion, not knowledge.

But what about Pluto? Is it a planet or isn't it? Are there eight planets or nine? These are, it would seem, simple matters of fact. If we had learned something new about Pluto such that it no longer qualified as a planet, this would be simply a case of correcting a mistake, and would not raise any epistemological issue. If instead a new planet had been discovered, bringing the total number to ten, that would have been astronomically exciting but of no epistemological concern. Alternatively, if Pluto had been destroyed in one of the scenarios suggested at the opening of this chapter, that would have been astronomically and psychologically dramatic but epistemologically ho-hum. What makes the new status of Pluto and new number of planets epistemologically interesting is that Pluto is still there, unchanged, and we are not reacting to any new information about it. The change is a matter of definition. As an objectivist, you might assume definitions sometimes need to be corrected, and in any event this is a rare and special case. Thus you see the problem of Pluto as an anomaly and preserve your objectivist epistemology.

But if you have enough experience with matters of this sort you may begin to see that many things are "a matter of definition," even in the so-called "hard" sciences. If basic facts of astronomy are just matters of definition, what does that say about knowledge in general? What does that say about the possibility of really having any knowledge at all? Further consideration of these matters may convince you that all knowledge is relative to definitions and concepts imposed by the knower. Facts, if we even call them that, are determined by our concepts and definitions; nothing is really true or false. Under one definition there are nine planets; under another there are eight. If we want there to be, say, 15 planets, we could come up with a set of criteria of planethood that would hold for 15 astronomical objects, or whatever number we desired. If Pluto is our favorite, we can use a definition that makes it a planet. If we think it's a puny upstart unworthy of being in the same class as Jupiter, we can define it out of that class. Planethood is just a matter of definition. Some people may prefer one definition to another, but such preferences are ultimately arbitrary. Sharp distinctions between truth and falsity have little or no basis. Knowledge is a matter of preferences and opinions, which are ultimately a matter of taste. Thus a subjectivist epistemology takes the domain of taste as paradigmatic of knowledge, if we even call it that. Subjectivism can take root in very general ways, with profound consequences for people's lives (Chandler, 1987; Chandler et al., 1990).

But subjectivists, in some cases, construct a rationalist epistemology that coordinates objectivity and subjectivity. Despite your encounter with the perils of Pluto you may reflect on subjectivity itself and find some basis for objectivity. The classification of Pluto and the number of planets do indeed depend on the definition of planet. Definitions are matters of conventional usage, rather than empirical claims, and thus cannot be evaluated as true or false. Given that no definition is the one true definition, there is no simple objective answer to the question of whether Pluto is a planet or the question of the number of planets in our solar system. But it does not follow that any answer is as defensible as any other. Some definitions, and thus some conclusions about planethood, are more justifiable than others. When the definition of planet was changed in 2006, this was not done on the basis of new empirical evidence about Pluto, but it did take into account new discoveries concerning the existence and nature of other astronomical objects in our solar system. Based on the accumulating evidence, there appeared to be no basis for classifying Pluto as a planet and excluding other objects, such as asteroids, that were as large as Pluto and no different in any characteristic that could reasonably be deemed relevant to planethood. Thus any definition that included all nine traditional planets would include additional objects, some already known and others perhaps yet to be discovered, with the result that there were at least 12 planets, and perhaps many more, in the solar system.

It was possible, however, to devise a parsimonious definition that included eight of the traditional nine planets, all but Pluto, and no other object that was already known or likely to be discovered. The official adoption of this definition by the International Astronomical Union did not make it the one true definition in any objective sense and thus does not justify an objectivist conclusion that we used to mistakenly believe there were nine planets including Pluto but now know there to be only eight. But the subjectivity of the definition does not justify a subjectivist conclusion that all definitions are equally good, or equally arbitrary, or the associated subjectivist conclusions that any object can be a planet or not, and that the number of planets in the solar system can be whatever we want it to be. We could retain the traditional set of nine planets by defining a planet as (a) any object that has the unique combination of characteristics of any one of the nine objects that were considered planets in the late 20th century or (b) any object that either meets the new 2006 definition or has a five-letter name beginning with "P." Such definitions would not be false. They are not inconsistent with evidence. Their arbitrariness, however, renders them less defensible than more parsimonious definitions based on astronomical criteria such as orbit, size, and gravitation. Thus we can reasonably conclude that there are precisely eight planets or that there are at least 12, but there appears to be no reasonable basis for concluding that there are nine. In deciding on a definition, astronomers were making a subjective choice within objective constraints. The rationalist sees this as typical of knowledge, thus situating knowledge within the domain of interpretation, neither purely objective nor purely subjective.

THE EPISTEMOLOGY OF HISTORY

Consider another example: history. A child of 9 or 10 years would readily understand the distinction between history and fiction. Both history and fiction involve stories but historical stories are true whereas fiction is not. If a work of history tells about Abraham Lincoln conquering Japan and freeing the Jews, it is presenting false information. Novels and short stories, in contrast, can tell any story they want. If you don't like the story, you are entitled to your opinion, but someone else may reasonably hold a different opinion. History is a matter of truth, whereas fiction is a matter of taste. Of course, our beliefs about what happened in the past can be distinguished from what actually happened, and the former may not correspond to the latter. But this only means we have made a mistake. It does not undermine the basic assumption that history is a matter of knowledge and that historical claims can thus, at least in principle, be judged true or false.

Consider a seemingly simple question: How many genocides have there been in human history? It might appear that, at least in principle, we could answer this question by determining whether each of the events in history was or was not a genocide and then counting the number of genocides. We might be unable to reach a definitive conclusion because there are historical events of which we are unaware, or about which we have insufficient knowledge to determine whether they should be classified as genocides. Even if we had substantial knowledge about every event in history, we might mistakenly classify some events due to gaps or inaccuracies in our knowledge. In principle, however, as the objectivist sees it, there is a right answer to the question of whether any given event was a genocide, and thus a right answer to the question of how many genocides have occurred in history.

But history cannot be objectively divided into some finite number of discrete events. Even to the extent that we can distinguish a particular event, whether it qualifies as a genocide depends on our definition of genocide. The literature of genocide is rife with disputes over the definition and conceptualization of genocide and the classification of various historical events. There is, it seems, no objective basis for parsing the flow of history into some specific number of discrete events and no objective basis for determining which such events, if we even agree in distinguishing them, constitute genocide. Definitions of genocide differ with regard to dimensions such as the nature of the perpetrator, the intent of the perpetrator, the nature of the victim group, the means of destruction, and the totality of destruction. Whether some portion of history can be differentiated as a discrete event, and whether that event is classified as genocide, is in the eye of the historian. Ultimately we see whatever stories we create for ourselves, in history as in fiction, and if some people prefer some stories to others, there is no reason to question their choices. Similarly, if some prefer to think of Pluto as a planet, or not, or prefer to believe there are some number of planets rather than some other number, who is to say who is right? Over the course of many such reflections in diverse domains, an objectivist may construct a subjectivist epistemology and thus become a subjectivist.

Further consideration of definitions of genocide may, at least initially, reinforce a subjectivist conception of knowledge. The legal definition of genocide in the 1948 United Nations Genocide Convention looks like a cobbled-together set of weirdly worded political compromises, which indeed it is. If you don't like it, however, no problem: you can choose a definition more to your liking. There are many to choose from, and they differ along many dimensions. If you are concerned about undermining the status of the Holocaust by acknowledging too many genocides, there are definitions that recognize only the Holocaust, or the Holocaust and a small number of other events, as genocides. If you are concerned about some other set of events that seem to you genocidal, you can find a definition that includes them. If you are concerned that some group is being falsely labeled a perpetrator of genocide, you can find a definition under which its actions, however unfortunate, are not genocidal. Defining genocide, it appears, is an arbitrary and political matter, and thus the entire study of genocide is necessarily arbitrary and political. If even astronomy—and even such basic factual matters as defining, identifying, and counting planets—is subjective, a function of definitions and conceptualizations, it is not surprising that matters of history would be subjective too.

But further examination of definitions and conceptualizations of genocide shows some degree of consensus and some indications of objectivity, or at least rationality (Moshman, 2001, in press). Among scholars of genocide, there appears to be a consensus that the 1948 Genocide Convention was strongly influenced by the politics of the era and that its definition is deeply flawed, at least for purposes of research in history and the social sciences. There appears to be a consensus that what is needed is a more parsimonious definition that hasn't been politically gerrymandered to include or exclude specific historical events of special concern. There appears to be a consensus that not just any definition will do and that some definitions are better than others. The lack of consensus on a specific definition is consistent with the subjectivist insight that there is no one true definition, but there are a small number of commonly used definitions that overlap substantially and there is agreement on the genocidal nature of many historical events, and on the nongenocidal nature of many others.

To the extent that diverse conceptions of genocide provide divergent perceptions of history, moreover, we can enhance our understanding of history by recognizing and coordinating those multiple perspectives. Some acts constitute genocide under every available definition, but many other acts of group destruction and mass killing are or are not genocides depending on what definition one uses. From an objectivist point of view, this might seem a serious problem and it might seem the study of genocide must either find the correct definition or acknowledge that genocide research is only a source of idiosyncratic perceptions and perspectives, not knowledge. A rationalist, in contrast, sees the diversity of reasonable perspectives as a potential source of objectivity. To the extent that definitional disagreements focus our attention on issues of perpetrator, intention, victim, process, and outcome—the dimensions along which they differ—we may better understand the actual events and their genocidal nature, and thus, without resolving the conceptual disagreements, attain greater objectivity through reflective coordination of our multiple subjectivities.

With "genocide" as with "planet," there may be more than one way to define what we have in mind, but not just any definition will do. Even to the extent that this leaves us with diverse definitions, moreover, our ability to coordinate and reflect on multiple definitions and conceptualizations may provide us with a metasubjective form of objectivity. To the extent that we recognize such a post-skeptical form of objectivity, we are constructing a rationalist epistemology. But in a world of epistemic peril, this may be a never-ending enterprise.

CONCLUSION

Epistemic development is the development of knowledge about knowledge. A central thesis of this chapter, following Chandler et al. (2002), has been that two levels of epistemic development can be distinguished, the first corresponding to childhood and the second to adolescence and adulthood. Childhood, I have suggested, is marked by the ongoing differentiation of three domains: a domain of truth, in which truth and falsity can be sharply distinguished; a domain of taste, in which no such distinction is possible or meaningful; and a domain of interpretation, in which the subjectivity of the mind is constrained by the reality of the object. Epistemic development in adolescence and adulthood, I have suggested, is largely a matter of determining which of these three domains is the domain of knowledge. Such development is neither universal nor tied to age, but it tends to proceed in the familiar sequence extending from objectivist to subjectivist to rationalist epistemologies.

We should be wary, however, of assuming there is a highest stage of epistemic development that we not only have attained but have fully understood. Rather than end on a complacent note of epistemic maturity, consider one last astronomical poser: What was the sixth planet to be discovered (and who discovered it, and when)? Thinking of discovery as an empirical process of finding what is there, one might readily surmise that the sixth planet to be discovered was likely the sixth from the sun, Saturn. But Saturn (along with Mercury, Venus, Mars, and Jupiter) is one of the classic five planets that have been known at least since the ancient Greeks. The sixth planet to be discovered was the planet Earth, which was discovered by Nicolaus Copernicus in the early 1500s when he determined that the five known planets all orbited the sun and that the Earth did as well, thus making it a planet and bringing the total number to six.

We need not look as far as Pluto, it seems, for epistemological trouble. There is an obvious sense in which the Earth was known to people long before Copernicus, who thus cannot be credited with discovering it. But there is also a sense in which the Earth as we know it is the planet Earth, which was indeed unknown prior to its discovery by Copernicus. Discovery is conceptual as well as empirical, rendering truth uncomfortably problematic. Development may tend toward rationalist epistemologies but we should not assume there exists—much less that we have attained—a mature and final state of knowledge about the nature and justification of knowledge.

ACKNOWLEDGEMENTS

I am grateful to Daniel Abbott, Deanna Kuhn, Rick Lombardo, Annick Mansfield, Matt Pearson, Yolanda Rolle, Martin Rowley, and Les Smith for feedback on a draft of this chapter.

REFERENCES

Carpendale, J. I., & Chandler, M. J. (1996). On the distinction between false belief understanding and subscribing to an interpretive theory of mind. *Child Development, 67*, 1686-1706.

Chandler, M. J. (1987). The Othello effect: Essay on the emergence and eclipse of skeptical doubt. *Human Development, 30*, 137-159.

Chandler, M., Boyes, M., & Ball, L. (1990). Relativism and stations of epistemic doubt. *Journal of Experimental Child Psychology, 50*, 370-395.

Chandler, M. J., Hallett, D., & Sokol, B. W. (2002). Competing claims about competing knowledge claims. In B. K. Hofer & P. R. Pintrich (Eds.), *Personal epistemology: The psychology of beliefs about knowledge and knowing* (pp. 145-168). Mahwah, NJ: Erlbaum.

Fabricius, W. V., & Schwanenflugel, P. J. (1994). The older child's theory of mind. In A. Demetriou & A. Efklides (Eds.), *Intelligence, mind, and reasoning: Structure and development* (pp. 111-132.). Amsterdam: North-Holland.

King, P. M., & Kitchener, K. S. (1994). *Developing reflective judgment*. San Francisco: Jossey-Bass.

King, P. M., & Kitchener, K. S. (2002). The reflective judgment model: Twenty years of research on epistemic cognition. In B. K. Hofer & P. K. Pintrich (Eds.), *Personal epistemology* (pp. 37-61). Mahwah, NJ: Erlbaum.

Komatsu, L. K., & Galotti, K. M. (1986). Children's reasoning about social, physical, and logical regularities: A look at two worlds. *Child Development, 57*, 413-420.

Kuhn, D. (2005). *Education for thinking*. Cambridge, MA: Harvard University Press.

Kuhn, D., Cheney, R., and Weinstock, M. (2000). The development of epistemological understanding. *Cognitive Development, 15*, 309-328.

Kuhn, D. & Franklin, S. (2006). The second decade: What develops (and how)? In D. Kuhn & R. Siegler (Eds.), *Handbook of child psychology, Vol. 2: Cognition, perception, and language* (6th ed.) (pp. 953-993) (W. Damon & R. Lerner, series eds.). Hoboken, NJ: Wiley.

Kuhn, D., & Weinstock, M. (2002). What is epistemological thinking and why does it matter? In B. K. Hofer & P. R. Pintrich (Eds.), *Personal epistemology: The psychology of beliefs about knowledge and knowing* (pp. 121-144). Mahwah, NJ: Erlbaum.

Lalonde, C. E., & Chandler, M. J. (2002). Children's understanding of interpretation. *New Ideas in Psychology, 20*, 163-198.

Mansfield, A. F., & Clinchy, B. M. (2002). Toward the integration of objectivity and subjectivity: Epistemological development from 10 to 16. *New Ideas in Psychology, 20*, 225-262.

Miller, S. A., Custer, W. L., & Nassau, G. (2000). Children's understanding of the necessity of logically necessary truths. *Cognitive Development, 15*, 383-403.

Moshman, D. (1990). The development of metalogical understanding. In W. F. Overton (Ed.), *Reasoning, necessity, and logic: Developmental perspectives* (pp. 205-225). Hillsdale, NJ: Erlbaum.

Moshman, D. (2001). Conceptual constraints on thinking about genocide. *Journal of Genocide Research, 3*, 431-450.

Moshman, D. (2004). From inference to reasoning: The construction of rationality. *Thinking & Reasoning, 10*, 221-239.

Moshman, D. (2005). *Adolescent psychological development: Rationality, morality, and identity* (2nd ed.). Mahwah, NJ: Erlbaum.

Moshman, D. (in press). Conceptions of genocide and perceptions of history. In D. Stone (Ed.), *The historiography of genocide*. Hampshire, UK: Palgrave Macmillan.

Moshman, D. (forthcoming). The development of rationality. In H. Siegel (Ed.), *Oxford handbook of philosophy of education*. Oxford, UK: Oxford University Press.

Nicholls, J. G., & Thorkildsen, T. A. (1988). Children's distinctions among matters of intellectual convention, logic, fact, and personal choice. *Child Development, 59*, 939-949.

Perry, W. G, (1970). *Forms of intellectual and ethical development in the college years: A scheme*. New York: Holt, Rinehart, and Winston.

Piaget, J. (1987). *Possibility and necessity*. Minneapolis: University of Minnesota Press.

Piaget, J. (2001). *Studies in reflecting abstraction*. Hove, UK: Psychology Press.

Piaget, J. (2006). Reason. *New Ideas in Psychology, 24*, 1-29.

Piéraut-Le Bonniec, G. (1980). *The development of modal reasoning: Genesis of necessity and possibility notions*. New York: Academic Press.

Pillow, B. H. (2002). Children's and adults' evaluation of the certainty of deductive inferences, inductive inferences, and guesses. *Child Development, 73*, 779-792.

Pillow, B. H., & Anderson, K. L. (2006). Children's awareness of their own certainty and understanding of deduction and guessing. *British Journal of Developmental Psychology, 24*, 823-849.

Pillow, B. H., & Henrichon, A. J. (1996). There's more to the picture than meets the eye: Young children's difficulty understanding biased interpretation. *Child Development, 67*, 803-819.

Rai, R., & Mitchell, P. (2006). Children's ability to impute inferentially based knowledge. *Child Development, 77*, 1081-1093.

Rowley, M., & Robinson, E. J. (in press). Understanding the truth about subjectivity. Social Development.

Schwanenflugel, P. J., Fabricius, W. V., & Noyes, C. R. (1996). Developing organization of mental verbs: Evidence for the development of a constructivist theory of mind in middle childhood. *Cognitive Development, 11*, 265-294.

Smith, L. (1993). *Necessary knowledge: Piagetian perspectives on constructivism*. Hillsdale, NJ: Erlbaum.

Sodian, B. & Wimmer, H. (1987). Children's understanding of inference as a source of knowledge. *Child Development, 58*, 424-433.

Wainryb, C., Shaw, L. A., Langley, M., Cottam, K., & Lewis, R. (2004). Children's thinking about diversity of belief in the early school years: Judgments of relativism, tolerance, and disagreeing persons. *Child Development, 75*, 687-703.

Wellman, H. M., Cross, D., & Watson, J. (2001). Meta-analysis of theory-of-mind development: The truth about false belief. *Child Development, 72*, 655-684.

In: Meta-Cognition: A Recent Review of Research...   ISBN: 978-1-60456-011-4
Editors: M.F. Shaughnessy et al. pp. 175-184   © 2008 Nova Science Publishers, Inc.

Chapter 10

METACOGNITIVE MULTICULTURAL EDUCATION

Virginia J. Mahan
South Plains Collete, Texas, USA

ABSTRACT

This chapter employs a social psychological and domain specific perspective vis-à-vis the use of metacognition as a tool to facilitate both teaching and learning in multicultural education. More specifically, it focuses on the explicit teaching of critical thinking and metacognitive skills as a means of detecting misunderstandings, inconsistencies in reasoning, and errors in logic. Such instruction seeks to (a) direct student attention to social judgments that have discriminatory impact, including stereotype and bias formation; and (b) increase students' self-awareness, including the appraisal/monitoring of their social judgments and control/management of discriminatory actions. Lastly, the chapter will examine the use of one paradigm of mental protection (Wilson, Gilbert, & Wheatley, 1998) as an instructional tool when exposing students to "unwanted influences."

INTRODUCTION

Romani, Artists, and Altruists ≠ Gypsies, Tramps, and Thieves

"Where did Gypsies originate? What do gypsies look like? Where do they live? What do they do for a living?" I ask my students on the first day of class immediately after playing a musical selection entitled "Divi, Divi, So Kerdjan" (Romanyi Rota, 2001). Although more diffident than they typically are later in the semester, students are generally eager to interact and take turns calling out descriptions, which may be encapsulated as follows: Unclean, dark-skinned, swarthy, tramp-like nomads who travel either in wagons or RV caravans and who subsist through thieving or, alternately, as fortune-tellers who read palms, tea leaves, tarot cards, and crystal balls. Moreover, students commonly describe a distinctive sartorial style for the women, who are known for their dancing to fiddle accompaniment: long, dark, wild, flowing hair; loose, tiered, ankle-length skirts; gaudy jewelry, including bangle bracelets and large hoop earrings; and bosoms bursting from low-cut, peasant blouses. Remarkably, one student declared with considerable assurance, "Gypsy women 'dance for the money they throw,'" without even realizing that she was in point of fact quoting the lyrics to Cher's old song, "Gypsies, Tramps, and Thieves" (1971). Unfailingly, no matter how often I conduct this exercise, I am astonished at the predictability and consistency of responses, the strong student consensus, and the students' high degree of confidence in the accuracy of their descriptions.

Then, I take careful aim and throw the first dart at their substantial confidence bubble. I ask the class: "How many of you have a spouse, relative, friend, classmate, co-worker, or neighbor who is Gypsy?" Blank expressions gaze back at me, and then I see it dawn on their faces. After all, exceedingly few students have had any contact with Gypsies, more accurately termed Romani. "How, then, did you acquire such similar and powerful images?" I query. Caught unaware, they, without fail, register surprise. After a moment or two, students take turns calling out: "T.V.," "books," "movies," "the media," "music." Moreover, when I launch the second barb to puncture their beliefs, students invariably register uneasiness as their certainty is further deflated. Indeed, I reveal that philanthropist 'Diamond Jim' Brady and former U.S. President William Jefferson Clinton, as well as actors Michael Caine, Charley Chaplin, Rita Hayworth, Bob Hoskins, and Freddie Prinze were all of Romani ancestry (Hancock, 2005). In addition, although unsubstantiated, other famous persons such as Pablo Picasso, Mother Teresa, and Yul Brynner are believed to have Romani heritage.

The aforementioned exercise is offered as an appetizer platter, a sampler, whereby students are dished up their first nibbles of metacognitive processes: thinking about (a) the influence of unconscious stereotyping, (b) the inaccuracy of stored information, (c) the need to monitor biases, and (d) the imperative for self-reflection, particularly with regard to cognition. Some students take their first taste of metacognition, find it agreeable, and immediately hunger for more. Others are, at first, unsure. Yet, over the course of time, these learners develop an acquired taste for metacognitive processes and subsequently crave increasingly heftier portions. Some students, however, get their first bite and find that it leaves a bitter aftertaste. They perceive metacognition as unpalatable, because it upsets their mental applecart, spilling cognitive ambiguity on the ground for them to trip over class after class. These students, of course, are the most difficult to bring round to routinely incorporating healthy servings of metacognition into their academic regimes.

Metacognition from a Social Psychological and Domain Specific Perspective

This chapter employs a social psychological and domain specific perspective vis-à-vis the use of metacognition as a tool to facilitate both teaching and learning in multicultural education. More specifically, it focuses on the explicit teaching and modeling of critical thinking and metacognitive skills. Metacognition has been referred to as a rather imprecise, "fuzzy" concept (Flavell, 1981, p. 37). What is more, according to Hacker (n.d.), the concept has become even hazier due to a swelling body of "research that has come from researchers of widely varying disciplines and for widely varying purposes" (p. 1). Although these studies have given rise to a variety of meanings, common and more succinct definitions include "knowledge and cognition about cognitive phenomena" (Flavell, 1979, p. 906), "the ability to reflect upon a process" (Banich, 2004, p. 589), or, in the simplest of terms, "people's cognitions about their own cognitions" (Nelson, 2002, p. ix); in other words, "thinking about thinking." In order to more precisely define, as well as refine, the term for my American Minorities Studies (AMS) students, I offer this operational definition: Metacognition provides a means of detecting misunderstandings, inconsistencies in reasoning, and errors in logic.

Course Objectives

The underpinnings of American Minorities Studies rest solidly in critical thinking: A logical, reasoned process of avoiding preconceptions by gathering factual data and verifying the information, detecting ingrained biases and assumptions, contemplating divergent viewpoints and evaluating alternatives, and only then drawing a conclusion (Smith, 1995). As cornerstones of the course, my objectives are (a) to develop knowledge of stereotyping and the formation of social biases, as well as self-awareness of its personal usage; (b) to increase the degree of self-monitoring and conscious deliberation that is exerted over biased thoughts, feelings, or actions; and (c) to slow down reflexive, impulsive, knee-jerk responses regarding social judgments. What is more, students are taught to carefully filter facts from mere opinions; to refrain from oversimplification; to tolerate ambiguity, transformation, and uncertainty; and to operate within an atmosphere of skepticism (Smith's, 1995).

Following Bigelow (1991), I teach students that textbooks frequently contain lies, myths, and deceitful instructional lessons (see also Loewen, 1992, 1996, 1999; Zinn, 2003). Therefore, it is their task to interrogate and cross-examine, not merely read, the printed word (Bigelow, 1991; 1998). Moreover, students are taught to examine what is included in textbook and media accounts, as well as what is purposely omitted from these accounts and why.

In addition, students are taught to employ dialectical thinking. Jameson described dialectical thinking as "an intensification of the normal thought processes," a type of "shifting of gears," in which the mind attempts "by willpower, by fiat, to lift itself mightily up by its own bootstraps" (1974, p. 307; n.d., p. 2). What is more, Jameson suggested that "an entire complex of thought is hoisted through a kind of inner leverage one floor higher" (n.d., p. 2), and "there is a breathlessness about this shift from the normal object-oriented activity of the mind to such dialectical self-consciousness—something of the sickening shudder we feel in an elevator's fall or in a sudden dip in an airliner" (n.d., p. 2). It is hardly surprising then that some students, particularly sensitive to these sudden cognitive jolts and unexpected nose-dives, experience a sense of discomfort, disequilibrium, or queasiness during their first encounters with metacognitive processes.

In comparison to Jameson, my own definition of dialectical thinking is far less eloquent: It requires a form of ongoing, continually evolving cognition in which each new thought (i.e., the thesis) generates an attentiveness to an opposing thought (i.e., the antithesis), which are both examined and then integrated into a coherent synthesis. Indeed, I model dialectical thinking by exposing students to an exchange of logical viewpoints and, ultimately, an integrative element. On the one hand, we are taught in elementary school that Columbus was the brave explorer who "discovered" America, and therefore a national holiday—October 12—has been designated to honor this hero (the thesis statement). As an opposing viewpoint, I teach that Columbus was a brutal invader who imperialistically took control of an already occupied land, economically exploited its inhabitants to obtain free gold and cotton, initiated the first Trans-Atlantic slave trade and, as viceroy and governor of the Caribbean Islands, played a major role in the mass genocide of aboriginal peoples (the antithesis; see, for example, Zinn, 2003). Indeed, inspection of the content of Columbus' personal journal reveals that, from the perspective of Native Americans, Columbus was an oppressor, the antithesis of a national hero. A fuller and more critical examination of the two perspectives leads students to a synthesis of historical perspectives.

The aforementioned objectives call for students to think about thinking: to reflect on (a) their preconceptions and faulty assumptions, (b) the construction of stereotypes and their inaccuracy, and (c) bias formation and the scope of unconscious biases (see Table 1). Students are pressed to question "truths" and unlearn erroneous "facts." Stated more succinctly, my personal instructional goal is remediation of biased cognitions, negative emotions, and discriminatory actions.

BACKGROUND

Students, of course, bring to a multicultural education course a body of pre-established assumptions, stereotypes, attitudes, and biases with regard to minority groups and their members, as well as towards dissimilar others. Recall that at the first of the semester in their initial descriptions of "Gypsies" and other subordinate groups, students effortlessly draw on their extant beliefs about social groups (e.g., persons with disabilities, race/ethnicity, religious affiliations, sexual orientation, etc.) and employ stereotypes with little awareness of their usage or accuracy. Moreover, many responses are so automatic that students have no conscious intention to use them in judgment of others (e.g., "What a gyp!" "I got gypped!" "I Jewed him down." "You're an Indian giver!" "That's mighty white of you." "We'll have to nigger rig it." "The police raided the party and hauled off the drunks in the paddy wagons."). Indeed, students are often taken aback when they must consciously consider their mechanical and unthinking use of such biased language.

In other words, by the time students enroll in a college level American Minorities Studies class, they hold unsound and flawed thinking processes, cleave to invalid beliefs, harbor strong negative motions, and exhibit biased behavior. My objective, then, is to diminish cognitive inaccuracies and reverse the prejudiced actions. Hatred toward minority groups is learned; thus, students can "unlearn" biases. However, it goes without saying: Some students are more resistant than others.

TRANSPOSING "PROTECTING OUR MINDS"
WITH EXPOSING THEIR MINDS

Wilson, Gilbert, and Wheatley (1998) have discussed theories vis-à-vis unwanted influences on a person's beliefs and emotions, focusing on the strategies the individual uses to protect his or her mind and guard against mental contamination, defined as "the process whereby a person has an unwanted judgment, emotion, or behavior because of mental processing that is unconscious or uncontrollable" (Wilson & Brekke, 1994, p. 117). Wilson et al. (1998) have proposed a "model of mental protection" (p. 174) which entails a series of five defenses against unwanted influences and mental contamination: (a) exposure control; (b) the use of mental preparation, such as "anticipatory counter arguing" (p. 179); (c) resistance; (d) remediation; and (e) behavior control. As a metacognitive tool to facilitate teaching, I, in essence, employ this paradigm in an attempt to counter students' use of the five mental protection strategies and to neutralize student resistance when exposed to unsettling new material.

Table 1. Sources of Social Bias

- Confirmation bias: Our tendency to search for, interpret, and even distort information in ways that verify our already extant beliefs, rather than to seek information that will refute these existing beliefs. Thus, when we encounter information that patently conflicts with our previously established beliefs, we are apt to disregard it.
- False consensus bias: The tendency to assume that others think just as we do. Thus, we presume that people agree with us to a far greater extent than they do in actuality.
- Fundamental attribution bias: The tendency to attribute our own behavior to external, situational causes, while attributing the behavior of others to internal, personal causes (e.g., I am receiving welfare assistance because the company for which I worked down-sized and let 100 workers go; "those people" are on welfare assistance because they are irresponsible, lazy, unmotivated, and "milking the system").
- Just world bias: The notion that life, as well as the world, is just and fair. Thus, people get what they deserve and, conversely, deserve what they get. This bias leads to victim blame, the tendency to condemn a person who has encountered misfortune for somehow having caused the trouble or, at the least, for not having actively taken steps to avoid or prevent it.
- Out-group homogeneity bias: Our tendency to perceive all members of an unfamiliar, subordinate group as similar to each other, although we perceive
- members of our own group as heterogeneous or reasonably diverse. Those *Asians/Blacks/Mexican Americans/gays/Jews/persons with disabilities/fill in the blank* all look alike or all act the same.
- Person positivity bias: Our tendency to evaluate individuals more positively than we evaluate the groups to which they belong. For example, a person who disparages a subordinate group may nonetheless have a close friend who is a member of that group, claiming it is because he or she is "different," not like those others, and somehow an "exception."
- Self-serving bias: Our tendency to attribute our successes to personal factors and our failures to situational or environmental factors.

Exposure Control: Channel Changes to Avoid Mental Contamination

Wilson et al. (1998) proposed that exposure control, "the decision whether to allow the stimulus to enter our minds" (p. 174), is a person's first line of defense against an unwanted influence. According to Wilson et al. (1998, p. 171), "it is not uncommon to avoid stimuli that we think will elicit negative emotions, such as closing our eyes at gory scenes in the movies or turning off the radio when our ex-lover's favorite song is played." Similarly, in the classroom it is not unusual for students to change, or even turn off, their cognitive channels when exposed to information that conflicts with their existing beliefs. As an example, most of us can easily regurgitate the information that we were fed during our primary years of education with regard to Helen Keller: She was a White woman from Alabama who was both blind and deaf, yet nonetheless successfully overcame these disabilities. Students who have been fed sanitized platefuls of bland facts about an ideal, heroified "woman who overcame" (Loewen, 1996, p. 33) may feel unsettled when they are subsequently served what some publishers still consider to be distasteful facts: Keller was a radical socialist, a founder of the American Civil Liberties Union (ACLU), a contributor to the National Association of Advancement of Colored People (NAACP), and a crusader for social class issues. The lack of correspondence between the two accounts—the truncated, antiseptic version and the expanded, yet more blemished, chronicle—creates considerable cognitive dissonance. Indeed, many students experience a queasy, unpleasant state of psychological tension and respond by protecting their minds. They grab hold of their mental remote control, quickly hit the "mute" button and are barely aware that the instructor's lips are moving, effectively ignoring the incompatible information. They may doodle, daydream, and temporarily tune out any dissonant information. However, in order to pass the exams, students will ultimately, at the very least, be required to recapitulate the material, whether or not they personally believe or agree with it. Thus, short of withdrawing from the class (which occasionally happens), exposure control as a mental protection strategy is not an option for students who need the course credit.

Similarly, when the sugar coating is scraped off other standard historical fare (e.g., "In fourteen hundred and ninety-two, Columbus sailed the ocean blue") to reveal an unpalatable portion of Columbus ("In fourteen hundred and ninety-three, Columbus stole all he could see" [Loewen, 1996, p. 38]), students are reluctant to digest the new information and thus enter self-protective mode. Indeed, the confirmation bias (see Table 1) involves our tendency to search for, interpret, and even distort information in ways that verify our already extant beliefs, rather than to seek information that will refute these existing beliefs. Thus, when students encounter information that patently conflicts with their previously established views, they find it hard to swallow and thus are apt to place the unfamiliar fare on the back burner of their brains.

Given that my personal instructional goal is to remediate biased cognitions, negative emotions, and discriminatory actions, how then can I best coax students to the table of metacognition? Wilson et al. (1998) have maintained that the most effective defenses against mental contaminants occur early on, rather than later in the sequence. Thus, repeated exposure to alternative perspectives and opposing viewpoints—indeed, an incessant barrage from the very first day of class—is my most successful offensive strategy to check students' exposure control.

Preparation: Anticipating Counterarguments

According to Wilson and his colleagues, "the second line of defense" or mental prophylactic strategy is preparation. Although exposure control is students' first line of defense against contaminating stimuli, they are nonetheless trapped in the classroom for 75-

minute time stretches. The best defense at this point, then, is for students to prepare themselves by reappraising the significance of the unwanted stimulus in a non-threatening manner: "I need the Humanities credits. I only have to endure this one semester. The semester will be over in no time."

When I began teaching American Minorities Studies, I encountered oppositional students far more frequently than I currently do. Puzzled, I was at first alarmed that students may simply be operating on a higher plane of apathy. However, when I expressed this concern to a colleague, he pointed out that I engage in "anticipatory counterarguments" akin to preemptory strikes. In other words, I employ the metacognitive teaching strategy of preparation by stockpiling cognitive ammunition in advance. Having over many years been exposed to a multiplicity of student opposing viewpoints (the theses), I have amassed a reserve of refutations of these positions (the antitheses). Generally, students are unprepared to effectively argue their position. At this preparation stage, I model dialectical thinking, as well as explicitly teach the students to place themselves in others' shoes and assume an opposing perspective.

Furthermore, I lay out the biases outlined in Table 1 on the first day of lecture and teach students to reflect upon and monitor these biases. Reflective writing assignments are effective in fostering critical thinking. For example, with regard to the out-group homogeneity bias: Pick five members of your own racial/ethnic/sex/gender or religious group. How are they the same? How are they different? Next, talk to five members of a racial/ethnic/sex/gender or religious group different than your own. How are they similar to each other? How do they differ? Reflect on the degree of inter- and intra-group variation (i.e., dissimilarities between the two groups, as well as within each group).

Resistance: From Here on, a Downhill Battle

Wilson et al. (1998) have suggested that the third mental protective strategy is resistance, a cognitive process that endeavors to stop an encoded message from having an unwanted effect. Taking "a very hard line on people's ability to resist attempts to change their beliefs" (1998, p. 180), Wilson et al. believe that people are unable to—it is simply impossible. Given that my goal is to amend biased cognitive processes, annul negative emotions, and upend discriminatory actions, this is encouraging. In line with Gilbert's writings (1993; Gilbert, Krull, & Malone, 1990), if students lack the motivation or mental ability to "unaccept" the information they have encoded in order to pass my exams, they cannot escape believing it. No matter how hard students may resist (e.g., attempt to switch off, deactivate, or neutralize the stimuli to which they have been exposed), their beliefs and emotions will inevitably be revised to some extent by the alternative perspectives and opposing standpoints to which they have been exposed, regardless of how unwelcome this new material may be. Indeed, students' attitudes can transform significantly without their realizing it (Wilson et al., 1998). As students will inevitably wind up in varying degrees of "contaminated" states, at this point, the instructional battle against student mental protection is downhill.

Remediation: Attempts to Undo the Damage

According to the Wilson et al. (1998) paradigm, remediation, which entails any mental operation that attempts to undo the damage done by a contaminant, is a fourth, albeit less effectual, line of defense. Gilbert's (1991; 1993) work suggests that remediation is only feasible when people have ample motivation and adequate mental capacity. Whenever students challenge and wish to "correct" the class lectures and readings, I encourage them to provide well-reasoned rebuttals, assuring them that they will be allowed class time to disprove the material I have presented. However, I stress that it is essential that students address their concerns point-by-point, provide supporting research data, and use recognized and reputable sources, rather than mere hearsay or opinions (or Wikipedia!). Thus, I encourage them to engage in dialectical thinking, one major instructional goal. Unfortunately, however, few students are either sufficiently organized or motivated to exert the time and effort required to engage in this type of remediation. Consequently, they are unable to effectively neutralize the mental contamination to which I have exposed them and only one more defensive strategy remains that students can deploy: behavior control.

Behavior Control: Just Tough it out

The fifth and least effectual defensive strategy that students would employ to protect their minds against unwanted beliefs is behavior control, the attempt to prevent unwelcome influences from impacting behavior in an undesired way. At this stage, students (a) have been exposed to the unwanted material and have had to regurgitate, employ, reflect upon, and synthesize this information in order to meet the requirements of exams and writing assignments, (b) have had their biased beliefs neutralized by an instructional salvo of preemptory counterarguments, (c) have mounted resistance, and (d) have been afforded the opportunity to offer a rebuttal, an antithesis backed by research data provided by recognized, reputable sources. As a last-ditch tactic, resistant students may simply decide to tough it out, a form of behavior control.

One very bright, although exceedingly bigoted, student, whom I suspected was a member of a hate group, spent an entire semester facing the wall to show his disdain for both me and the class. Just before the final exam in an ultimate display of contempt, the student informed me with that he would not take the final and thus simply settle for a C in the course, rather than the A that he could easily obtain. This was his ultimate behavioral protest. We chatted, and I told the student that I would hate to see him receive a C on a transcript when, with a bit of effort and very little difficulty, he could earn an A. I assured him that after demonstrating on the final that he had encoded the information from our last unit, he was free to flush all the unwanted beliefs down his cognitive sewer. Needless to say, I was exceedingly pleased when he showed up for the final, even more so when he attained an A. Why? By being exposed to the semester's lecture and readings, as well as the class discussions, the student had to think about and repeatedly reassess his extant stereotypes, biases, and beliefs, as evidenced by his high level of discomfort. If Wilson et al. (1998) are correct, this student, despite all his efforts to protect his original mental state, was ultimately influenced in some measure by the unwelcome information.

CONCLUSION

In teaching subject matter where the objective is to alter erroneous stereotypes and remedy biased beliefs, negative attitudes, and discriminatory behaviors, familiarity with Wilson and colleagues' (1998) model of mental protection may prove valuable. This paradigm of defensive mental strategies involves exposure control, preparation, resistance, remediation, and behavior control (1998, p. 174). These researchers have noted that "if people truly want to avoid unwanted beliefs, they are better off using early mental strategies such as exposure control and mental preparation" (1998, p. 181). Thus, since my instructional object is to alter biased belief systems, my teaching efforts are aimed largely at the first two stages: (a) exposing students to a barrage of research data, as well as (b) anticipating and preparing for student arguments, and bombarding them with preemptory strikes from an anticipatory stockpile of counterarguments. Students who continue to reject the class lecture material and readings and who are sufficiently sharp, as well as motivated, may reach the remediation stage of mental protection strategies. In this case, I encourage them to employ dialectical thinking and present rebuttals. In my experience, only rarely do students employ behavior control as a defensive strategy.

REFERENCES

Banich, M. T. (2004). *Cognitive neuroscience and neuropsychology.* Boston: Houghton Mifflin Company.

Bigelow, W. (1991). Discovering Columbus: Rereading the past. In W. Bigelow & B. Petersen (Eds.), *Rethinking Columbus: The next 500 years* (pp. 6-9). Portland, OR: Rethinking Schools.

Bigelow, W. (1998). Discovering Columbus: Rereading the past. In W. Bigelow & B. Peterson, (Eds.), *Rethinking Columbus: The next 500 years* (pp.17-21). Milwaukee: Rethinking Schools.

Flavell, J. H. (1979). Metacognition and cognitive monitoring: A new area of cognitive-developmental inquiry. *American Psychologist, 34,* 906-911.

Flavell, J. H. (1981). Cognitive monitoring. In W. P. Dickson (Ed.), *Children's oral communication skills* (pp.35-60). New York: Academic Press.

Gilbert, D. T. (1991). How mental systems believe. *American Psychologist, 46,* 107-119.

Gilbert, D. T. (1993). The assent of man: Mental representation and the control of belief. In D. M. Wegner & J. W. Pennebaker (Eds.), *Handbook of mental control* (pp. 57-87). Englewood Cliffs, NJ: Prentice-Hall.

Gilbert, D. T., Krull, D. S., & Malone, P. S. (1990). Unbelieving the unbelievable: Some problems in the rejection of false information. *Journal of Personality and Social Psychology, 59,* 601-613.

Hacker, D. J. (n.d.). Metacognition: Definitions and empirical foundations. Retrieved October 27, 2006, from http://www.psyc.memphis.edu/trg/meta.htm

Hancock, I. (2005). *We are the Romani people.* Hertfordshire, UK: University of Hertfordshire Press.

Jameson, F. (1974). *Marxism and form: Twentieth-Century dialectical theories of literature.* Princeton, NJ: Princeton University Press.

Jameson, F. (n.d.). Marxism and form: Twentieth-Century dialectical theories of literature. Excerpts from Presidential Lectures retrieved December 31, 2006, from http://prelectur.stanford.edu/lecturers/jameson/excerpts/marxform.html

Loewen, J. W. (1992). *The truth about Columbus: A subversively true poster book for a dubiously celebratory occasion.* New York: New Press.

Loewen, J. W. (1996*). Lies my teacher told me: Everything your American history textbook got wrong.* New York: Touchstone/Simon & Schuster.

Loewen, J. W. (1999). *Lies across America: What our historic sites get wrong.* New York: Touchstone/Simon & Schuster.

Nelson, T. O. (2002). Foreword: New theory and data on metacognitive monitoring and control in different contexts and by different individuals. In P. Chambres, M. Izaute, & P. Marescaux (Eds.), *Metacognition: Process, function and use* (pp. ix-x). Boston: Kluwer Academic Publishers.

Romanyi Rota. (2001). Diri, Diri, so kerdjan. On *Gypsy caravan* [CD]. New York: Putamayo World Music.

Smith, R. A. (1995). *Challenging your preconceptions: Thinking critically about psychology.* Pacific Grove, CA: Brooks/Cole Publishing Company.

Stone, B. (1971). Gypsies, tramps, and thieves. [Recorded by Cher]. On *Gypsies, tramps, and thieves* [record]. London, UK: Kapp Records.

Wilson, T. D., & Brekke, N. C. (1994). Mental contamination and mental correction: Unwanted influences on judgments and evaluations. *Psychological Bulletin, 116,* 117-142.

Wilson, T. D., Gilbert, D. T., & Wheatley, T. P. (1998). Protecting our minds: The role of lay beliefs. In V. Y. Yzerbyt, G. Lories, & B. Dardenne (Eds.), *Metacognition: Cognitive and social dimensions* (pp. 171-201). Thousand Oaks, CA: Sage Publications.

Zinn, H. (2003). Columbus and western civilization. In R. Kick (Ed.), In *You are being lied to: The Disinformation guide to media distortion, historical whitewashes and cultural myths* (pp. 205-213). New York: The Disinformation Company, Ltd.

In: Meta-Cognition: A Recent Review of Research...   ISBN: 978-1-60456-011-4
Editors: M.F. Shaughnessy et al. pp. 185-205   © 2008 Nova Science Publishers, Inc.

Chapter 11

THE RELATIONSHIP BETWEEN METACOGNITIVE AND COGNITIVE STRATEGIES AND READING COMPREHENSION IN SECOND LANGUAGE LEARNING

Seyed Mohammad Alavi and Mahyar Ganjabi

The Univrsity of Tehran

Tehran, Iran

ABSTRACT

This paper investigates the relationship of test-takers' use of cognitive and metacognitive strategies to the English as a Foreign Language (EFL) reading comprehension performance. The 150 students studying English literature at Iran Kermanshah Razi University took the TOEFL reading comprehension test, followed by a cognitive-metacognitive questionnaire on how they thought while completing the test. The subjects were divided based on their reading abilities into two groups (effective and ineffective readers) and based on their gender into males and females. Then, analyses were conducted on these divisions. The results suggested that first, the use of cognitive and metacognitive strategies had a positive relationship to reading test performance; second, effective readers reported significantly higher metacognitive strategy use than the ineffective readers; and third, no significant difference was found between males and females in the use of cognitive and metacognitive strategies. Discussion of the findings and implications for further research are articulated.

Keywords: Cognitive strategy, metacognitive strategy, comprehending strategy, retrieval strategy, planning strategy, monitoring strategy, reading skill

INTRODUCTION

A brief look at the history of language teaching and learning shows that in each era some factors have been dominant. In the early periods, the focus was on the teacher and teaching materials and little or no attention was paid to the learner and the learning process. Although the learner is the most important determiner of the language learning process, s/he was then the last factor to be considered. These views can be seen at the heydays of grammar translation and behavioristic methods (Richards & Rodgers, 2001). For example, from the grammar translation method perspective, it was the teacher and teaching materials that were believed to control the learning process. The learner was involved in mental gymnastics to increase his/her mental capacity. Thus, the learner was only responsible for grasping the material and nothing else was expected from him/her (Larsen-Freeman, 1986).

With the advent of cognitive and humanistic approaches, a changing approach emanated. There was no longer a rigid emphasis on the teacher and teaching process, but rather on the learner and learning process (Mitchell & Myles, 1998, Brown, 2000). At the onset, the learner was considered as the prime determiner of the whole learning process and it was believed that learning, which is the ultimate goal of teaching, was under the control of the learner (Widdowson, 1984). Therefore, learner characteristics such as attitude, motivation, gender, cultural background, strategies, styles, and so forth came into consideration as affecting the learning process (Brown, 2000).

As a result of such views on language learning, learner-centered and process-oriented approaches came into being. The implication of such approaches was that the amount of input would never determine the amount of intake (Izumi, 2003). It was assumed that there is a filter, namely the learner characteristics, between the input and intake which can have a determining effect on the process of internalization. A great deal of energy was devoted to examine the way language learners learn a foreign or second language. The results showed that the input and output were not of the same features and there was always a discrepancy between them (Izumi, 2003). This led researchers to conclude that something must happen inside the learners' minds resulting in such differences.

Among all the learner's factors affecting the learning process, strategies that the language learner users have received more attention, and every now and then new articles and books are published to shed light on different aspects of the strategies and their relationships with different aspects of language learning (Oxford 1990, O'Malley & Chamot, 1990; Purpura, 1997; Cohen, 2003). These publications show the importance of language learning strategies (LLS) in the learning process. It is conceived that language learning and use are mainly dependent on using such strategies (Oxford 1990; Purpura, 1998; Cohen, 2003). Bialystok (1990) elaborates on strategies used in communication (communication strategies) which in her opinion are responsible for bridging the gap between the learners' current competence and the linguistic demands of linguistic context. According to her, not only are strategies involved while the learner is using language for communication and building relations with others, but also while learning a language, that is, committing language or parts of language to memory. It is based on using such strategies that Bialystok (1990) identifies as language learning and use as 'strategic' that is, a language learner and user utilizes strategies "systematically, consciously, and intentionally".

The concept of 'strategy' has received different names over the past years such as "learner strategies", "learning strategies", "language learning strategies", and so forth. In this section, different definitions suggested by some well-known scholars in this area will be presented. Tarone (1977) as one of the pioneers in this area deals mainly with inter-language and therefore defines language learning strategies (LLS) in a way that contributes to inter-language development. She defines strategy as "an attempt to develop linguistic and sociolinguistic competence in the target language - to incorporate these into one's inter-language competence" (Tarone, 1983, p. 67, as cited in Lessard-Clouston, 1997).

Oxford (1990) as a prominent strategy researcher defines strategies as "specific actions, behaviors, steps, or techniques students use - often consciously - to improve their progress in apprehending, internalizing, and using the second language". Therefore, one of the distinguishing characteristics of strategies is being conscious, that is, it is under the learner's control at the beginning (Oxford, 1990; Yamamori, et. al. 2003). Also Oxford (1990, p.9) states that strategies should have the following characteristics:

1. contribute to the main goal, e.g. communicative competence;
2. allow learners to become more self-directed;
3. expand the role of teachers;
4. are problem-oriented;
5. are specific actions taken by the learner;
6. involve many aspects of the learner, not just the cognitive;
7. support learning both directly and indirectly;
8. are not always observable;
9. are often conscious;
10. can be taught;
11. are flexible; and
12. are influenced by a variety of factors.

In her influential book, Oxford (1990) deals with the strategies and considers them as tools which are important for increasing students' learning and developing communicative competence. She believes that one measure for the appropriateness of Language Learning Strategies (LLS) is their power and potential for developing communicative competence and consequently this leads to improved proficiency and greater self-confidence. Oxford (1990) adds that strategies are "operations employed by the learner to aid the acquisition, storage, retrieval, and use of information" (p.8).

O'Malley and Chamot (1990) define Language Learning Strategies as "the special thoughts or behaviors that individuals use to help them comprehend, learn, or retain new information" (p.1). They then use the taxonomy of declarative vs. procedural knowledge of Anderson (1985) to describe such strategies. They believe that at the early stages of language learning, strategies are consciously applied - that is they are under the careful control of learner. Therefore, they function as declarative knowledge. O'Malley and Chamot (1990) assert that strategies go through the "cognitive, associative, and autonomous stages of learning" (p.85). At the cognitive stage, the strategies still follow the rules of cognitive processing, that is, they are processed in short term memory. After a while, the strategies enter the procedural stage, the stage which is not extremely under the control of the learner and is performed automatically. At this stage, it is said that strategies are proceduralized. In their own terms, "strategies that have been used repeatedly are most likely operating as procedural knowledge" (p.87). Therefore, frequent practice and use is one essential factor for strategies to become proceduralized. After becoming proceduralized, strategies no longer operate under deliberate rule-based system.

Despite all these definitions provided by different researchers over the last few decades, Bialystok (1990) believes that none of them are satisfactory. Using 'strategic behavior' to refer to Language Learning Strategies, she says, "in the broadest sense, one might argue that each solution to a problem involves a strategy" (p.7). She presents some examples to show how differently this term is used in different contexts. For example, in sport, military, and management, the term 'strategy' has different meanings and is used in order to achieve some explicit and observable goals. Bialystok (1990) believes that these usages are quite different from that used in language learning and teaching which usually refers to an aspect of communication. However, she lists some aspects that she believes to be common among all definitions provided so far. They are as follows:

1. Effectiveness of strategies: "they are related to solutions in specific ways, and they are productive in solving the problem for reasons which theorists can articulate" (Bialystok, 1990, p.12).
2. Systematicity of strategies: strategies are not applied in a haphazard manner but are followed in a well-established orchestration.
3. Finiteness of strategies: strategies are limited and learner should make use of them differently according to the kind of problem and the context s/he is involved in to achieve a solution.

Following the previous ideas regarding intentionality of LLS, Allen (2003) lists some factors that she believes should be present in order for a strategy to be considered as strategy for the learner. The learner must:

1. have alternative strategies to choose according to the existing context;
2. think about the pros and cons of each strategy which s/he wants to use in relation to the task at hand; and
3. select strategy based on its effectiveness and appropriacy to the task or problem.

Najar (1998) defines strategies by referring to good language learners. He believes that research shows that using strategies is the main reason for the success of some language learners. He refers to transferability and appropriacy of strategies used by language learners as the two main factors involved in their success. According to him, a good strategy user has a host of strategies, many of which are specific to the domains in which they are expert.

To sum up these different viewpoints regarding strategy definition, a four-factor list proposed by Lessard-Clouston (1997) regarding the features common among all views will prove helpful:

> First, LLS are learner generated; they are steps taken by language learners. Second, LLS enhance language learning and help develop language competence, as reflected in the learner's skills in listening, speaking, reading or writing the L2 or FL. Third, LLS may be

visible (behaviors, steps, techniques, etc) or unseen (thoughts, mental processes). Fourth, LLS involve information and memory (vocabulary knowledge, grammar rules, etc).

Also, there are several types of strategy classifications in the literature. Some of these classifications are just restatements of the previous models. Selinker (1972) working on inter-language was among the first researchers who dealt with the role of strategy in language development. He distinguished between language learning strategies and communication strategies. This classification is conventional and is frequently referred to in the literature on strategies. Communication strategies are used by speakers intentionally and consciously in order to cope with difficulties in communicating in an second language or foreign language. The term Language Learning Strategy (LLS) is used more generally for "all strategies that second language and foreign language learners use in learning the target language and communication strategies are therefore one type of LLS" (Lessard-Clouston, 1999 p.).

Rubin (1981, as cited in O'Malley & Chamot, 1990, p.3) presented another classification which consists of two categories:

First primary category, consisting of strategies that directly affect learning includes clarification/verification, monitoring, memorization, guessing/inductive reasoning, deductive reasoning, and practice. The second primary category, consisting of strategies that contribute indirectly to learning, includes creating practice opportunities and using production tricks such as communication strategies.

Also, an alternative classification scheme was proposed by Naiman et. al. (1978) which differentiates between primary and secondary strategies. They believe that primary strategies are common to all language learners but secondary strategies are not. The primary strategies involve: "1)an active task approach; 2)realization of language as system; 3) realization of language as a means of communication and interaction; 4)management of affective demands; and 5)monitoring of second language performance" (Naiman, et. al. 1978, as cited in O'Malley & Chamot, 1990).

In another classification much similar to that of Naiman et. al. (1978) Dansereau (1985, as cited in O'Malley & Chamot, 1990) differentiated between primary strategies which are used "to operate directly on learning materials (e.g. comprehension and memory strategies)" and support strategies which help to establish "an appropriate learning attitude and aid in coping with distractions, fatigue, frustration, and so forth (e.g. concentration strategies)" (O'Malley and Chamot 1990, p.100).

Over the past few decades, some professionals have gone further and have introduced different classifications with much more complicated branches. One of these comprehensive models is that of Oxford (1990) which is very popular. Oxford's classification consists of differentiating between two general types of strategies: direct and indirect. According to her model, this type of classification is quite different from all the previous ones. It is more comprehensive and detailed, it is more systematic in linking individual strategies as well as strategy groups, with each of the four language skills; and it uses less technical terminology.

Direct strategies are directly applied on language, that is, they are in direct contact with language. These strategies are further divided into three types: memory, cognitive, and compensation strategies. Memory strategies fall into four subcategories: "creating mental linkages, applying images and sounds, reviewing well, and employing actions" (Oxford,

1990, p. 38). Compensation strategies are ones which "enable learners to use the new language for either comprehension or production despite limitations in knowledge" (Oxford, 1990, p. 47). That is, these strategies are intended to bridge the gap between the learner's current competence and the demands of linguistic context. These are of two types: "guessing intelligently in listening and reading and overcoming limitations in speaking and writing" (Oxford, 1990, p. 48). "Cognitive strategies", she believes, "are unified by a common function: manipulation or transformation of the target language by the learner" (p.43).

Indirect strategies are in indirect contact with language or have an execution function. These strategies consist of three categories: metacognitive, affective, and social strategies. Oxford (1990) calls these strategies "indirect" because "they support and manage language learning without (in many instances) directly involving the target language" (p.135). She believes that both direct and indirect strategies should work together to achieve goals. In addition, indirect strategies are applied in all four language skills. Regarding the affective strategies, the term 'affective' refers to emotions, attitudes, motivations, and values. "Affective strategies help to regulate emotions, motivations, and attitudes" (Oxford, 1990, p. 135). It is the influence of affective strategies that can turn an underachiever to an overachiever. It is usually reported that successful language learners are those who know how to manage their affective side. Affective strategies are divided into three branches: "lowering your anxiety, encouraging yourself, and taking your emotional temperature". Social strategies are necessary for each language learner and user. "[They] help students learn through interaction with others" (Oxford 1990, p. 135). These strategies consist of three categories: "asking questions, cooperating with others, and empathizing with others" (Oxford, 1990 p.145). She defines them in this way:

> Metacognitive means beyond, beside, or with the cognitive. Therefore, metacognitive strategies are actions which go beyond purely cognitive devices, and which provide a way for learners to coordinate their own learning process (p.136).

And finally, she divides metacognitive strategies into three strategy sets: "centering your learning, arranging and planning your learning, and evaluating your learning" (p.136).

O'Malley and Chamot's (1990) model consists of three broad categories with each one divided into further subcategories (p.46):

1. Metacognitive strategies
2. Cognitive strategies
3. Social/Affective strategies: they involve:
    a. Cooperation
    b. Questioning for clarification
    c. Self talk: "using mental redirection of thinking to assure oneself that a learning activity will be successful or to reduce anxiety about a task" (p.46).

This paper will use the classification suggested by Phakiti (2003). He divides cognitive strategies into comprehending and retrieval subcategories and metacognitive ones into planning and monitoring subcategories. According to him, this classification is based on Gagne et. al. (1993) and Purpura (1999). Retrieval strategies bring the stored information from long-term memory back to short-term memory for present utilization. Comprehending strategies are those which hold information in working memory long enough to be used for understanding the written text.

Planning strategies as one of metacognitive strategies refer to ''Second Language learners' actions of perceiving and overviewing tasks to develop directions to be done and how, and when to do it'' (Phakiti, 2003 p.). The second type of metacognitive strategies, monitoring, is ''learners' actions undertaken to check memory, and evaluate their thinking and reading performance'' (Phakiti, 2003 p.).

PURPOSE

This study investigates the nature of strategies used in reading comprehension. That is, it aims to illustrate the kind of strategies (i.e. cognitive and/or metacognitive) language readers use more frequently in reading. Moreover, this study seeks to determine the difference between effective and ineffective readers in terms of strategy use. Also in this study, the effect of gender (male or female) as a moderating variable will be accounted for by determining the significance of its effect on test-takers' performance.

RESEARCH QUESTIONS

This study focuses on the following research questions:

1   Is there any difference between cognitive and metacognitive strategies used by the test-takers in the TOEFL reading comprehension test(s)?
2   Is there any difference between effective and ineffective test-takers in their use of cognitive and metacognitive strategies?
3   Is there any difference between effective and ineffective test-takers in the use of cognitive strategy subcategories (comprehending and retrieval strategies) and metacognitive strategy subcategories (planning and monitoring strategies)?
4   Is there any difference between male and female test-takers in the use of each of these strategies in the reading comprehension test?

Table 1. Distribution of Subjects

Level of education	Male	Female	Total
2nd semester- daily class	10	30	40
2nd semester- evening class	10	28	38
8th semester- daily class	8	30	38
8th semester- evening class	12	22	34
Total	40	110	150

PARTICIPANTS

The participants of this study were all from Iran Kermanshah Razi University. From among 150 students participating in this study, 98 students provided the necessary data for the study. The participants were studying English literature at 2nd and 8th semesters (2 day and 2 evening classes). As a result, it was expected that they could understand both the TOEFL reading comprehension test and questionnaire. The rationale underlying using subjects from different semesters stems from the nature of research questions. That is, as the research questions show, the subjects should be of two different reading abilities (effective and ineffective). Therefore, it was assumed that freshman students would have lower ability in the TOEFL reading test and the senior students were assumed to be good at this test due to their higher exposure to different reading texts during their education. Table 1 shows the number of subjects enrolled in each semester.

INSTRUMENTATION

In this study, two devices were used: a cognitive-metacognitive questionnaire and the TOEFL reading test. The questionnaire used in this study is the one designed by Phakiti (2003) which seemed to be the most suitable for the purpose of this study because, first, it directly investigated reading skill and second, the wording of this questionnaire was more appropriate for the present subjects than other questionnaires. Phakiti (2003) notes that this questionnaire was drawn from the literature in reading, learning and test taking strategies and is much similar to the questionnaire developed by Purpura (1999). Also, he reports that two experts in strategies carefully examined this questionnaire and the reliability and validity of the survey was approved by them. Despite all these advantages, some changes were made on this questionnaire to make it more suitable for the Iranian learners. For example, some items were divided into two separate ones to make it more understandable for the present subjects and some confusing words were omitted. The total number of items after these changes was 33. Also, some items were deleted because it was assumed that they were either incompatible with the Test of English as a Foreign Language (TOEFL) reading test, or confusing for the subjects.

The questionnaire consists of four categories of strategies: comprehending, retrieval, planning, and monitoring. According to Phakiti (2003), this classification is based on Gagne et. al. (1993) and Purpura (1999). Furthermore, past tense was used in the questionnaire because it was given to the subjects after the TOEFL reading test. Based on Table 2, the type of each questionnaire item (comprehending, retrieval, planning, and monitoring) was determined.

Table 2- Strategy Questionnaire Items Classification

Processing	Subcategories	Number of items	Items used
Cognitive strategies	Comprehending	10	1,2,3,6,7,8,9,10,11,12
	Retrieval	6	4,5,13,14,15,21
Metacognitive strategies	Planning	11	14,16,18,21,22,24,25,26, 28,29,30,33
	Monitoring	9	17,19,20,23,27,31,32

The second instrument was the TOEFL reading test. This test was taken from the TOEFL CBT Success (2004). The test consisted of five passages, each followed by 10 questions. The time allocated to this part was determined according to the time specified in the original test (90 minutes). The test consisted of two types of questions:

1. Reading comprehension questions ask them to answer questions about the information given in the reading passages. There were a variety of questions about each reading passage, including main idea questions, directly answered detail questions, and implied detail questions.

2. Vocabulary questions asked them to identify the meaning of words in the reading passages. To answer these questions, they had to know the meanings of the words. They can also identify the meanings of some of the words by understanding the content surrounding the words, by using structural clues to identify the meanings of the words, or by breaking down the unknown words into known word parts in order to identify them.

To find out whether these instruments met the fundamental psychometric requirements, their validity and reliability had to be considered. The reliability of the TOEFL reading comprehension test was computed using Kuder-Richardson 21 (KR-21). The reliability turned out to be 0.84. It should be noted that this formula will generally yield a reliability coefficient that is lower than that given by KR-20. The validity of the TOEFL reading test and the questionnaire were computed using Factor Analysis (see tables 3 and 4). To examine the constructs of the instruments used in this study, a Principal Component Factor Analysis was performed. The result showed that two factors emerged as default that, as shown in Appendix 1, account for 77.25 cumulative percent of variances. The extracted default factors that appear in Table 3 show that cognitive strategies loaded under factor one and metacognitive strategies have loadings under factor two. This tends to explain the construct of the strategies tested by the questionnaire. The inclusion of TOEFL reading comprehension test in the Factor Analysis, as Table 4 shows, indicates that it tends to have a separate construct. Interestingly enough, the metacognitive monitoring strategies also loaded under Factor 3 indicating that monitoring has a kind of contribution to the test takers' ability in doing TOEFL reading comprehension test.

Table 3. Factor Analysis for Strategy Subcategories

Strategies	Component	
	1	2
Cognitive strategies	.994	
Comprehending strategies	.837	
Retrieval strategies	.817	
Metacognitive strategies		.995
Monitoring strategies		.805
Planning strategies		.774

Table 4. Factor Analysis for Strategy Types and TOEFL Reading Test

	Component		
	1	2	3
Cognitive strategies	.995		
Comprehending strategies	.840		
Retrieval strategies	.815		
Metacognitive strategies		.956	
Planning strategies		.884	
Monitoring strategies		.631	.590
TOEFL reading comprehension			.910

PROCEDURE

The TOEFL test and the questionnaire were administered to the students who were asked first to answer the reading test and then based on what they did in the reading test, fill in the questionnaire. The reading test took 90 minutes. The subjects were not allowed to use the dictionary or other sources so that their reading ability be manifested accurately. Also, the teachers were invited to be present at the research time to manage and regulate the subjects.

After answering the reading test, the subjects were asked to fill in the questionnaire. It should be mentioned that as this questionnaire makes use of a Likert Scale format, this posed some difficulty for the students. Therefore, a brief explanation was given to the students about what the Likert numbers represented.

After collecting the papers, the reading test was scored based on the traditional scoring scheme with each correct answer having one value. The total score of this test was 60, but no one achieved the highest score. Most of the subjects obtained middle scores from the reading comprehension test. The questionnaire was also scored using the Likert scale numbers. That is, the score given to each item was based on the number chosen for that item. Then based on the subjects' scores in the TOEFL reading test, they were divided into two groups (effective and ineffective).

Additionally, it should be mentioned that some students did not answer the test and the questionnaire and therefore, they were removed from this study. The number of subjects at the end was 98. In order to identify the effective and ineffective readers those subjects whose scores fell at + 0.5 standard deviations from the mean of the TOEFL reading test were considered as effective and those whose scores fell at - 0.5 standard deviations from the mean of the TOEFL reading test as ineffective ones. Also, the subjects were divided into two groups based on their gender (male or female) to determine the effect of gender on the strategy choice.

RESULTS AND DISCUSSION

To achieve the objectives of this study, the following statistical procedures were conducted. For the first question, a t-test was used because of the nature and the number of variables. For the other three questions, an ANOVA (repeated-measure and two-way) was selected.

Analysis No. 1: Cognitive and Metacognitive Strategies and Test-takers' Reading Comprehension

Table 5 shows the summary of descriptive statistics of cognitive and metacognitive strategies used by the test-takers in the TOEFL reading comprehension test.

The difference between cognitive and metacognitive strategies was put to t-test analysis (see table 6).

The result of t-test shows that there is a significant difference in the use of these strategy types by the test takers and the first null hypothesis is rejected (t (149) =3.577, p< .05). Therefore, all the test takers used these strategy types differently. As the means of cognitive and metacognitive strategies shows the metacognitive ones are used more by the subjects.

Analysis No. 2: Cognitive and Metacognitive Strategies among Effective and Ineffective Test-takers

The second null hypothesis is concerned with the fact as to whether there is any difference between effective and ineffective test-takers in the use of cognitive and metacognitive strategies. Therefore, effective and ineffective readers use of these strategies was put to analysis – in this case, a repeated measures ANOVA. In order to identify the effective and ineffective readers those subjects whose scores fell at + 0.5 standard deviations from the mean of the TOEFL reading test were considered as effective and those whose scores fell at - 0.5 standard deviations from the mean of the TOEFL reading test as ineffective ones. Table 7 shows the descriptive statistics for the two types of strategies used by the two groups.

Table 5. Descriptive Statistics for Cognitive and Metacognitive Strategies Used in the TOEFL Reading Comprehension Test (N= 150)

Strategy	Mean	std. deviation
Cognitive strategies	56.508	10.786
Metacognitive strategies	61.294	13.620

Table 6. T-test Results for the Difference between Cognitive and Metacognitive Strategies Used in the TOEFL Reading Comprehension Test

Strategy type	Mean differences	Std. deviation	Std. error mean	t	df	Sig. (2-tailed)
Cognitive vs. Metacognitive	4.828	16.386	1.338	3.577	149	.000

Table 7. Descriptive Statistics for Strategy Difference across Proficiency Levels

Proficiency	Effective readers			Ineffective readers		
Strategy	Mean	Std. deviation	N	Mean	Std. deviation	N
Cognitive	56.201	11.594	51	56.808	10.293	47
Metacognitive	66.320	9.689	51	55.894	16.614	47

Table 8. ANOVA Results for Strategy Difference across Proficiency Levels

	Type III sum of Squares	df	Mean Square	F	Sig.
Strategy	1036.469	1	1036.469	7.783	.006
Effective vs. ineffective	1178.908	1	1178.908	6.984	.010
Strategy vs. effective and ineffective	1488.756	1	1488.756	11.180	.001
Error	16204.366	96	168.795	-	-

As table 8 shows, there is a significant difference between effective and ineffective test-takers in the use of cognitive and metacognitive strategies.

As Table 4.6 shows, the effect of strategy is significant ($F (1, 96) = 7.783$, $p<.05$). That is, cognitive and metacognitive strategies influence the readers' ability to read. Also the proficiency level has a positive effect on the reader's ability to read ($F (1, 96) = 6.984$, $p<.05$). It means that the higher the learner's proficiency, the higher the reading ability will be. The interaction between the strategy type and proficiency level is also of significance ($F (1, 96) = 11.180$, $p<.05$). As descriptive statistics shows, effective readers used more metacognitive strategies than ineffective readers and fewer cognitive ones than ineffective readers. Therefore, one reason they were being more successful in reading skills was their higher use of metacognitive strategies.

The above analysis only shows that there is an interaction between strategy use and proficiency level. Now another question comes to mind as which effective and ineffective readers use, which cognitive and metacognitive strategies more significantly. A further analysis of the obtained data showed that metacognitive strategies are used more frequently by the effective readers than ineffective ones ($t (96) = 3.831$, $p< .05$). But no significant difference was found between effective and ineffective readers in terms of cognitive strategy use ($t (96) = .273$, $p> .05$).

Analysis No. 3: Effective and Ineffective Test-takers in Using the Subcategories of Cognitive and Metacognitive Strategies

For this analysis, a repeated-measures ANOVA was used. Table 9 shows the descriptive statistics for each of cognitive and metacognitive strategy subtypes used by effective and ineffective readers.

Table 9. Descriptive Statistics for Strategy subcategories across Proficiency Levels

Strategy type	Strategy subcategories	Effective readers			Ineffective readers		
		Mean	Std. deviations	N	Mean	Std. deviations	N
	Comprehending	43.882	11.259	51	44.723	11.162	47
Cognitive strategy	Retrieval	38.071	8.147	51	38.475	8.193	47
	Planning	55.803	11.908	51	50.468	16.935	47
Metacognitive strategy	Monitoring	40.728	9.104	51	31.580	11.050	47

As Table 10 shows, the difference between cognitive and metacognitive strategy subcategories is not significant. That is, effective and ineffective readers used these subcategories equally.

As the above shows, the effect of strategy is significant. That is, the type of strategy subcategories used, whether cognitive or metacognitive, has a positive effect on the ability of readers (F (1, 96) = 28.413, p<.05). The proficiency level of subjects has no correspondence with the type of cognitive strategies used by either two groups (F (1, 96) = .146, p>.05). It means that both effective and ineffective readers used the cognitive strategy subtypes equally. The interaction between the cognitive strategy types and proficiency levels is also not significant (F (1, 96) = .037, p>.05).

On the other hand, the proficiency level has a positive effect on the type of metacognitive strategy used (F (1, 96) = .13.232, p<.05). This may be one reason for their partial success in reading. Like the cognitive strategy, the interaction between metacognitive strategy subtypes and proficiency levels is not significant (F (1, 96) = 1.492, p>.05).

Table 10. ANOVA Results for Strategy Subcategories Differences across Proficiency Levels

Strategy subcategories		Type III sum of Squares	df	Mean Square	F	Sig.
Cognitive subcategories	Strategy	1778.328	1	1778.328	28.413	.000
	Effective vs. ineffective	18.936	1	18.936	.146	.703
	Strategy vs. effective and ineffective	2.344	1	2.344	.037	.847
	Error	121468.964	96	129.885	-	-
Metacognitive subcategories	Strategy	14106.795	1	14106.795	118.451	.000
	Effective vs. ineffective	2565.452	1	2565.452	13.232	.000
	Strategy vs. effective and ineffective	177.704	1	177.704	1.492	.225
	Error	18612.354	96	193.879	-	-

Table 11. Descriptive Statistics for the Degree of Strategy Use across Gender

Gender Strategy	Male			Female		
	Mean	Std. deviation	N	Mean	Std. deviation	N
Cognitive	55.968	11.338	40	56.704	10.625	110
Metacognitive	61.794	12.824	40	61.112	13.951	110

Analysis No. 4: Male and Female Test-takers' Use of Cognitive and Metacognitive Strategies in the Reading Comprehension Test

This question investigates the effect of gender (male or female) on using cognitive and metacognitive strategies. Table 11 presents the descriptive statistics for difference between males and females in terms of using cognitive and metacognitive strategies.

In order to achieve more reliable results, a two-way ANOVA was used. Table 12 shows the results.

Table 12. ANOVA Results for Strategy Difference across Gender

Source	Type III sum of squares	df	Mean square	F	Sig.
Strategy	1535.846	1	1535.846	10.114	.002
Gender	.043	1	.043	.000	.987
Strategy vs. gender	29.475	1	29.475	.194	.660
Error	44947.999	296	151.851	-	-

As the above results show, the effect of strategy is significant ($F_{(1, 148)}$ =10.114, p <.05). That is, the type of strategy used by the either males or females can affect their performances. The effect of gender on the performance of students is also significant ($F_{(1, 148)}$ = .000, p>.05). But the interaction between gender and strategy is not significant ($F_{(1, 148)}$ = .194, p>.05). This finding is supported by the result obtained from descriptive analysis. The descriptive means show that there is not much difference between males or females in their use of either type of strategies.

CONCLUSION

The basic findings in the present study mainly relied on the ways the terms were defined and the method of data gathering and data analysis. For example, strategy items intended to assess particular cognitive and metacognitive strategies might have turned out to assess others, for example, due to wording of the strategy items and the test-takers' misinterpretations of the items meaning. Regardless of some limitations to the study, the nature of cognitive and metacognitive strategies in relation to reading performance could be elaborated on and discussed with caution. Cognitive and metacognitive strategies might need to be viewed as two interactive facets of the same mental process that do not occur independently of each other. There are difficulties distinguishing cognitive strategies from metacognitive strategies as suggested in the literature. As pointed out by Purpura (1999, p. 127, cited in Phakiti 2003), "cognitive strategy use seems to function in concert with metacognitive strategy use, which functions in an executive capacity".

Despite all shortcomings, some findings were achieved which are in line with other studies done in this area. The findings in this study, in general, suggest that cognitive and metacognitive strategy use can explain variation in reading test performance. The use of cognitive and metacognitive strategies across achievement groups (effective vs. ineffective) differed quantitatively. The participants in this study used metacognitive strategies more than cognitive ones. That is, they made more use of metacognitive strategies no matter whether they are effective or ineffective.

The present study shows that the use of strategies is a key to second language readers success. The present study divided the second language readers into two groups based on their knowledge of English (effective and ineffective readers), and accordingly it turned out that there are some differences between cognitive and metacognitive strategies used by these two groups. As the results showed, effective readers used metacognitive strategies more than ineffective ones. This may be one reason for the relative success of the expert readers.

This study also revealed that the subcategories of metacognitive strategy (planning and monitoring strategies) were used more than the subcategories of cognitive strategy (retrieval and comprehending strategies). The results also showed that planning and monitoring strategies are used more by effective readers, than ineffective ones. Monitoring strategies are used more by effective readers than planning and monitoring strategies. This shows the main role of metacognition as "cognition of cognition" (Phakiti, 2003). That is, the key to reader's success is their ability to monitor their performance throughout the process of reading. The monitoring strategies enable the readers to evaluate and reevaluate their performance until their peak achievement is achieved.

To sum up, this study leads to the following rather generalizable remarks. First, to achieve success in reading comprehension, metacognitive strategies (planning and monitoring) can be considered as a key factor. This is also supported by Phakiti (2003) in his study on the effect of cognitive and metacognitive strategies on reading comprehension. He came to the conclusion that highly successful test-takers use more metacognitive strategies. Second, unlike Phakiti (2003), this study showed that there is no difference between male and female readers in the use of cognitive and metacognitive strategies. But Phakiti (2003 b) showed that male test-takers use metacognitive strategies more than female ones.

PEDAGOGICAL IMPLICATION

Learning strategies, as useful tools that prove the more reliable and less confusing ground for successful language learning, would assist learners to make the most of their capability to handle language learning in general. Thus, they should be provided with the means to achieve the desired objectives. The findings of this study have many pedagogical implications for instruction and curriculum development as well as teaching. First, learners of English as a foreign language should learn to recognize the strategies they are using and be advised to select the most appropriate techniques for instructional environment. Successful language learners may serve as informants for students experiencing less success in language learning regarding strategies, techniques, and study skills. Through monitoring each other, students can take an active part in not only learning, but also teaching.

Second, teachers should become aware of the strategies and styles that students are (or are not) using so that teachers can develop teaching styles and strategies that are compatible with their students' way of learning.

Third, teachers can help students identify their current learning strategies by means of a variety of data collection methods such as surveys, group discussions, diaries, think-aloud procedure and so forth. Teachers need to know the advantages and disadvantages of each method.

Fourth, language curricula, materials and instructional approaches should incorporate activities to accommodate the various characteristics of the learners found in the foreign language classroom. In addition, use of appropriate learning strategies can enable students to take responsibility for their own learning by enhancing the learner autonomy, independence and self-direction (Dickinson, 1987).These factors are important because learners need to keep on learning when they are no longer in formal classroom setting (Oxford, 1990). Unlike most other characteristics of the learner such as aptitude, motivation, personality, and general cognitive styles, learning strategies are teachable. Thus teachers can help their students learn quicker, easier and more effectively by weaving learning strategy training into regular classrooms.

Almost all the research studies sought and mentioned in this study have a way of promoting strategy training and suggesting different ways of implementing strategy training for more successful learning and teaching. As for the strategy training, instruments such as the SILL (Strategy Inventory for Learning Language) could be starting point for such research studies, providing a general idea of which strategies have a significant degree of association with proficiency. It would then be necessary to establish what these strategies actually mean to students in their particular learning situation, and then to find a way of converting them into teachable techniques, the effect of which could be measured over a period of time with different groups of learners. The SILL provides a snapshot, but only using more longitudinal approaches will give us an idea of the possible effects that language learning strategies have on proficiency.

Since the results of most studies show that metacognitive strategies are used more often by good and successful language learners, attempts should be made by teachers and syllabus designers to aim at developing this particular strategy in all the learners. Moreover, with the same aim, the use of memory strategies used more often by less proficient students should be replaced to help them become better learners.

Researchers must re-conceptualize second language learning strategies to include the social and affective side of learning along with the more intellectual sides. In strategy training, teachers should help students develop affective and social strategies, as well as intellectual related strategies, based on their individual learning styles, current strategy use and specific goals (Oxford, 1990).

Research should be replicated so that more consistent information becomes available within, and across, groups of learners. Particularly important is information on how students from different cultural background use language learning strategies. Second language teachers need to feel confident that the research is applicable to their students.

In addition, some research studies on factors affecting strategy choice would be helpful. Learning style is an important factor, along with gender, age, nationality, ethnicity, beliefs, previous educational and cultural experiences and learning goals. Additionally, it is likely that different kinds of learners (e.g. analytic vs. global or visual vs. auditory) might benefit from different modes of strategy training.

Teachers must have training relevant to their own instructional situations in three areas: identifying students' current learning strategies through surveys, interviews, or other means; helping individual students to discern which strategies are most relevant to their learning styles, tasks and goals; and aiding students in developing orchestrated strategy use rather than a scattered approach.

SUGGESTION FOR FURTHER RESEARCH

The following hints can be helpful for the future research:

1 Iranian students served as the subject of the study. Would we come to the same results if subjects came from different cultural backgrounds?
2 Language learners come to learning contexts with their own ways of learning. Would the learning style of learners affect the results of such studies?
3 In order to generalize the findings of the study, the number of subjects under should be increased.
4 The range of age, here is between 19 and 23. Could age be a factor in the choice of strategies?
5 Can we transfer the results of this study in a foreign language context to second language context?
6 Would strategies which proved to be effective in reading comprehension be conducive to enhancing the general second language proficiency?

APPENDIX I: FACTOR ANALYSIS

Total Variance Explained

Component	Initial Eigenvalues			Extraction Sums of Squared Loadings			Rotation Sums of Squared Loadings		
	Total	% of Variance	Cumulative %	Total	% of Variance	Cumulative %	Total	% of Variance	Cumulative %
1	2.596	43.266	43.266	2.596	43.266	43.266	2.389	39.817	39.817
2	2.039	33.988	77.254	2.039	33.988	77.254	2.246	37.437	77.254
3	.727	12.123	89.377						
4	.615	10.256	99.634						
5	1.157E-02	.193	99.827						
6	1.041E-02	.173	100.000						

Extraction Method: Principal Component Analysis.

APPENDIX II: COGNITIVE AND METACOGNITIVE QUESTIONNAIRE

Directions: A number of statements, which people use to describe themselves when they were taking a test are given below. Read each statement and indicate how you thought during the test. Choose 1 (Never), 2 (Sometimes), 3 (Often), 4 (Usually) and 5 (Always).

Your thinking	1	2	3	4	5
1. I made short notes during the test.	1	2	3	4	5
2. I underlined the main ideas during the test.	1	2	3	4	5
3. I translated the reading texts into Farsi.	1	2	3	4	5
4. I used my own English structure knowledge to comprehend the text.	1	2	3	4	5
5. I spent more time on difficult questions.	1	2	3	4	5
6. I tried to understand the texts regardless of my vocabulary knowledge.	1	2	3	4	5
7. I tried to understand the questions regardless of my vocabulary knowledge.	1	2	3	4	5
8. I tried to find topics and main ideas by scanning.	1	2	3	4	5
9. I tried to find topics and main ideas by skimming.	1	2	3	4	5
10. I read the texts several times to better understand them.	1	2	3	4	5
11. I read the questions several times to better understand them.	1	2	3	4	5
12. I used my prior knowledge to help understand the reading test.	1	2	3	4	5
13. I tried to identify easy and difficult test components.	1	2	3	4	5
14. I determined which parts were more important than others before starting the test.	1	2	3	4	5
15. When I started to complete the test, I planned how to complete the test and followed the plan.	1	2	3	4	5
16. I was aware of what and how I was doing in the test.	1	2	3	4	5
17. I checked my own performance and progress while completing the test.	1	2	3	4	5
18. I attempted to identify main points of the given reading texts.	1	2	3	4	5
19. I thought through the meaning of the test questions before answering them.	1	2	3	4	5
20. I would correct mistakes immediately when found.	1	2	3	4	5
21. I asked myself how the test questions and the given texts related to what I already knew.	1	2	3	4	5
22. I determined what the test questions required me to do.	1	2	3	4	5
23. I was aware of how much the test remained to be completed.	1	2	3	4	5
24. I tried to understand the questions adequately before attempting to find the answers.	1	2	3	4	5

25. I made sure I understood what had to be done.	1	2	3	4	5
26. I made sure I understood how to do the test.	1	2	3	4	5
27. I was aware of my ongoing thinking process when answering to questions.	1	2	3	4	5
28. I made sure to clarify the goal and know how to complete the test.	1	2	3	4	5
29. I checked my accuracy as I progressed through the test.	1	2	3	4	5
30. I determined how to do the test.	1	2	3	4	5
31. I carefully checked the answers before submitting the test.	1	2	3	4	5
32. I thought about how I had completed the test.	1	2	3	4	5
33. I saved time for checking my responses.	1	2	3	4	5

REFERENCES

Allen, S. (2003). An analytic comparison of three models of reading strategy instruction. *iral*, 41(4), 319-339.

Bialystok, E. (1990). *Communication strategies*. (Oxford: Basil Blackwell)

Brown, H.D. (2000). *Principles of language learning and teaching*. Fourth Edition. (White Plains, NY: Pearson Education)

Cohen, A.D. (2003). The learner's side of foreign language learning: Where do styles, strategies, and tasks meet?. *iral*, 41(4), 279-291.

Dickinson, L. (1987). *Self-imitation in language learning*. (Cambridge, MA: Cambridge University Press)

Gagne, E. D., Yekovich, C. W., and Yekovich, F.R. (1993). *The cognitive psychology of schooling learning*. (New York, NY: Hyper Collins College Publishers).

Izumi, S. (2003). Comprehension and production processes in second language learning: In search for the psycholinguistic rationale of the output hypothesis. *Applied Linguistics*, 24(2), 168-196.

Larsen-Freeman, D. (1986*). Techniques and principles in language teaching*. Oxford: Oxford University Press.

Lessard-Clouston, M. (1997). Language learning strategies: An overview for L2 teachers. *The Internet TESL Journal*, 3(12). Retrieved September 10, 2004, from: http://www.oteslj. org/Articles/Lessard-Clouston-Strategy.html

Naiman, N., Fronchlin, M., Stern, H.H. & Todesco, A. (1978) The Good Language Learner. Toronto,: Modern Language Center, Ontario Institute for Studies in Education.

Mitchell, R. and Myles, F. (1998). *Second language learning theories*. (New York: Oxford University Press).

Najar, R.L. (1998). A study of cognitive learning strategy use on reading tasks in the L2 classroom. Retrieved December 6, 2004 from: http://www.aare.edu.au/98pap/naj 98081.htm

O'Malley, J.M. and Chamot, A.U. (1990). *Learning strategies in second language acquisition*. (New York: Cambridge University Press).

Oxford, R.L. (1990). *Language learning strategies: What every teacher should know.* (New York: Newbury House).

Phakiti, A. (2003). A closer look at the relationship of cognitive and metacognitive strategy use to EFL reading achievement test performance. *Language Testing,* 20(1), 26-56.

Purpura, J.E. (1997). An analysis of the relationship between test takers' cognitive and metacognitive strategy use and second language test performance. *Language Learning,* 47(2), 289-325.

Purpura, J.E. (1999).*Learner strategy use and performance on language tests: a structural equation modeling approach.* (Cambridge: Cambridge University Press).

Richards, J.C. and Rodgers, T.S. (2001). *Approaches and methods in language teaching.* Second Edition. (Cambridge: Cambridge University Press).

Selinker, L. (1972) The Interlanguage. IRAL 10, 209-230.

Tarone, H.G. (1977) Conscious Communication Strategies in Interlanguage: A progress report. In H.D. Brown, C.A. Y0orio & R. Crymes (Eds.), on TESOL 77 : Teaching and Learning ESL (pp .194-230) Washington, DC: TESOL.

Widdowson, H.G. (1984) Learning Purpose and Language Use. Oxford OUP.

Yamamori, K., Isoda, T., Hiromori, T. and Oxford, R.L. (2003). Using cluster analysis to uncover L2 learner differences in strategy use, will to learn, and achievement over time. *iral,* 41(4), 381-411.

In: Meta-Cognition: A Recent Review of Research...   ISBN: 978-1-60456-011-4
Editors: M.F. Shaughnessy et al. pp. 207-220   © 2008 Nova Science Publishers, Inc.

Chapter 12

GIFTEDNESS: PREDICTING THE SPEED OF EXPERTISE ACQUISITION BY INTELLECTUAL ABILITY AND METACOGNITIVE SKILLFULNESS OF NOVICES

Marcel V. J. Veenman[*]

Dept. of Developmental and Educational Psychology, Leiden University
Wassenaarseweg 52, 2333 AK Leiden, the Netherlands

ABSTRACT

This chapter addresses the relation between two key factors that affect the speed of novices' knowledge acquisition. Both intellectual and metacognitive skills appear to be profound predictors of learning outcomes. It remains unclear, however, whether metacognitive skills are part of intelligence or to what extent they have their own virtue in novice learning. Over the past two decades we have conducted a number of studies in which participants of different age and from different educational backgrounds performed a variety of tasks in several school domains. Metacognitive activities, such as planning, monitoring, and reflection, were assessed by analyzing thinking-aloud protocols. Although correlated to intelligence, metacognitive skills appear to have a robust additional value for the prediction of novice learning on top of intelligence. Apparently, being gifted not only implies a high intelligence level, but also requires a well-developed repertoire of metacognitive skills that may help you to cope with new, unfamiliar learning tasks. Implications for the development of metacognitive skills over age and for the instruction of those skills are being discussed.

INTRODUCTION

It is hard to think of an infant (even of an infant prodigy) being a grand-master chess player, a successful architect, or a professor in psychology. Knowledge and cognitive skills

[*] Veenman@fsw.leidenuniv.nl

are gradually acquired over a long period of time. Therefore, it takes many hours of training to become an expert in a certain domain. Estimates of this training period range from about 5000 hours (Elshout, 1985) to 10 years or more (Chase & Simon, 1973). For instance, the surprising skillfulness of the Polgar sisters, who in their early teens wiped the floor with many (grand-)master chess players, resulted from extensive training from their early youth on. Evidently, the factors that determine a rapid acquisition of expertise are of main interest to psychologists and educational researchers. Although more factors are involved in gifted performance (e.g., motivational aspects of task interest and persistence; cf. Heller, Mönks & Passow 1993), intelligence and metacognitive skillfulness stand out as crucial ones. One way of studying the role of giftedness in the acquisition of expertise is to present novices with an unfamiliar task in a particular domain to find out what person related factors predicting fast learning.

Not all novices are alike; some, as if they were baron Munchausen, are capable of pulling themselves out of the swamp of unknowing ('bootstrapping' in terms of Bereiter, 1985). Schoenfeld and Herrmann (1982) and Elshout (1985) simultaneously introduced the notion of the 'expert-novice': a novice who rapidly acquires expertise in a domain. The expert-novice is characterized by both a high level of intellectual ability (Elshout, 1985; Hunt, 2006; Sternberg, 1990), as well as a high level of metacognitive skillfulness (Cheng, 1993; Elshout, 1985; Feltovich, Prietula & Ericsson, 2006; Schoenfeld & Herrmann, 1982; Sternberg, 1990). A major issue, then, is whether the rapid progression of expert-novices results from their higher intelligence, their better metacognitive skills, or from a weighed sum of both characteristics.

Metacognitive Skillfulness

Metacognition has been recognized as a most relevant predictor of learning (Brown, 1978; Flavell, 1976, 1979; Glaser, 1990; Veenman, Van Hout-Wolters & Afflerbach, 2006; Wang, Haertel & Walberg, 1990). Metacognitive skillfulness is distinguished from metacognitive knowledge (Alexander, Carr & Schwanenflugel, 1995; Baker, 1994; Schraw & Moshman, 1995; Veenman & Elshout, 1999). The latter concerns the declarative knowledge one has about the interplay between personal characteristics, task characteristics and the available strategies in a learning situation (Flavell, 1979). Such knowledge does not automatically lead to the appropriate task behavior. For instance, a student may *know* that planning one's activities is necessary and yet refrain from doing so for various reasons. The task may be uninteresting or too difficult, or the student may lack the necessary knowledge and skills for mastery of the task. Metacognitive skills, on the other hand, concern the procedural knowledge that is required for the actual regulation of, and control over one's learning activities (Brown, 1978; Brown & DeLoach, 1978; Flavell, 1992; Kluwe, 1987). Task analysis, planning, monitoring, checking, and recapitulation are manifestations of such skills. These skills can be acquired and eventually executed implicitly (Baker, 1994; Reder, 1996), though some argue that awareness of their metacognitive nature is a prerequisite (Nelson, 1996; Schnotz, 1992).

Nelson (1996) gave an initial impetus to a unified theory of metacognition. Basically, he distinguished an "object-level", at which level cognitive activity takes place, from a "meta-level" which governs the object-level. Two general flows of information between both levels are postulated. Information about the state of the object-level is conveyed to the meta-level through monitoring processes, while instructions from the meta-level are transmitted to the object-level through control processes. Thus, if errors occur on the object-level, monitoring processes will give notice of it to the meta-level and control processes will be activated to resolve the problem. According to Nelson's model, metacognition can be seen as a *bottom-up* process, where anomalies in task performance trigger monitoring activities, which in turn activate control processes. As an extension of Nelson's model, metacognition could also take the perspective of a *top-down* process of self-instructions for the regulation of task performance (Veenman, 2006). Apart from being triggered by task errors, the latter top-down process can also be activated as an acquired program of self-instructions whenever the learner is faced with task performance. Quite in line with Nelson's model, these self-instructions evoke various cognitive activities at the object level.

Intellectual Ability as the Repertoire of Cognitive Skills

There exist many conceptions of intelligence (see e.g. Brody, 1992; Carroll, 1993; Sternberg, 1990). Here I adopt a rather pragmatic point of view. Intelligence may be perceived as the magnitude and quality of the human cognitive toolbox, which contains basic cognitive operations (Elshout, 1983). The contents and qualities of this toolbox are not only determined by the biological substratum (e.g. hereditary factors or brain damage), but increasingly by the opportunities one seeks and what the environment offers for acquiring useful cognitive strategies (e.g., at home or in educational settings). In the same vein, Humphreys (1968, 1989) and Snow (1989; Snow & Lohman, 1984) regard intelligence as the acquired repertoire of intellectual or cognitive skills that is available to a person at a particular point of time. An intelligence test samples this repertoire. The main question here is whether metacognitive skills are essentially part of this cognitive toolbox or repertoire. Sternberg (1990; Davidson, Deuser & Sternberg, 1994), for instance, regards metacognitive skills as a core process component in his triarchic theory of intelligence. Metacognitive skills, however, may also develop relatively independent from intellectual skills. Slife, Weiss and Bell (1985) adequately formulated this research issue: "The question is whether metacognition can be reduced to cognition".

Intellectual Ability and Metacognitive Skillfulness

There are three mutually exclusive models for describing the relation between intellectual ability and metacognitive skillfulness as predictors of learning (Veenman & Elshout, 1991; Veenman, Elshout & Meijer, 1997). The first model regards metacognitive skillfulness as a manifestation of intellectual ability, or as an integral part of the intellectual toolbox. According to this 'intelligence' model, metacognitive skills cannot have a predictive value for learning, independent of intellectual ability. Some support for the intelligence model was obtained by Elshout and Veenman (1992) in an experiment with novices working with a computer-simulated environment for learning calorimetrics. Several other researchers (Cheng, 1993; Hannah & Shore, 1995; Shore & Dover, 1987; Span & Overtoom-Corsmit, 1986; Zimmerman & Martinez-Pons, 1990) reported significant differences in the usage of metacognitive strategies between intellectually gifted and average students. These differences were, however, rather small and they were not consistently obtained for all metacognitive strategies reported (cf. Alexander et al., 1995). Moreover, correlations with learning performance scores were often not available or not presented. Slife et al. (1985) showed that the metacognitive functioning of students with learning disabilities was less adequate relative to regular students, although both groups were matched on intelligence and domain knowledge. Apparently, the last results do not support the intelligence model.

According to the second contrasting model, intellectual ability and metacognitive skillfulness are entirely independent predictors of learning, that is, as entirely separated toolboxes. This is referred to as the 'independency' model. Allon, Gutkin and Bruning (1994) reported low correlations between WISC-R intelligence and metacognition obtained retrospectively by questioning participants about their problem solving activities. Swanson (1990) claimed to obtain further support of the independency model for children performing two Piagetian tasks. His experimental design, however, which forced intelligence and metacognition to be orthogonal factors, does not permit the conclusion that both predictors are *fully* independent (Veenman & Elshout, 1991). Indeed, follow-up studies (Maqsud, 1997; Swanson, Rubadeau, & Christie, 1993) showed that metacognition was only partially independent of intelligence.

The last model is a mergence of the aforementioned two models. According to this 'mixed' model, metacognitive skillfulness is related to intellectual ability to a certain extent, but it also has a surplus value on top of intellectual ability for the prediction of learning. This mixed model has been corroborated by several studies. Berger and Reid (1989) concluded from their study with mentally retarded individuals, high or low intelligent students with learning disabilities, and normal achieving adults that "IQ mediates metacognition, but does not explain it". Although Bouffard-Bouchard, Parent, and Larivee (1993) found that intellectually gifted students only tended to exhibit better metacognitive strategy use during concept-formation task relative to intellectually average students, gifted students outperformed average ones on learning performance. Moreover, if intelligence was partialled from the correlation between metacognitive strategy use and learning performance, a significant correlation of .40 remained. Stankov (2000) argued that metacognition is partly independent of fluid intelligence. Minnaert and Janssen (1999), on the other hand, could not decide between the independency and mixed model when predicting freshmen's academic performance. They, however, used a questionnaire (i.e., LERQ), an off-line method for assessing metacognitive skillfulness that appears to be less valid relative to on-line methods, such as the analysis of thinking-aloud protocols and behavioral observations (Veenman, 2005).

Since 1987, these three models have been put to the test in a number of studies by our research group. The major research question was whether metacognitive skillfulness is entirely part of intellectual ability, or to what extent metacognitive skillfulness has its own virtue in learning processes.

METHOD

Participants. The 439 participants from the 11 studies differed in age, educational background, and type of task they had to perform. Seventy-two secondary education students ranging from the ages of 12 to 14 had to solve a series of mathematical word problems (Veenman, Kok, & Blöte, 2005; Veenman & Spaans, 2005). Another 111 participants of different age groups (ranging from 9 to 22 years old) performed an inductive learning task in the domains of biology and geography (Veenman, Wilhelm, & Beishuizen, 2004). Fourty-eight first-year psychology students studied texts on forensic psychology and geography (Veenman & Beishuizen, 2004). Sixteen first-year psychology students performed a learning-by-doing task in physics, as they learned to solve a series of thermodynamic problems while being able to request various forms of help from the computer (Veenman & Elshout, 1999). Another sixteen technical university students had to construct a mathematical model of the outburst of a contagious disease on a isolated island (Veenman & Verheij, 2003). Finally, 176 first-year psychology students performed a discovery-learning task in computerized simulation environments for physics, statistics, or psychology (Elshout & Veenman, 1992; Veenman & Elshout, 1991; Veenman, Elshout, & Busato, 1994; Veenman et al., 1997). It should be acknowledged that participants were novices in each domain, as tasks were unfamiliar to them or the level of task difficulty was highly challenging their present capacity as assessed by pretests.

Intellectual Ability

For secondary school students a standardized Dutch intelligence test was administered (Groninger Intelligence Test; Kooreman & Luteijn, 1987), which is appropriate for that age group. The GIT is a standardised Dutch Intelligence test that has been sufficiently validated against Wechsler scales (Evers, van Vliet-Mulder, & ter Laak, 1992). This paper-and-pencil intelligence test consists of three subtests: mathematical speed (measuring the number factor); a spatial filling-out task (measuring the visualisation factor); and verbal analogies (measuring the inductive and deductive reasoning factor; Carroll, 1993). Internal consistencies of the separate tests ($.75 \leq$ alpha $\leq .87$) as well as of the entire GIT (alpha $= .87$) were adequate.

For university populations a series of intelligence tests were administered (Elshout, 1976). These tests included Vocabulary (difficult word meanings), Verbal Analogies (verbal reasoning), Linear syllogisms (symbolic reasoning), Number series (numerical reasoning), Number speed (of simple arithmetic procedures), Embedded figures (spatial ability), and a word-pair memory task. These tests represent six primary intelligence factors from the survey of factor-analytic studies by Carroll (1993): inductive reasoning, quantitative reasoning, sequential reasoning, verbal ability, closure flexibility, and memory span.

Finally, for the various age groups in the study by Veenman, Wilhelm, and Beishuizen (2004), a Number Series Test (Elshout, 1976) assessed inductive reasoning (Carroll, 1993), and a Concrete Syllogisms Test tapped deductive reasoning (Carroll, 1993). For the spatial reasoning factor, both the Hidden Figures Test (Flanagan, 1951), and the Spatial Insight subtest of the Differential Aptitude Test (Evers & Lucassen, 1983) measured flexibility of closure (Carroll, 1993). Moreover, numerical fluency was covered with a Math Word Problems Test (adapted from Elshout, 1976, parallel to a WISC-R subtest). Test instructions were simplified so that all age groups could capture the meaning of the tests.

All these intelligence subtests can be traced back to standardized intelligence tests like the WAIS, the WISC, or tests used by Sternberg (1990), or those reviewed by Carroll (1993). For all studies, an overall Intellectual Ability score, which forms an IQ equivalent (Veenman

& Elshout, 1999), was obtained by calculating the unweighted mean of the standardized scores on the tests.

Learning Environments

Various types of tasks from different domains were presented to participants. Secondary school students were presented with realistic math word problems, such as: "At 10 a.m. Mr. Smith leaves Amsterdam for Brussels by car. Maximum speed of his car is 90 miles per hour. He drives to Brussels with a mean speed of 50 miles per hour. The distance from Amsterdam to Brussels is 140 miles. One hour after Mr. Smith has left, Mr. Jones leaves Brussels by car. Mr. Jones takes his time and drives to Amsterdam with a mean speed of 40 miles per hour. At what time do Mr. Smith and Mr. Jones meet?"

The inductive learning task of Veenman et al. (2004) required students to experiment with variables that might affect, for instance, plant growth: watering once or twice a day, using insecticides or not, putting dead leaves in the pot, having a large or a small pot, and placing the plant on the balcony, indoors, or in a glasshouse. Some variables did not affect plant growth (insecticides and dead leaves), one variable had a linear effect (placing the plant), and two variables interacted (pot size and the amount of water).

The texts for first-year psychology students (Veenman & Beishuizen, 2004) concerned the topic of decision making about taking legal actions or not, and the topic of problems with the rice growth on Java (Indonesia). Both were quite substantial texts, introducing various new concepts.

In the case of learning to solve a series of thermodynamics problems (Veenman & Elshout, 1999), 20 problems about the changing relation between temperature, pressure, and volume were presented to subjects on the computer. They could voluntarily ask the computer for help: To give them a hint for one specific step, to give them instructions for how to solve the entire problem while performing the actions themselves, to perform one specific step for them, and to show how to solve the problem all the way.

In another study, technical students had to solve a problem of how to build a model of an ecological valid situation of the outbreak of a contagious disease on an island (Veenman & Verheij, 2003). This was a paper and pencil task in preparation of a computerized model of the problem.

Finally, in a number of studies first-year psychology students had to perform a discovery-learning task by experimenting in computerized simulation environments. These environments concerned calorimetry, electricity, statistics, instrumental conditioning, and the explosive power of chemical substances (Elshout & Veenman, 1992; Veenman & Elshout, 1991; Veenman, et al., 1994, 1997).

Metacognitive Skills

Metacognitive skillfulness was operationalized in terms of an organized set of metacognitive activities for passing through all phases of the task in an orderly way (orientation, planning, evaluation and reflection; Veenman & Elshout, 1995; Veenman & Verheij, 2003). Certain metacognitive activities, such as orienting on the task, preferably should be performed in an early stage of task performance. Others, such as planning and monitoring, need to be employed throughout the task. Both evaluation and reflection should at least re-occur at the end of the task. These metacognitive skills appear to be highly interdependent (Veenman et al., 2004). Good orientation leads to good planning and systematic behavior, which in turn, allows for more monitoring and evaluative control. Finally, reflection builds on the outcome of the aforementioned skills.

During all tasks participants were requested to think aloud, a research method often used for the study of cognitive processes (Ericsson & Simon, 1993; Pressley & Afflerbach, 1995). Participants were instructed to merely verbalize their thoughts during task performance. In case they fell silent, they were urged to "keep on talking" by the experimenter. Merely verbalizing one's ongoing thoughts differs from non-concurrent self-reports or introspections, as the latter two require a reconstruction of, or a retrospective reflection upon one's thought processes. Such reconstructions or reflections may distort the thought processes reported (Ericsson & Simon, 1993; Nisbett & Wilson, 1977; Pressley & Afflerbach, 1995). Thinking aloud, as concurrent verbalization of one's thoughts does not interfere with those thought processes in general (Ericsson & Simon, 1980, 1993); or, more specifically, with ongoing regulatory processes (Veenman, Elshout & Groen, 1993). Thinking aloud, however, may slightly slow down those processes.

The thinking-aloud protocols were judged on the quality of metacognitive activities by at least two judges. Orientation activities were judged on analyzing the task assignment, activating prior knowledge, goal setting, and generating predictions or test expectations. Planning was scored on designing an action plan, systematic execution of that plan, not haphazardly getting involved in trial-and-error behavior, and orderly note taking. Evaluation was judged on comprehension and progression monitoring during task performance, detecting and repairing mistakes, checking outcomes, and attending to whether the goal is reached. Finally, reflection was scored on recapitulating, drawing conclusions, generating explanations, and taking notice of what can be learned for future occasions. With slight adjustments these metacognitive activities could be assessed for all learning tasks, including problem solving, discovery learning, and text studying. It must be emphasized that metacognitive activities were judged on the quality of performing regulatory activities, *not* on the quality of information these activities produced. For instance, participants generating well-considered, though incorrect predictions scored high on orientation. Similarly, participants drawing elaborated, yet incorrect conclusions scored high on elaboration while accumulating incorrect knowledge. An overall score for metacognitive skillfulness was calculated by adding up the scores of the four categories of metacognitive activities (orientation, planning, evaluation, and reflection).

In order to enhance the validity of this assessment method, other measures for metacognitive skillfulness were obtained in six studies with a multi-method design ($N = 119$ in total). These other measures included rating the same protocols separately on the frequency of metacognitive activities, rating activities that were registered by the computer in log-files, and observational data. Quality of metacognitive skills as assessed from thinking-aloud protocols correlated .87 on the average with the other measures (for a more detailed overview, see Veenman, 2005). Nevertheless, it was decided to resort to the qualitative analysis of thinking-aloud protocols because this method allows for the distinction between shallow and deep metacognitive processes. For instance, a participant detecting a mistake without repairing it may be regarded as showing signs of shallow metacognitive skillfulness, whereas those participants who do repair the mistake demonstrate deeper metacognitive skillfulness.

Learning Performance

In all studies learning performance was assessed independent of, and subsequent to the learning environment sessions. Learning measures included multiple-choice and open-ended questions for assessing domain-specific declarative knowledge, structured interviews, and problems similar to those presented in the learning environment, and reasoning problems that went beyond those presented in the learning environment. A composite measure of learning performance was obtained by calculating the unweighted mean of learning measures within each study.

Statistical Procedures

Within each study data for intellectual ability, metacognitive skillfulness, and learning performance were transformed to z-scores in order to make them comparable across experiments. Next, all data of the 439 participants were gathered in one data file. On this overall data file correlational and regression analyses were performed. As the data were transformed to z-scores *within* each study, no significant differences between the data from separate experiments can be established, neither for age, nor for type of task.

RESULTS

First, the semipartial correlation was calculated with intellectual ability partialled from the correlation between metacognitive skills and learning performance (Nunnally, 1967). This semipartial correlation of .42 (see Table 1) reflects the predictive value of metacognitive skills for learning performance, independent of intellectual ability.

Table 1. Correlations for novices (N = 439)

	Intel. Ability	Meta-skills	Semipartial Meta-skills
Learning Perf.	.57**	.63**	.42**
Meta-skills	.45**		

** means $p < .01$.

Using regression-analytic techniques for the partitioning of variance (Pedhazur, 1982), the unique and shared sources of variance in learning performance was subdivided for intellectual ability and metacognitive skillfulness. Firstly, the squared multiple correlation of intellectual ability and metacognition for predicting learning performance was calculated from the correlation between intelligence and learning and the semipartial correlation of metacognitive skillfulness and learning presented in Table 1 ($R^2 = (.57)^2 + (.42)^2 = .50$). Apart from the semipartial correlation between metacognition and learning performance with intellectual ability partialled from metacognition (.42, see Table 1), the semipartial correlation between intellectual ability and learning performance with metacognition partialled from intellectual ability ($r = .32$) was calculated. The proportion of variance shared by both predictors could be calculated by subtracting both squared semipartial correlations from the squared multiple correlation (shared $r^2 = .50 - (.32)^2 - (.42)^2 = .22$). Consequently, it was estimated that intellectual ability uniquely accounted for 10% of the variance in learning performance, metacognition uniquely accounted for 18% of the variance, while both predictors had 22% of variance in common. In total, both predictors accounted for 50% of variance in learning.

DISCUSSION

Evidently, both intellectual and metacognitive abilities accounted for learning performance. Metacognitive skillfulness was significantly correlated to intellectual ability, and this result leads to the rejection of the independency model. Metacognitive skillfulness, however, also uniquely accounted for a substantial proportion of variance in learning performance. These results corroborate the mixed model, while rejecting the intelligence model. Obviously, it really takes two to tango. The expert-novice is characterized by a high intelligence *and* a high level of metacognitive skillfulness. At a lower, intermediate pace of expertise acquisition, however, intelligence and metacognition may even compensate for one another to a certain extent. Relatively low-intelligent students may plan their activities step-by-step and keep a close watch on what they are doing. High-intelligent students with poor metacognitive skills, on the other hand, may reveal a chaotic pattern of learning activities, but still be able to distill some essential ideas from that chaos (for a more detailed description, see Veenman & Elshout, 1991).

Elsewhere (Veenman, 1993, 2006), I have argued that a general task schema of self-instructions represents the metacognitive skills that are involved in cognitive performance in *novel* situations. Upon entering a new domain the general task schema needs to be attuned to that particular task or domain. The task-specific schema that results from this specialization process contains the planning and control structure for the execution of problem solving and learning strategies that are (more or less) tailored to the specific task at hand. Consequently, the general task schema is trans-situational (cf. Brown & DeLoache, 1978), whereas the task-specific schema obviously is not. An important implication is that at the onset of a new type of tasks, novices have to "learn" to construct a task-specific schema through specialization of their general task schema. This additional task puts high demands on the cognitive resources of novices. In the course of the specialization process metacognitive skills are improved, refined, and integrated with the domain-specific knowledge that increasingly becomes available. Finally, if this specific task is frequently encountered and adequately dealt with, the task-specific schema may be automated and stored in long-term memory independent of the general task schema. Apparently, this is the case with experts or advanced subjects in a particular domain.

Some evidence for such a task-specific schema has been found by Veenman and Elshout (1999) and by Veenman, Elshout and Hoeks (1993). Apart from novices, they also included a total of 31 advanced students in physics. Participants either had to solve thermodynamics problems or discover principles of calorimetry in a computer-simulated environment. Metacognitive skillfulness appeared to be hardly correlated to intellectual ability, whereas metacognition was highly correlated to prior knowledge and learning outcomes. In the same vein, Prins, Veenman and Elshout (2006) presented advanced students in physics with easy or more complex assignments in a simulation environment for optics. Learning performance on the easy task correlated zero with intellectual ability, (cf. Elshout, 1987), and rather low with metacognitive skillfulness. In the results for the far more complex task, however, the mixed model reemerged. Due to the complexity of this task, they had to call upon their general task schema again.

In conclusion, giftedness pertains to high levels of both intellectual and metacognitive skills that are equally important in speeding up the acquisition of expertise. Moreover, the role of both types of skills may change along the trajectory of gaining expertise. These conclusions have relevant implications. Metacognitive skills do not necessarily develop parallel to intellectual skills (Alexander et al., 1995). Intelligence only gives students a head start in metacognition, but it does not further affect its developmental course (Veenman et al., 2006). Moreover, metacognitive skills can be trained effectively (e.g. Baker, 1994; Veenman et al., 1994). Cognitive training aimed at raising the intelligence level, however, often confounds the nature of such training by including components of metacognitive skills as well (Sternberg, 1990). This chapter provides a good argument for studying the separate effects of training intellectual and metacognitive skills in order to determine who profits from what. Finally, we should bear in mind that motivational factors, such as task interest, persistence, and self-efficacy (Bouffard-Bouchard et al., 1993; Zimmerman & Martinez-Pons, 1990) may still co-vary with intellectual and metacognitive skills as determinants of giftedness.

REFERENCES

Alexander, J. M., Carr, M., & Schwanenflugel, P. J. (1995). Development of metacognition in gifted children: Directions for future research. *Developmental Review*, *15*, 1-37.

Allon, M, Gutkin, T. B., & Bruning, R. (1994). The relation between metacognition and intelligence in normal adolescents: Some tentative but surprising findings. *Psychology in the Schools*, *31*, 93-97.

Baker, L. (1994). Fostering metacognitive development. In H. W. Reese (Ed.), *Advances in child development and behavior. Volume 25* (pp. 201-239). San Diego: Academic Press.

Bereiter, C. (1985). Toward a solution of the learning paradox. *Review of Educational Research*, *55*, 201-226.

Berger, R. S., & Reid, D. K. (1989). Differences that make a difference: Comparisons of metacomponential functioning and knowledge base among groups of high and low IQ learning disabled, mildly mentally retarded, and normal achieving subjects. *Journal of Learning Disabilities*, *22*, 422-429.

Bouffard-Bouchard, T., Parent, S., & Larivee, S. (1993). Self-regulation on a concept-formation task among average and gifted students. *Journal of Experimental Child Psychology, 56*, 115-134.

Brody, E. B. (1992). *Intelligence. Nature, determinants, and consequences* (2nd ed.). New York: Academic Press.

Brown, A. L. (1978). Knowing when, where, and how to remember: a problem of metacognition. In R. Glaser (Ed.), *Advances in instructional psychology, Vol. 1* (pp. 77-165). Hillsdale, NJ: Erlbaum.

Brown, A. L., & DeLoache, J. S. (1978). Skills, plans, and self-regulation. In R. S. Siegel (Ed.), *Children's thinking: What develops?* (pp. 3-35). Hillsdale, N.J.: Erlbaum.

Carroll, J. B. (1993). *Human cognitive abilities. A survey of factor-analytic studies.* Cambridge: Cambridge University Press.

Chase, W. G., & Simon, H. A. (1973). Perception in chess. *Cognitive Psychology, 4*, 55-81.

Cheng, P. (1993). Metacognition and giftedness: The state of the relationship. *Gifted Child Quarterly, 37*, 105-112.

Davidson, J. E., Deuser, R., & Sternberg, R. J. (1994). The role of metacognition in problem solving. In J. Metcalfe, & A. P. Shimamura (Eds.), *Metacognition* (pp. 207-226). Cambridge: MIT Press.

Elshout, J.J. (1976). *Karakteristieke moeilijkheden in het denken [Characteristic difficulties in thinking]*. Amsterdam: University of Amsterdam.

Elshout, J. J. (1983). Is measuring intelligence still useful? In S. B. Anderson, & J. S. Helmick (Eds.), *On educational testing* (pp. 45-56). San Francisco: Jossey-Bass.

Elshout, J. J. (1985). Een goed begin is het halve werk: over determinanten van effectief beginnersgedrag (Well begun is half done: about determinants of effective novice problem solving behavior). In: F. J. Mönks, & P. Span (Eds.), *Hoogbegaafden in de samenleving* (pp. 201-210). Nijmegen: Dekker & v.d. Veght.

Elshout, J. J. (1987). Problem solving and education. In: E. de Corte, H. Lodewijks, R. Parmentier, & P. Span (Eds.), *Learning and instruction* (pp. 259-273). Oxford: Pergamon Books Ltd. Leuven: University Press.

Elshout, J. J., & Veenman, M. V. J. (1992). Relation between intellectual ability and working method as predictors of learning. *Journal of Educational Research, 85*, 134-143.

Ericsson, K. A., & Simon, H. A. (1980). Verbal reports as data. *Psychological Review, 87*, 215-251.

Ericsson, K. A., & Simon, H. A. (1993). *Protocol analysis; verbal reports as data.* Cambridge: MIT Press.

Evers, A., & Lucassen, W. (1983). *Differentiële Aanleg Testserie*. Lisse: Swets & Zeitlinger.

Evers, A., Van Vliet-Mulder, J. C., & Ter Laak, J. (1992). *Documentatie van tests en testresearch in Nederland [Documentation of tests and test research in the Netherlands]*. Assen: Van Gorkum / Dutch Institute of Psychologists (NIP).

Feltovich, P. J., Prietula, M. J., & Ericsson, K. A. (2006). Studies of expertise from psychological perspectives. In K. A. Ericsson, N. Charness, Feltovich, P. J., & R. R. Hoffman (Eds.), *The Cambridge handbook of expertise and expert performance* (pp. 41-67). Cambridge: Cambridge University Press.

Flanagan, J. C. (1951-1956). *Flanagan Aptitude Classification Tests.* S.R.A.

Flavell, J. H. (1976). Metacognitive aspects of problem solving. In L. B. Resnick (Ed.), *The nature of intelligence* (pp. 231-235). Hillsdale N.J.: Erlbaum.

Flavell, J. H. (1979). Metacognition and cognitive monitoring: A new area of cognitive-developmental inquiry. *American Psychologist, 34*, 906-911.

Flavell, J. H. (1992). Perspectives on perspective taking. In H. Beilin, & P. Pufall (Eds.), *Piaget's theory: prospects and possibilities* (pp. 107 - 141). Hillsdale, NJ: Erlbaum.

Glaser, R. (1990). The reemergence of learning theory within instructional research. *American Psychologist, 45*, 29-39.

Hannah, C. L., & Shore, B. M. (1995). Metacognition and high intellectual ability: Insights from the study of learning-disabled gifted students. *Gifted Child Quarterly, 39*, 95-109.

Heller, K. A., Mönks, F. J., & A. H. Passow (1993). *International handbook of research and development of giftedness and talent.* Oxford: Pergamon.

Humphreys, L. G. (1968). The fleeting nature of the prediction of college academic success. *Journal of Educational Psychology, 59*, 375-380.

Humphreys, L. G. (1989). Intelligence: Three kinds of instability and their consequences for policy. In R. L. Linn (Ed.), *Intelligence* (pp. 193-216). Urbana: University of Illinois Press.

Hunt, E. (2006). Expertise, talent, and social encouragement. In K. A. Ericsson, N. Charness, Feltovich, P. J., & R. R. Hoffman (Eds.), *The Cambridge handbook of expertise and expert performance* (pp. 31-38). Cambridge: Cambridge University Press.

Kluwe, R. H. (1987). Executive decisions and regulation of problem solving behavior. In F. E. Weinert, & R. H. Kluwe (Eds.), *Metacognition, motivation, and understanding* (pp. 31-64). Hillsdale, N.J.: Erlbaum.

Kooreman, A. and Luteijn, F. (1987). *Groninger Intelligentie Test. Schriftelijk verkorte vorm.* Lisse: Swets & Zeitlinger.

Maqsud, M. (1997). Effects of metacognitive skills and nonverbal ability on academic achievement of high school pupils. *Educational Psychology, 17*, 387-397.

Minnaert, A., & Janssen, P. J. (1999). The additive effect of regulatory activities on top of intelligence in relation to academic performance in higher education. *Learning and Instruction, 9*, 77-91.

Nelson, T. O. (1996). Consciousness and metacognition. *American Psychologist, 51*, 102-116.

Nisbett, R. E., & Wilson, T. D. (1977). Telling more than we know: Verbal reports on mental processes. *Psychological Review, 84*, 231-259.

Nunnally, J. C. (1967). *Psychometric theory.* New York: McGraw-Hill.

Pedhazur, E. J. (1982). *Multiple regression in behavioral research* (2nd Ed.). New York: Holt, Rinehart and Winston.

Pressley, M., & Afflerbach, P. (1995). *Verbal protocols of reading: The nature of constructively responsive reading.* Hillsdale, NJ: Erlbaum.

Prins, F. J., Veenman, M. V. J., & Elshout, J. J. (2006). The impact of intellectual ability and metacognition on learning: New support for the threshold of problematicity theory. *Learning and Instruction, 16*, 374-387.

Reder, L. M. (1996). *Implicit memory and metacognition.* Mahwah: Erlbaum.

Schoenfeld, A. H., & Herrmann, D. J. (1982). Problem perception and knowledge structure in expert and novice mathematical problem solvers. *Journal of Experimental Psychology: Learning, Memory & Cognition, 8*, 484-494.

Schnotz, W. (1992). Metacognition and self regulation in text processing: Some comments. In M. Carretero, M. L. Pope, R. J. Simons, & J. I. Pozo (Eds.), *Learning and instruction.*

European research in an international context, Volume 3 (pp. 365-375). Elsmford, NY: Pergamon Press.

Schraw, G., & Moshman, D. (1995). Metacognitive theories. *Educational Psychology Review, 7*, 351-371.

Shore, B. M., & Dover, A. C. (1987). Metacognition, intelligence and giftedness. *Gifted Child Quarterly, 31*, 37-39.

Slife, B. D., Weiss, J., & Bell, T. (1985). Separability of metacognition and cognition: Problem solving in learning disabled and regular students. *Journal of Educational Psychology, 77*, 437-445.

Snow, R. E. (1989). Aptitude-treatment interaction as a framework for research on individual differences in learning. In P. L. Ackerman, R. J. Sternberg, & R. Glaser (Eds.), *Learning and individual differences* (pp. 13-59). New York: Freeman.

Snow, R. E., & Lohman, D. F. (1984). Toward a theory of cognitive aptitude for learning from instruction. *Journal of Educational Psychology, 76*, 347-376.

Span, P., & Overtoom-Corsmit, R. (1986). Information processing by intellectually gifted pupils solving mathematical problems. *Educational Studies in Mathematics, 17*, 273-295.

Stankov, L. (2000). Complexity, metacognition, and fluid intelligence. *Intelligence, 28*, 121-143.

Sternberg, R. J. (1990). *Metaphors of the mind: Conceptions of the nature of intelligence.* Cambridge: Cambridge University Press.

Swanson, H. L. (1990). Influence of metacognitive knowledge and aptitude on problem solving. *Journal of Educational Psychology, 82*, 306-314.

Swanson, H. L., Christie, L., & Rubadeau, R. J. (1993). The Relationship between metacognition and analogical reasoning in mentally retarded, learning disabled, average, and gifted children. *Learning Disabilities Research, 8*, 70-81.

Veenman, M. V. J. (1993). *Intellectual ability and Metacognitive skill: determinants of discovery learning in computerized learning environments.* Dissertation. Amsterdam: University of Amsterdam.

Veenman, M. V. J. (2005). The assessment of metacognitive skills: What can be learned from multi-method designs? In C. Artelt, & B. Moschner (Eds), *Lernstrategien und Metakognition: Implikationen für Forschung und Praxis* (pp. 77-99). Münster: Waxmann.

Veenman, M. V. J. (2006). *Metacognitive skills as self-instructions.* Paper presented at the 2nd meeting of the EARLI SIG on Metacognition, Cambridge.

Veenman, M. V. J., & Beishuizen, J. J. (2004). Intellectual and metacognitive skills of novices while studying texts under conditions of text difficulty and time constraint. *Learning and Instruction, 14*, 619-638.

Veenman, M. V. J., & Elshout, J. J. (1991). Intellectual ability and working method as predictors of novice learning. *Learning and Instruction, 1*, 303-317.

Veenman, M. V. J., & Elshout, J. J. (1995). Differential effects of instructional support on learning in simulation environments. *Instructional Science, 22*, 363-383.

Veenman, M. V. J., & Elshout, J.J. (1999). Changes in the Relation between Cognitive and Metacognitive Skills during the Acquisition of Expertise. *European Journal of Psychology of Education, 14*, 509-523.

Veenman, M. V. J., Elshout, J. J., & Busato, V. V. (1994). Metacognitive mediation in learning with computer-based simulations. *Computers in Human Behavior, 10*, 93-106.

Veenman, M. V. J., Elshout, J. J., & Groen, M. G. M. (1993). Thinking aloud: Does it affect regulatory processes in learning. *Tijdschrift voor Onderwijsresearch, 18*, 322-330.

Veenman, M. V. J., Elshout, J. J., & Hoeks, J. C. J. (1993). Determinants of learning in simulation environments across domains. In D. Towne, T. de Jong, & H. Spada (Eds.), *Simulation-based experiential learning* (pp. 235-248). Berlin: Springer Verlag.

Veenman, M. V. J., Elshout, J. J., & Meijer, J. (1997). The generality vs. domain-specificity of metacognitive skills in novice learning across domains. *Learning and Instruction, 7,* 187-209.

Veenman, M. V. J., Kerseboom, L and Imthorn, C (2000). Test anxiety and metacognitive skillfulness: Availability versus production deficiencies. *Anxiety, Stress, and Coping, 13,* 391-412.

Veenman, M. V. J., Kok, R., & Blöte, A. W. (2005). The relation between intellectual and metacognitive skills at the onset of metacognitive skill development. *Instructional Science, 33,* 193-211.

Veenman, M. V. J., & Spaans, M. A. (2005). Relation between intellectual and metacognitive skills: Age and task differences. *Learning and Individual Differences, 15,* 159-176.

Veenman, M. V. J., Van Hout-Wolters, B. H. A. M., & Afflerbach, P. (2006). Metacognition and Learning: Conceptual and Methodological Considerations. *Metacognition and Learning, 1.* 3-14.

Veenman, M. V. J. & Verheij, J. (2003). Technical students' metacognitive skills: Relating general vs. specific metacognitive skills to study success. *Learning and Individual Differences, 13,* 259-272.

Veenman, M. V. J., Wilhelm, P., & Beishuizen, J. J. (2004). The relation between intellectual and metacognitive skills from a developmental perspective. *Learning and Instruction, 14,* 89-109.

Wang, M. C., Haertel, G. D., & Walberg, H. J. (1990). What influences learning? A content analysis of review literature. *Journal of Educational Research, 84*, 30-43.

Zimmerman, B. J., & Martinez-Pons, M. (1990). Student differences in self-regulated learning: relating grade, sex, and giftedness to self-efficacy and strategy use. *Journal of Educational Psychology, 82*, 51-59.

In: Meta-Cognition: A Recent Review of Research...   ISBN: 978-1-60456-011-4
Editors: M.F. Shaughnessy et al. pp. 221-227   © 2008 Nova Science Publishers, Inc.

Chapter 13

AN INTERVIEW WITH JOHN FLAVELL

Michael F. Shaughnessy
Eastern New Mexico University, USA

Q: What are you currently working on, writing, researching?

A: Not much. Actually, I have been retired for about four years now. I am still reviewing things and occasionally writing something, but that's about it. I recently taught a course on a one-time fill-in basis, but I'm not doing any formal research at all and no longer have a grant.

Q: Historically, who has influenced you and why?

A: Piaget, of course, but also Heinz Werner. Werner was an old-school, Piaget-like developmental psychologist from Germany who came and taught at Clark University, where I got my Ph.D. He was a developmentalist in much the Piagetian, classical sense. I would never have been interested in development if I had not gone to Clark and been one of his students. He certainly helped set the direction of my life. I have also been influenced by Chomsky, who gave us ideas about innate constraints on development. Also, when I first came to the University of Minnesota in 1965 James Jenkins was a powerful intellectual stimulus for me. I think I owe a lot to him. Undoubtedly, there have been other people who influenced me, but those are the ones that come to mind.

Q: What do you mean by "theory of mind" research? How does it impact metacognition?

A: Theory of mind and metacognition have overlapping meanings. Theory of mind means basically what people understand either explicitly or implicitly about the mind, their own and other people. Do they understand what it is to have a memory? Do they know what a desire is or what a belief is? Do they have a representational conception of the mind? Metacognition is the earlier concept and was defined as cognition about cognition. It mostly involved cognition about your own cognition that might help you learn something - knowledge of memory and study strategies, for example. Work on metacognition began in the 1970s and has continued to the present day. Then, in the early 1980s, theory of mind research came along. Theory of mind, as I said, has more to do with understanding minds in general - what the mind is, what beliefs are, what the creatures that inhabit the minds are all about. The two areas overlap, but they have a somewhat different focus.

Q: How do children go about constructing higher level knowledge, and for kids, what do you mean by higher level knowledge for children?

A: Well, I guess what I mean is all the things you need to learn between the time you are a child and the time you are an adult - knowledge of the world, what things are like, knowledge of numbers, knowledge of space, knowledge of people, knowledge of objects, etc.; thus, all the knowledge that would go into cognitive development. Higher order of knowledge of children would certainly include theory of mind, concrete and formal operations á la Piaget, and general world knowledge. This knowledge is acquired via a variety of processes and mechanisms. For example, I was recently talking to a student who was doing her thesis on children's question-asking, a mechanism of development. It is one of the ways the child makes intellectual progress, by asking questions and getting answers. The child is unclear about something, an example of Piaget's disequilibrium; the child may then get to a new and higher understanding or equilibrium by getting an answer to a question, maybe with the help of follow-up questions.

Modeling, in which a parent, teacher or somebody else shows you how to do something, is another important developmental mechanism.

Q: Metamemory. Why is it important? Why should we study it?

A: Well, it was the first kind of metacognition that was studied. Since remembering things is very important for all of us, and certainly important for children going through school;, and memorizing things and remembering things involves studying, involves using study and memory strategies to acquire, hold, and retain and reuse information, it is part of the whole educational enterprise. Everyone agrees that memory is important, and memory development is important. Metamemory was another way of looking at it, another way of studying it that had not been previously done. Memory development, in general, is clearly the development of information capacity. It occurs through biological and neurological development and also through the effects of knowledge on memory. If you know more, then you can remember more things. In addition to that, one also needs memory strategies, some general metamemory knowledge, and some general knowledge about what your mind is like as a memorizer. Those things are all what would be comprised in the process of memory development.

Q: Where do mnemonics fit in?

A: Mnemonics are clearly memory strategies. If you are using mnemonics, you are trying to use something to improve your memory. For example, rehearsing would be a mnemonic. Categorizing things would be another. Self-testing - testing yourself to see if you understood something and have learned it - would be another one.

Q: Going way back to 1971, what is memory development the development of?

A: It's basically what I just said, I think. Memory development includes all those things – first, basic processes and changes in the basic size of your memory box, acquired partly through biological maturation and partly through experience. Second, the acquisition of memory strategies. Third, general knowledge about memory, or metamemory. Those are the basic things I see as comprising memory development. Those are the things that develop when memory develops.

Q: I am here sitting in Portales, New Mexico with a Band-Aid box. Can you guess what is in it, and why is this kind of question important to cognitive development?

A: Well, you are referring to the most famous task in the whole area of theory of mind development. In this task, you show the child a Band-Aid box and ask the child what is in it. The child says Band-Aids, of course. You open it up and it turns out to have only pencils in it. You close it up again and you say, "Now if your little friend comes in, and she has not seen this before, what will she think is in there?" What you typically find in this very robust and well-studied task is that 3-year-olds will typically say pencils; they will report the reality of what is there. Whereas, by the time they get to be 4 or 5, they understand that you are talking about a person's belief - false belief in this case. They will correctly say, "She will think it is Band-Aids." What did you think when you first came in? "Oh, I thought it was Band-Aids, too." In contrast, the 3-year-old will just go right to the actual reality contents. That has been taken to be a benchmark task in assessing developmental change in children's understanding of a very important mental concept, namely belief - what beliefs are and how they can be at odds with how things really are.

Q: How would you say it relates to object permanence?

A: I think probably not at all. Object permanence would be the elementary knowledge that Piaget identified during infancy a long time ago, namely, that an object continues to exist even when it is out of sight. This knowledge is not tested for in the false belief task. A child who fails the false belief would clearly have had object permanence long since. He knows that things continue to exist when out of sight. For example, take the Band-Aid box case. Suppose you show the box empty, then you show them one Band-Aid, then you put the Band-aid in the box and close up the box. The object permanence question would ask whether the children know that there is a Band-Aid in there, and of course they would.

Q: It is almost rigid categorization.

A: Which is?

Q: That the child can only see the Band-Aid box holding Band-Aids.

A: Well, I don't think it is quite that. The essence of the task is that the child comes in and makes the very reasonable guess that the box has Band-Aids in it, but then finds that it doesn't. I don't see any question of rigidity here. It is just that, when you ask what somebody else would think it contains, he gets it wrong because he does not really grasp the fact that the other person is going to have a mental representation based upon the information the other person has, which is provided only by the appearance of the box. The understanding of what a belief is, which is supposed to be at stake in this task, is not a matter of rigidity, as I see it. I don't think you would measure rigidity in that way at all.

Q: In 1963, you published The Developmental Psychology of Piaget. It is now almost 2007, now more than 40 years later. In retrospect, what has changed?

A: Well, a lot. First of all, two things about Piaget. Clearly he was the father of the field, and the most important figure we have ever had. All of us continue to admire what he has done. Furthermore, a number of his tasks and findings have proven to very robust. People still replicate them. What have changed are two things, I think. On the one hand, our theories or ideas about how development proceeds, and what happens when, have changed in a number of ways.

On the other hand, we now have so much more research information about children's cognitive development than Piaget had access to. One of the main things that people no longer believe in the same way that Piaget seems to have is that stages are relatively rigid things across the board. When you get to be 6 or 7 or 8, you are clearly in the concrete operational stage, and you will think consistently at that level in lots and lots of different tasks, Piaget argued. Nowadays we think that things are more task specific. Children are less consistent in their level of reasoning across tasks during any given age period. So, the consensus now is that stages are not the general, unitary things that Piaget thought they were. Consequently, people in the field don't talk much about general stages anymore.

Q: Role taking and communication skills: why are these skills important, and what has your research shown?

A: Well, role-taking means adopting, or otherwise taking into account of, the perspective of another person; understanding in some sense, at some level, the perspective of the other person. Although I did not fully realize this when I was doing that work on role taking, it is really fundamental. You can't even hold a conversation with somebody without doing at least some implicit role taking. More generally, interpersonal relations won't go anywhere if you don't have any role taking and communication skills. You can't understand what other people are saying, they won't understand you, and you can't converse on a common topic and have what they call 'common ground' in your interaction. Personal relations are based upon role taking and communication at one level or another.

Back in the 1950s and 1960s, we did some work just testing children's ability to take perspective of another person and also their ability to communicate in a perspectival way, that is, to communicate appropriately depending on the other person's perspective - what the other person does and doesn't know. Since then, during the 1970s and 1980s mostly, we did some work on perceptual role taking – for example, testing whether young children realize that, if I hold up a card with a picture of a dog on their side and a picture of a cat on mine, I see the cat, and they see the dog. Do they realize that their visual experience and mine are different in such situations? That is a very basic, elementary form of perceptual perspective taking.

Q: Why study this appearance reality distinction?

A: That is a very good question! When we first did the appearance-reality stuff, the fake rock that looks like a rock and was really a sponge- what we thought we were getting at, and still do to some extent, is whether preschool aged children understand that a given thing can be thought of in two different ways, as being this in appearance and that in reality;- in this case, as a rock in appearance and a sponge in reality. We thought that the research suggested that children don't understand that;, that they construe the thing as having only a single, undifferentiated "is". We now think that view is only partly right, at best. There is now evidence suggesting that the appearance and reality questions have traps of their own for young children. Part of it is a failure to truly understand what you are asking. That is not the whole story, most likely, but there is some recent research suggesting that it may be important. Here is the way I think of it, though I am not sure I'm right. Children do learn something about the appearance-reality distinction. They do develop the ability to think of the same thing in more than one way. On the other hand, the task we use probably underestimates what children know because of its verbal demands. Children may be acquiring the appearance-reality distinction and related things, but they may be acquiring it earlier than we thought, and the reason they don't pass the task when they are age three, let's say, may not be entirely because of their lack of understanding of the appearance reality distinction, but because of their failure to understand the test questions properly.

Q: What kind of metacognitive activities or experiences should parents or maybe even teachers be fostering?

A: Well, let me think about that one for a minute. One thing they should do, I think, is to encourage their children to think about their own functioning, to be self-reflective, to monitor and regulate their own activity, to look before they leap and think before they act when appropriate. Also to call their attention to the child's own mind and say, "You may think this, but you could be wrong. Maybe you have to look a bit further. Maybe you should be a bit more careful in coming to that conclusion" or whatever it may be. I think, generally, conveying more mental things to the child, within reason, by the teacher and by the parent, can be useful. For example, I do some tutoring with second graders right now; very simple stuff. I just have them reading to me. Nowadays, and this would not have been true years ago, the teacher gives the second graders a whole list of study strategies, a whole list of reading strategies. The kind of thing where you break up the word into pieces, see if there is anything else in the picture or page of the book that will give you a clue as to what it means, or sound it out; about 12 different strategies all together Years ago, like when you and I were kids, they would not have done that. I think these are some of the results of the metacognition research. People in education are very much aware of metacognition, and they are putting it into practice. Parents, similarly, can do the same. You try to help your child be more self reflective in the theory of mind area, to pay more attention to how the other feels when you do this to her. Why does this child not like what you did? Why does that child think this or that? In other words, encourage the child to do more perspective taking. I think all of those are important uses by parent and teacher of metacognitive and theory of mind ideas.

Q: Would you want to comment on the contributions of some of your colleagues - maybe, Dave Moshman, Robbie Case, and Deanna Kuhn?

A: Deanna Kuhn has been very important for her groundbreaking research on adolescent and adult scientific reasoning, among other things. Robbie Case was a very important man in cognitive development. He had a neo-Piagetian model of development that was quite influential, both in the field in general but also in education. He was significant because he tried to find a way to combine modern thinking about information processing cognitive psychology with Piaget's theory. Dave Moshman wrote a very good, comprehensive chapter on adolescent reasoning a few years ago. He has also done major research in that area.

Q: Whom have I missed?

A: There are many other developmental psychologists who have made major contributions. My colleague, Ellen Markman, is a superb developmental psychologist. I also think of Henry Wellman, Michael Tomasello, Josef Perner and many others.

Q: Would disequiibration trigger metacognitive activity?

A: Yes. That was a central assumption of Piaget's theory. If you are going along on some problem and everything seems to be going smoothly, and then, suddenly, you come across some fact or idea that just throws your previous theory out of whack, into disequilibrium, then presumably, one thing you ought to do is be reflective and jump up a level and say to yourself "Hey, maybe I have been thinking about this wrong. Maybe I better check this; Maybe I better check that." All of these would be metacognitive responses to a state of cognitive disequilibrium. Just being consciously puzzled is metacognitive in a way ! You realize that you don't understand and that you need to learn more or think things out differently.

Q: Since children cannot see adults thinking, how do they come to understand that adults are, in fact, thinking about them, about absent objects and about emotional issues?

A: A whole lot of that is acquired through conversation between children and adults. People talk about mental states, both to the child and to each other in the child's hearing. The adult will say, "Do you want this? Do you think that?", and the child learns something about desires and beliefs thereby. Just from conversation alone the child can acquire a great deal. She can realize that somebody else has a different perspective than she does, etc. Clearly, language in the broadest sense - language as it occurs in communication - is one very important avenue to acquiring theory of mind.

Q: Some have indicated, to get ahead, get a theory. Others have indicated, I think it was Dave Moshman, to really get ahead, get a metatheory. Which is more important? Having a theory about something or having a big metatheory?

A: I don't know. Do you mean for the child or for us?

Q: I guess for us as developmental psychologists to have a theory about perhaps inferencing for example as a skill.

A: I think that is the name of the game. That is what science is trying to do, to create plausible theories and then test them. I suppose metatheory would be, in a way, knowing what constitutes good theory; being able to evaluate the theory as such and maybe even have a theory about what makes a good theory. That would be, I guess, metatheory. I am not quite sure what he had in mind when he said that, so I am not sure that my answer is responsive to what lies behind that quote.

Q: Could you now meta-review your work and its contributions to cognitive development?

A: I can think of a number of things that I have done that seem to have been very important and got me where I am. I am a member of the National Academy of Sciences, for example. Some of the things I am going to mention briefly must have been responsible for that. One of them clearly was writing a book about Piaget, because that helped introduce Piaget and popularize Piaget among development psychologists everywhere, certainly in the English-speaking world; that is one thing. A second one would be, I suppose, the role taking communication research you referred to earlier. More important than that, no doubt, would be metacognition. I coined the term, or else Ann Brown and I coined the term, I am not really quite sure which of us did it, but one of us did. Not that the idea was totally original, but certainly we brought it into prominence and sparked all of this stuff on metamemory and all the rest of the things we have been talking about. So, the Piaget book is one contribution. Concept and work on metacognition would be a second one. A third one probably would be in the general theory of mind area, particularly the appearance reality research. Those would certainly be, I think, the main ones.

Q: I stole this from Edith Neimark: how did you come to think about thought? What got you interested in it?

A: I don't really know exactly. I was trained as a clinical psychologist, but I also had all this training from Heinz Werner on development and most of that was on cognitive development. Right from the beginning I was interested in thinking. I did my thesis on schizophrenic thinking, for example. When I started studying developmental psychology I found myself less drawn to personality and social development than to intellectual development. Also, I did not have any training in linguistics so developmental psycholinguistics was an option. I guess that is how I came to be interested in cognitive as opposed to all these other forms of developmental research.

Q: What question have I neglected to ask you?

A: Well, you might have asked whether I have had a happy academic and general life. The answer would be, absolutely. I have loved being an academic. Doing research, teaching, and working with students has been a really satisfying career. Although I think I do most things at a pretty mediocre level, there are a few I think I can do quite well, and I was lucky enough to get into the field - quite possibly the only field - that would allow me to do them. I have also had a very supportive family life. In short, I am a happy person who feels that he has been extremely lucky in life!

INDEX

D

E

F

G

H

I

J

K

L

M

Q

R